Max Weber and the Theory
of Modern Politics

Max Weber and the Theory of Modern Politics

DAVID BEETHAM

Lecturer in Government, Manchester University

London . George Allen & Unwin Ltd

Ruskin House   Museum Street

ISBN 0 04 329018 3

Printed in Great Britain
in 10 point Times Roman type
by Alden & Mowbray Ltd
at the Alden Press, Oxford

Contents

Acknowledgements *page* 9

Abbreviations 11

1 MAX WEBER AS POLITICAL THEORIST 13
Weber's political writings 17
Politics and theory 22
Politics and academic sociology 25
References 31

2 WEBER AS PROTAGONIST OF BOURGEOIS VALUES 36
Economic change and the national interest 36
Freedom and the Russian revolution 44
Bureaucracy and political leadership in wartime Germany 49
Weber as a theorist of bourgeois politics 55
References 59

3 THE LIMITS OF BUREAUCRATIC RATIONALITY 63
The irresistible advance of bureaucratic administration 67
Bureaucracy as a power group 72
Bureaucracy as a status stratum 79
Socialism, stagnation and slavery 82
References 89

4 PARLIAMENT AND DEMOCRACY 95
Parliament as a training ground for political leadership 96
Mass democracy and elites 102
Parliament as a protector of liberty 113
References 116

5 NATIONALISM AND THE NATION STATE 119
The concept of the nation 121
Germany as a 'Machtstaat' 131

Nationalism and the proletariat   144
References   147

6 SOCIETY, CLASS AND STATE: GERMANY   151
The social basis of the authoritarian state   152
A strategy for bourgeois democracy   164
War and revolution   170
Politics and class   177
References   179

7 SOCIETY, CLASS AND STATE: RUSSIA   183
The outlook for bourgeois democracy   184
The pathology of absolutism   192
Revolution and Bolshevism   198
The conditions for liberal democracy   203
References   210

8 CLASS SOCIETY AND PLEBISCITARY LEADERSHIP   215
Politics in capitalist society   218
The plebiscitary leader   226
Max Weber and the theory of bourgeois politics   240
References   245

9 SOCIAL SCIENCE AND POLITICAL PRACTICE   250
Practical analysis and historical sociology   252
Social science as ideology   261
References   276

Bibliography   280

Index   285

Acknowledgements

I am glad to acknowledge a debt to two German scholars. Professor Johannes Winckelmann, the editor of Weber's works, accorded me the hospitality of the Max Weber Institute in Munich for two periods in 1971–2, to study the extensive secondary literature on Weber. Professor Wolfgang Mommsen, well known for his writings on Weber's political thought, gave me the opportunity of discussing Weber with him, and made helpful comments on Chapter 5 of the present study. Although in the following pages I am critical of both scholars, this does not lessen my debt to their work.

I am grateful to colleagues in Manchester, in particular to Geraint Parry and Norman Geras, for their comments and criticisms on various drafts of this work. Mrs Thelma Wright did a splendid job in typing the manuscript, and my wife Margaret gave me untiring support in the course of its production.

Abbreviations

The following abbreviations are used in the text. The translations from Weber's work are my own. [In the few cases where I have used that of others, the English work precedes the German in the footnotes.]

GARS	*Gesammelte Aufsätze zur Religionssoziologie* (Tübingen, 1920–1).
GASS	*Gesammelte Aufsätze zur Soziologie und Sozialpolitik* (Tübingen, 1924).
GASW	*Gesammelte Aufsätze zur Sozial- und Wirtschaftsgeschichte* (Tübingen, 1924).
GAW	*Gesammelte Aufsätze zur Wissenschaftslehre*, 2nd edn (Tübingen, 1951).
GPS	*Gesammelte Politische Schriften*, 2nd edn (Tübingen, 1958).
WG	*Wirtschaft und Gesellschaft*, 5th edn (Tübingen, 1972).
ES	*Economy and Society* (New York, 1968).
GM	Gerth and Mills, eds, *From Max Weber* (London, 1948).
MSS	*Methodology of the Social Sciences* (New York, 1959).
PE	*The Protestant Ethic and the Spirit of Capitalism* (London, 1930).
Jugendbriefe	*Jugendbriefe* (Tübingen, 1936).
Lebensbild	Marianne Weber, *Ein Lebensbild* (Tübingen, 1926).
SVS	*Schriften des Vereins für Sozialpolitik.*

Chapter 1

Max Weber as
Political Theorist

As a major contributor to the development of sociology, Max Weber needs no introduction. As a political commentator and propagandist, he is less well known to English readers. Besides his work as an academic sociologist, Weber involved himself actively in the politics of his time. In her biography of her husband, Marianne Weber devotes as much space to his political views and activities as she does to an account of his academic work.[1] At the outset of his career, she tells us, he expressed a clear preference for the active over the contemplative life;[2] on more than one occasion politics beckoned as a serious possible alternative to scholarship;[3] on the last of these occasions, at the end of the war, it was only the shortsightedness of others that prevented him attaining the position of national leadership that his gifts of statesmanship merited.[4] Admittedly, here as elsewhere, Marianne Weber carries her devotion too far. Her husband's commitment to academic values was too deeply rooted for a transition to the role of politician to have been a natural one. As he explained himself in a letter to Karl Petersen at the time of his resignation from the national committee of the German Democratic Party in 1920:

> The politician has to make compromises; that is his job. But my calling is that of a scholar. . . . The scholar may not compromise, or allow 'nonsense' to remain unexposed.[5]

Yet if Weber regarded the values of the scholar and the role of the politician as incompatible, he was nevertheless active throughout his life as a political commentator and polemicist, an 'exposer of nonsense'. The scope of his writings in this field is remarkable, ranging from his early analyses of social and political change in East Prussia, through book-length articles on the 1905 Russian revolution, to his sustained polemics on the reform of the German constitution in the wartime and postwar period. These writings remain mostly untranslated, yet they are important to any complete assessment of Weber as a social and political theorist.

The purpose of this book is to provide a systematic account of Weber's theory of modern politics, in which primacy of emphasis is given to these writings on contemporary politics and political issues, rather than to the more familiar sociological work of *Economy and Society*. These writings have received close attention in the German literature on Weber, where they have been the subject of considerable controversy. Wolfgang Mommsen's book on Max Weber and German politics,[6] published in 1959, provoked a sharp reaction to its emphasis on the nationalist and elitist elements in Weber's political thought.[7] This disagreement was reinforced at the Weber centenary meeting of the German Sociological Association in 1964, in response to Raymond Aron's paper 'Max Weber und die Machtpolitik',[8] and it has continued ever since. The issues involved in this debate are of some importance, and will be discussed at various points in the present work; indeed, it is impossible to write about Weber's political thought without taking up a position on the genuineness of his commitment to parliamentary democracy, and on the relative strengths of the liberal and nationalist element in his political philosophy. In relation to this controversy the present study will argue that both sides to the debate suffer from being over-simplistic. The character of Weber's nationalism was more subtle than Mommsen allows, while on the other side Weber's defenders fail to make clear what kind of 'liberalism' he was committed to, and ignore the tension between this liberalism and his other values.

At the same time it should be said that this controversy over Weber's political values has had the effect of concentrating attention on one aspect only of his political writings: on what they reveal of his political outlook, and of the particular standpoints he adopted on the changing issues of German politics. In the process their significance as examples of political analysis, and for what they show of Weber as an empirical theorist of politics, has been largely ignored. No systematic study of Weber's political writings from this point of view has yet been made, to show how he analyses the interplay of social forces in a particular society, and to elucidate the general assumptions embodied in this analysis: assumptions about the possible forms of government and political activity, about the relationship between society and state, about the character of modern politics in general. It is this aspect of the political writings that is especially relevant to a total assessment of Weber as a political theorist, since it transcends the particular issues of German politics that he was concerned with. Just as Karl Marx's occasional writings ('The Eighteenth Brumaire,' etc) provide important evidence about his method of political analysis and the character of his political theory, the same is true of Weber also.

The significance of Weber's political writings gains additional emphasis in view of the limited framework within which politics is considered in his major work on sociological theory, *Economy and Society*. This work is broadly historical in conception, and its treatment of politics is dominated by two contrasting models which Weber regarded as being of fundamental historical significance: first, the contrast between traditional and rational forms of social structure, which served to define the characteristic uniqueness of modern society; secondly, the more universal contrast between the 'Alltag' (everyday) and the 'Ausseralltag' (exceptional), between the routine structures of everyday administration on the one hand, and the innovative power of charisma on the other. From both sets of perspectives, bureaucratic administration is defined as the central phenomenon of modern society, and understanding its character as a central issue in sociological theory. There is no wish here to deny the importance of Weber's analysis of bureaucracy in *Economy and Society*, but at least it can be said that it does not amount to a theory of politics. In the whole work there is little about politics as Weber himself defined it ('the struggle to share or influence the distribution of power, whether between states or among the groups within a state'),[9] little about social conflict or the way this is mediated or suppressed by different systems of government. There is little even about the wider social and political context in which modern bureaucracy operates.

It is here that the significance of Weber's political writings is most apparent. They are rich in themes that are absent from his sociological work: on the struggle for power within society; on the development of political leadership; on the character of modern democracy; on the effects of international conflict on national political structures and vice versa. Above all, Weber's writings on the politics of Germany and Russia offer an analysis, unique in Weber, of the interaction between society and state. The importance of this can be readily shown in his treatment of bureaucracy. In *Economy and Society* bureaucracy is presented as an abstract model, considered largely in isolation from the social and political process. In the political writings bureaucracy is set in its social and political context, and in so doing Weber develops a theory of its inherent limitations and of its interaction with other social

forces and groups. Such material can not only be seen as complementary to Weber's academic work; it also raises questions about
the nature and limitations of his sociology, and emphasises the
different view of society he held, when seen from the standpoint
of political practice.

In order to demonstrate the theoretical significance of Weber's
political writings, their treatment in the present work will be
thematic, rather than historical, as in Mommsen's book, or anec-
dotal, as in the books by J P Mayer and Ilse Dronberger.[10] This
does not mean that questions of historical context or of the
development in Weber's thought will be ignored, only that such
questions will be treated within an overall synoptic framework.
The central theme of the book will be that of modern politics
itself: what Weber considered its distinctive features and problems
to be. If it may seem odd to look to his political as much as his
academic writings for such a theory, it is important to remember
that, for Weber, knowledge was not merely the preserve of a
scientific context; it also formed a necessary basis for effective
action. A reiterated concern of his political writings was the
necessity of achieving a clear understanding of the character of
modern politics as a prerequisite to realistic policy and practice.
In what follows, central elements in Weber's conception of the
modern state and modern politics will be considered in turn from
this standpoint: bureaucratic administration; mass political
involvement; national conflict; the social context of capitalism
and class. Separate chapters will be devoted to each of these
themes. They will not, however, be treated solely on an empirical
level, as if they could be divorced from the explicitly evaluative
framework of Weber's political concerns. It is not only what Weber
saw as characteristic of modern politics that will be considered,
but what he saw as problematic about it from the standpoint of
his own values.

In this work, then, we are interested in Weber's political
writings, not primarily as a chronicle of the successive positions
he took up on the issues of German politics, but for what they
reveal of Weber as a political theorist. We are interested in them
as examples of political analysis, and for what that analysis shows
about Weber's conception of modern politics and what he conceived to be problematic about it. The book will aim to discuss
these themes in a systematic way, so as to facilitate comparison
with Weber's more familiar treatment of politics in his sociological
work. The last chapter will offer a critique of Weber's sociology
on the basis of that comparison.

Before proceeding, however, it is necessary to answer a number of preliminary questions. First, what are the political writings which are being discussed here? Secondly, how far can they be treated in the theoretical manner outlined? Thirdly, what kind of relationship is being argued for here between Weber's political and academic writings? These questions will be considered briefly in the remainder of this chapter.

WEBER'S POLITICAL WRITINGS

The political writings which form the main subject of this book embrace a diversity of types of writing, from brief items of correspondence to extended articles of book length. There is no simple principle of classification in terms of which they can be considered. One distinction commonly made in German is between issues of 'Sozialpolitik' and 'Staatspolitik', between writings on the 'social question' (the condition of the working class) and those on political subjects proper, involving the interests and structure of the state. The collected volumes of Weber's works, edited posthumously by his wife, are ordered according to this distinction. It was, however, a characteristic of Weber's approach, that issues which others regarded as exclusively social became for him essentially political, so the distinction can at best be only a rough and ready one.

The overlap between the two kinds of question is evident in Weber's writings on East Prussia, and these will provide a convenient starting point. The two sets of investigations Weber completed in the early 1890s for the Verein für Sozialpolitik (Association for Social Policy) and the Evangelisch-soziale Kongress (Protestant Social Congress) were decisive for establishing his academic reputation.[11] Conceived initially as studies on social policy—the condition of agricultural labourers—they developed into a wide-ranging socio-political analysis of the changing relationship between landowners and labourers under the influence of capitalism, and the consequences of this change for the structure of the state and for national interests in the face of Polish immigration. The amount of material Weber derived from these investigations is impressive. Besides the publication of the massive Verein study itself, he devoted a succession of academic articles to setting out its wider implications;[12] and the material also formed the basis for a number of weighty political speeches, ranging from an address to the Protestant Social Congress on the nature of capitalism and the aspirations of the working class,[13] to his inaugural lecture at Freiburg on the significance of the national interest as a goal for political economy.[14] As examples of socio-political analysis, as well as an expression of Weber's political values, these early articles and speeches are important, and will be considered at various points in the present study. At the same time, something should be said here about the two organisations which provided the context for Weber's early work, the Verein für Sozialpolitik and the Evangelisch-soziale Kongress respectively.

Weber's association with the Verein für Sozialpolitik and his concern with the 'social question' date from 1887, and mark a decisive break with the National-liberal orientation of his father.[15] The Verein was an association dominated by academics, whose purpose was to promote peaceful social reform by research and propaganda for a social policy which lay midway between the 'extremes' of laissez-faire Manchesterism and revolutionary Marxism.[16] It prided itself on being above class and party, though its members showed a general commitment to improving the lot of the working class, as being the only means to close the gap between the social strata and avoid the dangerous alienation of the workers from society. Its chosen instrument was the research monograph, and over the years its members produced an impressive documentation of social conditions in Germany, an 'enormous sandheap of social knowledge' as Rosa Luxemburg unkindly described it.[17] The biennial conferences, besides providing a forum for discussing the weighty volumes of research, were also the scene of intense political debate. In the words of Gustav Schmoller, a founder and father figure of the association, the Verein existed 'to bring the truth to light, to create a greater awareness of social affairs among all parties and classes . . . to smooth the way for those ideals of practicable social reform that are so eminently justifiable'.[18]

The history of the Verein was one of some tension between its academic and propagandist purposes. In practice, the refusal of the association to ally itself with any party or class denied it the political effectiveness such as the Fabians achieved in Britain, while its practical orientation offended those, like Max Weber in his later period, who believed that an academic association should not be confined to people who shared one political viewpoint, however broadly defined. Weber's disaffection with the Verein in his later years, which culminated in his helping to found the German Sociological Society in 1909 and in the famous debate on value freedom, are the best known aspects of his relationship with the association.[19] Yet the Verein also served as an important context for the development and expression of Weber's political views. Some of his most significant pronouncements on bureaucracy, on socialism and social democracy, on industrial relations and the character of the German state, were made in speeches to meetings of the Verein between 1905 and 1911.[20] The memorandum he sent to members of the Verein in 1912, seeking to stimulate a new initiative in welfare legislation, forms his most complete statement on social policy.[21] And other articles he wrote on aspects of social affairs, even where not under the aegis of the Verein itself, can best be understood against the background of the association and the controversy between its different political groupings.

These controversies have been analysed in a book by Dieter Lindenlaub, which is accepted as the definitive work on the Verein für Sozialpolitik in Weber's period, and is important for understanding the background to his political theory.[22] Lindenlaub distinguishes two main lines of controversy in the Verein. The first was within the older generation of founder members, between a dominant 'conservative' wing, whose chief exponents were Gustav Schmoller and Adolf Wagner, and a 'liberal' wing led by Lujo Brentano.[23] Although agreed on the broad aim of improvement for the working class, they disagreed about what this meant and how it could be achieved. The conservatives favoured a policy of protection for agriculture, and believed a balance between the classes could best be secured from above by bureaucratic control over industry and industrial relations. The liberals sought to free the expanding German industry from state regulation; the central plank of social policy for them was the removal of legal obstructions to the operation and effectiveness of the trade unions, and, to a lesser extent, the reform of the suffrage. The liberals wanted the workers to achieve by their own efforts what the conservatives sought to achieve for them by state regulation. Of the two wings, the conservatives remained dominant in the Verein until the late 1890s.[24] At that point the emergence of a younger generation (including Sombart, Toennies, Alfred and Max Weber), who were more sympathetic to the liberal direction, brought a sharpening of political controversy within the association.[25] They also raised a fresh issue—that of the correct attitude to Marx's work—which united them against the older generation, Brentano included. The younger generation agreed in taking Marx seriously, and held that capitalism and the class conflict it generated formed the constitutive element of modern social relations. The refusal of their elders to accept the concept of capitalism, except for the analysis of some marginal economic problems, meant that, in the eyes of the younger generation, their social analysis was at best superficial. Modern society could only be understood by those who had come to terms with Marx.[26]

Both these controversies are important in providing the context for Weber's political thought. The views of the older generation of conservatives, particularly their idealisation of Prussian bureaucracy and their acceptance of paternalism in society and state, provided a focal point in opposition to which Weber's own political views came to be defined. At the same time he was in the forefront of the younger generation in accepting capitalism as 'the most fateful force'[27] of modern life, a view which, though partly obscured in his later sociology, he never in fact seriously departed from. Both sets of issues are central to the subject of this book.

The other organisation Weber was involved in at the time of his studies on East Prussia, the Protestant Social Congress, was in the long term less important to him, though its meetings in the mid 1890s provided the scene for his most forthright speeches on the nature of capitalism and the need for German industrialisation and imperial expansion.[28] The first meeting of the Congress was called in 1890 to press for the recognition of the 'legitimate demands of the working class' in both church and state.[29] Its membership overlapped considerably with that of the Verein,[30] but it had a more single-mindedly agitational purpose. Weber, never a committed Christian, became involved through friendship with two of its leading figures, Pastors Gohre and Naumann, and he contributed frequently to Naumann's journal, *Die Hilfe*, and to *Christliche Welt*. Friedrich Naumann was to become a politician of some consideration, and his career was strongly influenced by Weber; to some extent he reflected in practical activity Weber's own political thinking. It is generally accepted, for instance, that Weber's inaugural speech at Freiburg was a decisive factor in Naumann's shift from a Christian to a more nationalist brand of socialism, which culminated in the formation of the National Social Party in 1897.[31] Although Weber was critically disposed towards this project,[32] he attended its inaugural meeting, while his mother put up the money for Naumann's candidacy for the Reichstag.[33] On the collapse of the party in 1903 and Naumann's subsequent election as a left liberal deputy, Weber became his 'constant adviser'.[34] His letters to Naumann in this period contain his earliest systematic critique of the German system of government and its limitations.[35] Weber brought to questions of social policy a strongly political approach derived from his family tradition, and there remained a difference of emphasis between Naumann and himself, summarised by Marianne Weber in her statement that 'for Naumann, the national power state was a means to social reform, whereas, on the contrary, for Weber social and political justice were a means to the security of the nation state.'[36] How far this is a fair assessment will be discussed later.

Weber's speeches and writings for the Verein für Sozialpolitik, then, and to a lesser extent for the Evangelisch-soziale Kongress, form one important body of material that will be considered here. Alongside this, there are writings of a more exclusively political character, dating from the wartime and postwar period, most of which were published initially as articles in the *Frankfurter Zeitung*. These are of two kinds. First, up to 1917, are a number of articles and papers on German foreign relations, critical both of prewar policy and of the conduct of the war itself, in particular the government's definition of war aims.[37] These are significant for Weber's conception of the nation state and of the international context of national politics. Then, from 1917 onwards, Weber turned his attention to questions of internal political reform. The two extended series of articles he wrote on the democratisation of the constitution, which received wide circulation in pamphlet form, are among the most weighty of his political writings.[38] Although part of a general movement for democratisation current at the time, these articles are distinctive both in the character of their argument for democracy and for the wide range of issues handled. Weber's political activity was not confined to the writing of articles, however. He formulated specific proposals for reform to put before the Parliamentary commission in 1917,[39] and was himself a member of the committee that advised on the new constitution at the end of the war.[40] He also campaigned vigorously for the newly formed Democratic Party in the winter elections of 1918–19, making speeches throughout the country, and after the elections kept up his campaign for a presidential system of government.[41] These many articles and speeches from the period after 1915 comprise the main bulk of the German editions of Weber's collected political writings, and form a second important body of material for this study.

Weber's political interests were not confined to issues of German politics alone. He visited both the USA and Britain, and studied the workings of their politics from Ostrogorski and others. The systems of government of both countries served him in different ways as models for his critique of German politics, and references to both abound in his writings.[42] It was Russia, however, that of all foreign countries attracted his most sustained interest. He wrote two extensive studies of the Russian revolution in 1905–6 for the *Archiv für Sozialwissenschaft und Sozialpolitik*,[43] as well as a short article on the February revolution in 1917.[44] These studies have been universally ignored in all discussions on Weber, yet together they constitute his most substantial exercise in political analysis. They will be given corresponding emphasis in this book.[45] Apart from these articles, there are also a number of writings on general political themes to be considered, the most important being the two lectures he gave in the winter of 1918–19, the first to a group of army officers in Vienna on 'Socialism', the second to a student association in Munich on 'Politics as a Vocation'. The latter, which combines an empirical analysis of the conditions of modern politics with an explicitly normative account of the politician's role, is justly one of the most famous of Weber's political writings.

The writings briefly sketched out above, together with Weber's voluminous correspondence on politics,[46] amount to a substantial body of political comment and analysis. The term used to describe them in German—writings on 'Tagespolitik', or occasional writings—aptly expresses their character. They were mostly written in response to a specific occasion, whether a political event, such as the Russian revolution, or some momentary request for a talk from a specific group. They are also for the most part explicitly evaluative and critical. This brings us to the second question raised above: how far is it possible to treat such writings in a theoretical manner, as providing material for a theory of politics?

POLITICS AND THEORY

A common, though superficial, view of Weber's political writings is that, in contrast to the 'scientific objectivity' of his sociological work, they contain nothing but a tissue of subjective value judgements. Hans Maier, for example, sees the increasing objectivity of Weber's scientific work after the early period as balanced by the corresponding irrationality of his political valuations. 'It is impossible,' he writes, 'to find any continuity amidst the strudel of [his] highly emotional utterances on the politics of the day.'[47] This is not only an inadequate assessment of these writings; it also misconceives the relationship Weber himself posited between empirical analysis and political practice. Although he strove to prevent a subordination of social science to practical goals, and to maintain a clear distinction between the activities of analysis and propaganda, at the same time he always insisted that a correct apprehension of reality was a precondition of successful political practice. Correct empirical analysis was as important for politics as for science; the ability to recognise inconvenient facts as much a virtue in the politician as in the academic. This is pointed out clearly by von Schelting, in what is still the most comprehensive analysis of Weber's methodology. The attainment of responsible political action, he writes, 'stands or falls with the possibility of achieving objectively valid knowledge of the empirical relationships pertaining in those areas of social and economic life which are relevant for the standpoint of the actor. . . . No one knew this better than Max Weber.'[48]

The political virtue most frequently emphasised by Weber was thus that of 'Sachlichkeit'—matter of factness, realism.[49] The ideal politician of 'Politics as a Vocation' is one who combines passion with objectivity.[50] A frequent target of his political writings are those Weber scornfully terms 'Literati', ideologists, whether of Right or Left, who showed a profound ignorance of the political facts of life.[51] Weber's writings themselves are as much aimed to awaken others to these realities as to propagate his own values—whether it be instructing a gathering of socially committed Christians that the development of capitalism had rendered the individual personal relationships of the religious ethic obsolete,[52] or pronouncing certain socialist ideals inconsistent with modern bureaucracy,[53] or urging the Right that great power status was incompatible with Germany's authoritarian political system.[54] Of course, Weber's brand of realism needs to be treated with some scepticism. It was reality presented so as to persuade. At times realism itself became elevated into a principle which was destructive of all ideals.[55] Nevertheless, it remains true that for Weber political advocacy involved empirical analysis as much as moral exhortation; the starting point of political argument was an informed awareness of social reality.

This being so, it is not surprising that we can find in Weber's political writings a good deal of material of an analytical kind. In the first instance it is analysis of the particular social and political structure of Germany or Russia. However, as one would expect with someone of Weber's sociological insight, wider theoretical implications are never far from the surface. Thus his concern with the problem of political leadership in Germany involved the problem of how leadership was possible at all in the face of bureaucratic administration; and the attainment of freedom in Russia was linked with the question of its attainment in societies characterised by large-scale capitalism in general. Even where his concern was with the distinctive features of German or Russian politics, these are often defined by contrast with political arrangements elsewhere. Weber demonstrates a theoretical grasp even in the most 'occasional' of contexts, and this makes it possible to use such writings as evidence for a theory of politics, particularly where the material has been carefully worked over, as in his more extended articles.

An interesting illustration of the theoretical content of Weber's political writings is provided by Winckelmann's edition of the *Staatssoziologie*.[56] Starting from the recognition that Weber never lived to complete his sociology of the state, Winckelmann argues that there is firm evidence available of the topics he intended to treat in such a work.[57] He then proceeds to make good the gap with extracts from Weber's political writings, in particular 'Politics as a Vocation' and the articles on 'Parliament and Government in a Reconstructed Germany'; these extracts are reorganised according to topics—political leadership, democracy, parliamentary government, etc—and 'all value judgements are eliminated'.[58] The finished product is then published as Weber's posthumous 'Sociology of the State', and it appears as such in the fourth and fifth German editions of *Economy and Society*.[59]

Such a project serves to emphasise the extent of theoretical content in Weber's political writings. It also illustrates the possible dangers of treating Weber's work in this way. In the first place, in eliminating Weber's value judgements Winckelmann is not removing an extraneous irrelevance, but that which sets the context and gives the analysis its whole significance. However rich in theoretical content it may be, a polemic such as 'Parliament and Government' cannot simply be treated as a preliminary sketch for *Economy and Society*—as a 'preparation for the completion of the manuscript of his great sociological work'[60]—without fundamentally changing its character. Secondly, Weber was himself explicit that what he was engaged in in his political articles was not science, and should not be accorded the authority of science. In the introduction to the articles on Germany's future constitution, for instance, he wrote that they were 'purely political works of the moment, without any pretensions at all to "scientific" validity,'[61] a judgement which applied also to the articles on 'Parliament and Government'.[62] This was not only a question of their occasional character, but also of their context being a practical political one, rather than an academic. 'Science,' for Weber, meant more than merely empirical analysis; it involved a particular way of organising empirical material, a particular sophistication in the definition and use of concepts; it meant also that the problems for inquiry were mediated, if no more, through the tradition and perspective of a scientific community. Weber's political writings do not meet these criteria, even if all the value judgements could somehow be spirited away.

Winckelmann is surely right to emphasise the important theoretical elements in Weber's political writings. The present study will explore these elements, but at the same time seek to avoid the difficulties of Winckelmann's approach. First, Weber's value concerns will be regarded as an integral part of his theory, and not extraneous to it. Discussion will remain within the context of Weber's values and the problems posed for these values by his understanding of contemporary society. Secondly, although it will be argued that Weber's writing has a significance beyond the immediate historical context, this context will not be ignored, especially where it is important to the development of Weber's theory.[63] Thirdly, there can be no suggestion that the theory discussed here was, or might have been, Weber's 'scientific' sociology of politics. Indeed it will be argued that the aspects of politics which Weber found significant from the academic and practical standpoints diverged as much as they coincided.

What is meant then by 'theory' in this book, and by Weber's 'theory' of politics, is something more than a mere succession of particular analyses and evaluations, but something less than 'science'. This brings us to the final question to be considered in the present chapter: what relationship do Weber's political writings hold to his academic sociology?

POLITICS AND ACADEMIC SOCIOLOGY

The question of the relationship between Weber's political and sociological writings has received a good deal of attention in the literature on Weber. It has usually been treated as a question of what light knowledge about Weber's political situation and standpoint can throw on the character and purpose of his academic writings. One of the earliest and most thoroughgoing attempts to deduce conclusions about Weber's sociology from his political situation is a work by Christoph Steding, *Politik und Wissenschaft bei Max Weber* (Politics and Science in Max Weber), published in 1932.[64] Steding argues that the key to Weber's academic work is to be found in the dilemma of bourgeois liberalism in an age when its individualist ideals had been overtaken in the economic sphere by the cartellisation of industry, and in the political sphere by the advent of mass democracy and socialism. According to Steding, this dilemma is the key both to Weber's failure in politics and to a proper understanding of his sociological work, which reveals him as a politician *manqué*, an academic 'against his will'.[65] Thus *The Protestant Ethic and the Spirit of Capitalism* is an expression of 'the bourgeoisie come to self-consciousness'—but too late, because its spirit belongs to a past world.[66] The concept of charisma embodies Weber's own ideal of 'independence from all constraints except those of one's inner calling.'[67] His account of Judaic prophecy in the sociology of religion reflects his own prophecies of doom against the Kaiser during the war, and so on.[68] On Steding's view, all Weber's sociology finds its proper interpretation in his political situation and values; indeed, the distinction between politics and sociology disappears.

Few critics since Steding have been as thoroughgoing in their attempt to derive Weber's sociology from his politics, though on a different level Arthur Mitzman has attempted to show that the key to Weber's academic work lies in his family situation: the struggle for independence from his father, and his supposed failure to consummate his marriage.[69] Most critics have been more modest in their approach, contenting themselves with drawing out parallels in a few specific areas. Thus Mommsen shows how the purely instrumental approach to constitutional issues of Weber's political thought is reflected in his sociological category of legal authority, and how the emphasis on leadership in his political writings is reflected in the central place assigned to charisma in his sociology[70] —the latter also a theme in a recent study by Anthony Giddens.[71]

The weakness of all these approaches is that they rarely spell out exactly what they are claiming to have shown about Weber's scientific work, by evidence adduced from his political context or standpoint. The cruder versions depend upon the implausible assumption that, when Weber was writing about the Protestant ethic or about emigration from the estates of East Prussia, he was really writing about something else: the pathos of the modern bourgeoisie, or his desire to be free of his father's household. The more restrained versions, while avoiding such crudities, remain less than explicit about the purpose of the connections they are making, or how knowledge about Weber's political position can help our assessment of his scientific conclusions or categories. As is often pointed out, questions about the origin and the validity of scientific work are separate questions; knowledge about the first does not entitle us to conclude the second. Only where we already have independent evidence for challenging the validity of a scientific conclusion or category does it become illuminating to refer to the author's political views or context for an explanation. But the latter kind of inquiry, while useful in its proper place, is not a substitute for the former.[72]

The same considerations apply to the account of Weber's work given by Georg Lukacs, who locates it within the context of a general critique of sociology in Wilhelmine Germany.[73] The main problem of sociology in this period, he argues, was how to provide an account of the origins and structure of capitalism which would challenge the Marxist position. This Weber does in *The Protestant Ethic* with an account of the development of capitalism in which the economic motives for capital accumulation are played down, and in his other works with an analysis of contemporary capitalism according to the general categories of rationality and calculability, which obscure what is problematic about it: the phenomena of exploitation and class conflict. From this point of view the whole methodological basis of Weber's sociology—the separation of science from practical commitment, the ideal type method, the development of abstract categories—can be seen as a way of evading the problems posed by the 'dialectic of social reality'.[74] At the same time, however, Weber's categories cannot help reflecting this reality. Thus his general categories of social action 'are nothing more than the abstractly formulated psychology of the calculating individual of the capitalist system', and his account of the irreconcilability of the different value spheres shows him 'stumbling on the problem of the *Communist Manifesto*, that history is the history of class struggle'.[75] Although parts of what Lukacs says have plausibility, his account in general rests on the assumption that the arguments Weber himself uses, for example to justify his methodological position, can be happily ignored, and that his intentions can be assumed without question to be primarily political rather than academic.[76] But for this Lukacs offers no sustained evidence.

A different approach to Weber's academic and political writings, which at the same time offers some account of the logic of their relationship, is provided by writers such as Karl Löwith[77] and Gunter Abramowski.[78] Their approach is much more sympathetic to Weber. They claim to discover, behind all the variety of his academic work, a self-conscious unity of purpose of an ethical or existential kind. The character of this purpose is then clarified by appeal to his non-academic writings, where these value issues are discussed more explicitly. A justification for this approach can be given in terms of Weber's own methodology. For Weber, the activity of the social scientist was only possible within a context of values which both provided the criterion for what was worth studying and also gave the object of investigation its significance. One implication of this is that the critique of a social scientist's work will involve not only an examination of its empirical claims, but also an elucidation of its underlying 'existential' purpose.[79]

Both Löwith and Abramowski discern the unifying principle of Weber's academic work in the theme of rationalisation. Löwith's 1932 articles on Weber and Marx have had a special influence on subsequent interpretation. Central to his argument is the parallel he draws between Weber's concept of rationalisation and Marx's analysis of capitalism through the concept of alienation. Where Marx, argues Löwith, saw the dilemma of modern man in the alienating power of capitalism—whereby the products of man's creation came to dominate man the producer—Weber located this 'perversion' in the process of rationalisation as such. Wherever men seek to increase their freedom by making life more predictable, the structures they create take on a life of their own and come to limit that freedom.[80] Löwith's argument is that, in their scientific writings, both Marx *and* Weber transcended the purely scientific to embrace questions of human existence and dignity, and were in this sense philosophical writers. But whereas the terms of Marx's analysis enabled him to offer a transformation of man's situation through revolution, Weber could only provide an understanding of the dilemma so that men could come to terms with it. 'Where Marx offered a therapy, Weber offered only a diagnosis.'[81] Abramowski follows Löwith[82] in arguing that behind all Weber's scientific analyses, behind all his researches into universal history, stands an existential question: what does this process of rationalisation signify for our humanity? 'How, under the conditions of increasing . . . bureaucratisation, of the scientific disenchantment of the world, are human freedom, responsible action and meaningful existence possible?'[83] Abramowski accepts with Löwith that it was only from a value standpoint, that of 'the freedom of independent decision and action for the individual', that this process of rationalisation took its significance for Weber.[84]

The attraction of this approach is that it appears to provide a way of treating Weber's academic and political writings together, which can find justification in terms of Weber's own methodology.

On this view knowledge of Weber's political values is not merely interesting additional information, but integral to understanding the existential purpose of his academic work. However, it must be questioned how far the interpretation of Weber's methodological position which underlies this approach is in fact correct. Although the issues raised here are too complex to be dealt with satisfactorily in a brief space, one simple point can be emphasised. It is true that, for Weber, knowledge in the sphere of the 'cultural' sciences had to meet a criterion of significance as well as of validity, and that this significance was determined by 'the values which dominate the investigator and his age.'[85] But it does not follow from this that the significance of Weber's academic work is to be found in his own *personal* hierarchy of values. In his article on 'Objectivity' Weber identified a spectrum of value significance, from an interest in a family chronicle at one extreme to 'the greatest cultural phenomena, common to a nation and mankind over long epochs,' at the other.[86] The characteristic of his own work was that he was concerned with the latter kind (capitalism, bureaucracy, etc), that is with phenomena to which his own society as a whole attached significance, and not merely a contemporary or transient significance, but a *universal* one.[87] The fact that he drew sharply articulated conclusions from these phenomena for his own value standpoint in his political speeches, and even in asides in his academic writing, does not entitle us to conclude that these personal judgements defined the real significance of his academic work.[88]

What holds for the subjects of Weber's work, applies also to the concepts in terms of which he treated them. Abramowski is right to say that the concept of 'rationalisation' formed a central preoccupation of Weber's work. But it is not true, as he claims, that it gained its 'real significance' from the problem it posed to human freedom.[89] For Weber, the concept of rationalisation defined a constitutive element of modern society in contrast with traditional societies, and thus had a significance which transcended the particular value orientation of the individual sociologist. Indeed, in the preface to the first volume of the *Grundriss der Sozialökonomik*, of which Weber's own *Economy and Society* formed but a part, he was explicit that, despite the variety of value standpoints and methodological positions of the different contributors, they were united in the view that 'the development of economic activity must be conceived before all else as a special manifestation of the universal rationalisation of life.'[90] One can only be sceptical therefore of attempts to treat Weber's academic work from within the framework of his own personal political values. There is no doubt that Löwith and Abramowski provide illuminating insights into Weber's conception of his own society; but at the same time they offer a less than adequate account of his academic work and its purposes.[91]

As can be seen, attempts to draw connections between Weber's political situation and values on the one hand, and his academic sociology on the other, tend to prove unsatisfactory. This is because they are based on inadequate methodological premises. Either, as in the case of Steding, they fail to specify how a knowledge about the origins of a writer's work can provide a test for the adequacy of its conclusions. Or else, as in the case of Lukacs, they make assumptions about the intentions of Weber's academic work which far outrun any evidence. Or else, finally, as in the case of Löwith and Abramowski, their argument rests on a mistaken interpretation of Weber's method and his concept of 'value relevance'. The result is thus to reduce Weber's work to a specious unity, which does justice neither to the variety of his academic purposes, nor to the complexity of his value position.

This is not to deny that such approaches can produce useful insights. It is a contention of the present study that the question of the relationship between Weber's political writings and his academic sociology is an important one, and that significant features of the latter can be shown to be 'ideological'. But the duty of the critic who seeks to characterise aspects of Weber's work in this way is to be thoroughly explicit about what he is claiming by doing so, and his methodological justification for claiming it. To adapt a phrase of Weber's, such a judgement is only acceptable if it forms the conclusion, and not the starting point, of analysis.

The starting point must be the recognition that, at any rate after his early period, Weber drew a self-conscious distinction between doing science and engaging in political propaganda, between his academic and political roles. Any account of Weber's work which is to make sense must at least begin by taking this distinction seriously. This means that the point of his political writings is to be sought in a political context, and that of his sociology, in the first instance at least, within a particular scientific tradition. Only in this way can a clear understanding be gained of each. If it is misleading to look for the key to Weber's academic work in his bourgeois political standpoint, it is equally misleading to treat his political writings as a kind of preliminary to the achievements of his systematic sociology.

The present study will therefore seek to maintain a clear distinction between Weber's scientific and non-scientific work, on the assumption that each is to be considered on its own terms. The main part of the book will explore systematically the conception of modern society and politics that is to be found in his political writings. Material from *Economy and Society* used here will be mainly for the purpose of conceptual clarification only. When, however, this account of Weber's political theory has been given, the final chapter will return to the question of its relationship to his academic sociology. On the one hand, a contrast will be drawn between the questions, content and methods of analysis in the two types of writing, which will help to clarify what kind of activity Weber understood social science to involve. On the other hand, a number of features in his academic sociology will be identified which acted as a support to his political standpoint, and these will be examined to see in what sense they can be characterised as 'ideological'.

This must wait till the end. The first task is to gain a clear understanding of Weber's social and political values, since these will provide a framework for the discussion of his political theory. This will form the subject of the following chapter.

REFERENCES

1 Marianne Weber, *Ein Lebensbild* (Tübingen, 1926), hereafter cited as *Lebensbild*.
2 ibid, pp 173–6. *Jugendbriefe*, p 326.
3 *Lebensbild*, pp 236–7, 566–7, 652–6.
4 ibid, p 656.
5 The letter is published in B B Frye, 'A letter from Max Weber', *Journal of Modern History*, vol 39 (1967), pp 124–5.
6 W J Mommsen, *Max Weber und die deutsche Politik, 1890–1920* (Tübingen, 1959).
7 Examples are the critiques of Mommsen by R Bendix, P Honigsheim and K Loewenstein in *Kölner Zeitschrift für Soziologie und Sozialpsychologie*, vol 13 (1961), pp 258–89.
8 O Stammer, ed, *Max Weber und die Soziologie heute* (Tübingen, 1965), pp 103–56. English translation *Max Weber and Sociology Today* (Oxford, 1971), pp 83–132.
9 GPS, p 494; GM, p 78.
10 J P Mayer, *Max Weber and German Politics*, 2nd edn (London, 1956). I Dronberger, *The Political Thought of Max Weber* (New York, 1971).
11 The main study was 'Die Verhältnisse der Landarbeiter im ostelbischen Deutschland', *Schriften des Vereins für Sozialpolitik*, vol 55 (1892). Weber's report to the Verein meeting is in vol 58 (1893), pp 62–86, 128–33; also GASW, pp 444–69. *Lebensbild*, p 136, tells of the impression the monograph made. It was supplemented by a further study for the Protestant Social Congress, reported in *Christliche Welt*, vol 7 (1893),

cols 535–40. For an account in English see V K Dibble, 'Social Science and Political Commitments in the Young Max Weber', *Archives Européennes de Sociologie*, vol 9 (1968), pp 92–110; also R Bendix, *Max Weber* (New York, 1962), ch 2.

12 'Die Erhebung des Vereins für Sozialpolitik über die Lage der Landarbeiter', *Das Land*, vol 1 (1893); 'Entwicklungstendenzen in der Lage der ostelbischen Landarbeiter', *Preussischer Jahrbücher*, vol 77 (1894), pp 437–73, reprinted in GASW, 470–507.

13 *Verhandlungen des 5. Evangelisch-sozialen Kongresses* (1894), pp 61–82, 92–4.

14 'Der Nationalstaat und die Volkswirtschaftspolitik', GPS, pp 1–25.

15 *Jugendbriefe*, pp 273, 298; *Lebensbild*, p 131.

16 A straightforward account of the Verein, with a summary of its debates, is given by its last general secretary, F. Boese, *Geschichte des Vereins für Sozialpolitik, 1872–1932* (Berlin, 1939). For the recent study by Dieter Lindenlaub, see page 19 and n 22 below. The nearest to an account in English is J J Sheelan, *The Career of Lujo Brentano* (Chicago, 1966).

17 R Luxemburg, *Gesammelte Werke*, vol 1, pt 2 (Berlin, 1970), p 388.

18 Boese, op cit, p 254. Schmoller's opening address to the twenty-fifth anniversary meeting of the Verein in 1897 provides a classic statement of its *raison d'être*; it is reprinted in Boese, op cit, pp 253–69.

19 *Lebensbild*, pp 422–30; Boese, op cit, pp 133–7, 145–8. There is a somewhat garbled account in T S Simey, 'Max Weber: Man of Affairs or Theoretical Sociologist', *Sociological Review*, vol 14 (1966), pp 303–27.

20 These are reprinted in GASS, pp 394–430.

21 'Rundschreiben', 15.11.1912 (copy in the Max Weber Institute, Munich); it is published with a commentary in Bernard Schäfer, 'Ein Rundschreiben Max Webers zur Sozialpolitik', *Soziale Welt*, vol 18 (1967), pp 261–71.

22 Dieter Lindenlaub, *Richtungskämpfe im Verein für Sozialpolitik (1890–1914)*, 2 vols (Wiesbaden, 1967).

23 ibid, ch 3, especially pp 85–95, 196–237.

24 ibid, pp 153–5.

25 ibid, pp 272–3.

26 ibid, pp 274–91.

27 GARS, vol 1, p 4. The phrase is in fact a late one. For an analysis of capitalism in Weber's early writings, see page 219. On the basis of these writings Dibble rightly concludes that 'Weber took Marx seriously', and Mommsen arrives at the same judgement. Dibble, op cit, p 99; Mommsen, op cit, p 29. The Marxian influence is much underrated in Guenther Roth, 'The Historical Relationship to Marxism' in R Bendix and G Roth, *Scholarship and Partisanship* (Berkeley, 1971), pp 227–52.

28 *Verhandlungen des Evangelisch-sozialen Kongresses*, 5 (1894), pp 61–82, 92–4; 7 (1896), pp 122–3; 8 (1897), pp 105–13, 122–3; also 'Was heisst Christlich-sozial?', *Christliche Welt*, vol 8 (1894), cols 472–7.

29 *Lebensbild*, pp 139–40.

30 Out of fifty or so members of the Verein mentioned as most important in the 1890s by Lindenlaub (op cit, pp 11–12), twelve were regular attenders at the Congress, and six were on its committee, including Weber. (See appendices to the proceedings mentioned in note 28.)

31 *Lebensbild*, pp 143, 231–6. The contrast between Naumann's reflections on a Christian social programme in 1893 and his national social catechism

of 1897 is a truly remarkable one. Friedrich Naumann, *Gesammelte Werke* (Frankfurt, 1967), vol 5, pp 62–73, 199–233.

32 GPS, pp 26–9.

33 *Lebensbild*, p 235.

34 ibid, p 412. Weber's letters to Naumann are in fact more tentative than this phrase would suggest; see ibid, p 403.

35 GPS, 1st ed (München, 1921), pp 451–8; *Lebensbild*, pp 403–10. Two of the letters appear in E Baumgarten, *Max Weber, Werk und Person* (Tübingen, 1964), pp 485–9.

36 *Lebensbild*, p 235.

37 'Bismarcks Aussenpolitik und die Gegenwart', 'Zur Frage des Friedenschliessens', 'Der Verschärfte U-Bootkrieg', 'Deutschland unter den europäischen Weltmächten', 'Deutschlands äussere und Preussens innere Politik'. GPS, pp 109–86.

38 'Wahlrecht und Demokratie in Deutschland', 'Parlament und Regierung im neugeordneten Deutschland', GPS, pp 231–79, 294–431. Most of the latter is translated in ES, pp 1381–462.

39 *Lebensbild*, pp 599–600.

40 See page 232; also 'Deutschlands künftige Staatsform', GPS, pp 436–71.

41 'Das neue Deutschland', 'Der Reichspräsident', GPS, pp 472–5, 486–9.

42 For America see W J Mommsen, 'Die Vereiningten Staaten von America im politischen Denken Max Webers', *Historische Zeitschrift*, vol 213 (1971).

43 'Zur Lage der bürgerlichen Demokratie in Russland', 'Russlands Übergang zum Scheinkonstitutionalismus', op cit, vol. 22 (1906), Beiheft, pp 234–353 and vol 23 (1906), Beiheft, pp 165–401. (Cf. Ch 2, n 44.) Extracts from the two articles appear in GPS, pp 30–108.

44 'Russlands Übergang zur Scheindemokratie', GPS, pp 192–210.

45 See Chapters 2 and 7.

46 Though a good deal of this is lost, some are preserved in GPS, 1st edn, pp 451–88, while lengthy extracts from others are given in *Lebensbild*. For the rest, I have relied unashamedly on extracts quoted by Mommsen from the Weber 'Nachlass' in Merseburg.

47 Hans Maier, 'Max Weber und die deutsche politische Wissenschaft' in K Engisch, B Pfisten, J Winckelmann, eds, *Max Weber. Gedächtnissschrift* (Berlin, 1966), pp 174–5.

48 A von Schelting, *Max Webers Wissenschaftslehre* (Tübingen, 1934), p 9; cf W Schuchter, *Wertfreiheit und Verantwortungsethik* (Tübingen, 1971), p 32, and H H Bruun, *Science, Values and Politics in Max Weber's Methodology* (Copenhagen, 1972), pp 268–72.

49 See index to GPS, p 585.

50 GPS, pp 533–4; GM, p 115.

51 In a typical passage Weber describes their characteristics as 'absence of "Sachlichkeit", lack of political proportion, deliberate blindness in the face of realities.' GPS, p 258.

52 *Verhandlungen des 5. Evangelisch-sozialen Kongresses* (1894), pp 72–3.

53 GPS, pp 319–20; GASS, pp 498–9.

54 GPS, p 282.

55 'Abandon all hope,' Weber says in the Inaugural Address to those who dream of peace and happiness; cf 'Politics as a Vocation': 'No summer's bloom lies ahead of us, but a polar night of icy darkness.' GPS, pp 12, 547.

56 Max Weber, *Staatssoziologie*, ed J Winckelmann (Berlin, 1956).
57 ibid, Introduction, pp 7–15.
58 ibid, p 11.
59 WG, 2. Halbband, kapitel IX, Abschnitt 8: 'Die rationale Staatsanstalt und die modernen politischen Parteien und Parlamente (Staatssoziologie)'.
60 Winckelmann, ed, *Staatssoziologie*, p 9.
61 GPS, p 436.
62 ibid; cf GPS, p 294.
63 This is the objection Mommsen emphasises most strongly to Winckelmann's strategy. See Mommsen, op cit, pp x–xi.
64 C Steding, *Politik und Wissenschaft bei Max Weber* (Breslau, 1932). A discussion of some of the works mentioned here, though from a political rather than a methodological standpoint, is to be found in G Roth, 'Political Critiques of Max Weber', *American Sociological Review*, vol 30 (1965), pp 213–23; also in R Bendix and G Roth, op cit, pp 55–69.
65 Steding, op cit, p 20.
66 ibid, pp 17–23.
67 ibid, pp 29, 45.
68 ibid, pp 31–4.
69 A Mitzmann, *The Iron Cage* (New York, 1970).
70 See particularly the two articles by W J Mommsen: 'Zum Begriff der "plebiszitären Führerdemokratie" bei Max Weber', *Kölner Zeitschrift für Soziologie und Sozialpsychologie*, vol 15 (1963), pp 295–322; and 'Universalgeschichtliches und politisches Denken bei Max Weber', *Historische Zeitschrift*, vol 201 (1965), pp 557–612.
71 A Giddens, *Politics and Sociology in the Thought of Max Weber* (London, 1972). Giddens is the first writer in English to raise the question discussed here, though the shortness of his work prevents him from engaging the issues at any real depth.
72 An example which takes as its starting point a discussion of the inadequacy of a Weberian concept, and then seeks to account for this in terms of Weber's political context is C von Ferber, *Die Gewalt in der Politik* (Stuttgart, 1970); von Ferber's starting point, however—the place of violence in Weber's account of politics—involves a misinterpretation of Weber. See page 216. Von Ferber explicitly links his inquiry with that of Steding, though not uncritically so: op cit, pp 39–42.
73 G Lukacs, *Die Zerstörung der Vernunft*, Werke, vol 9 (ed Luchterhand), pp 521–37.
74 ibid, p 533.
75 ibid, pp 531, 533. A more recent attempt to locate the problems of Weberian method in the conflicts of capitalist society is W Lefèvre, *Zum historischen Charakter und zur historischen Funktion der Methode bürgerlicher Soziologie* (Frankfurt, 1971).
76 e.g. 'aus gesellschaftlichen und *demzufolge* aus methodologischen Gründen' (my italics). Lukacs, op cit, p 533.
77 K Löwith, 'Max Weber und Karl Marx', *Archiv für Sozialwissenschaft und Sozialpolitik*, vol 67 (1932), pp 53–99, 175–214, partially translated in D Wrong, ed., *Max Weber* (New Jersey, 1970), pp 101–22.
78 G Abramowski, *Das Geschichtsbild Max Webers* (Stuttgart, 1966).
79 See particularly chapter 4 of Abramowski's book, entitled 'Die aktuelle Perspektive und das ethische Motiv der universalhistorischen Forschungen Max Webers', op cit, pp 160–85.

80 Löwith, op cit, pp 77–90.
81 ibid, pp 61–2.
82 The debt to Löwith is an explicit one: Abramowski, op cit, p 10, n 4.
83 ibid, p 14.
84 ibid, p 162.
85 GAW, p 184; MSS, p 84.
86 GAW, p 183; MSS, p 83.
87 Why only in Western civilisation, Weber asks, 'have cultural phenomena appeared which (as at least we like to think) lie in a line of development having *universal* significance and value?', GARS, vol 1, p 1; PE, p 13.
88 An example of such a conclusion in recent English writings is an article by Alan Dawe, who makes out the concept of value relevance to mean the propagation by the sociologist of his own personal values, a conclusion as far as it could be from Weber's purpose: A Dawe, 'The relevance of values', in A Sahay, ed *Max Weber and Modern Sociology* (London, 1971), pp 37–66.
89 Abramowski, op cit, p 184.
90 *Grundriss der Sozialökonomik* (Tübingen, 1914). 1. Abteilung, p vii.
91 Their interpretation also overlooks the development in Weber's later work of a conception of sociology as a generalising science, and begs the question of how far the concept of value relevance, designed to meet the problem of the uniqueness of historical phenomena, is applicable to a science which 'seeks *general* laws of events' (WG, p 9).

Chapter 2

Weber as Protagonist of Bourgeois Values

'After long experience,' Weber wrote to a friend in 1918, '... I am convinced that the individual can only come to know what his own will really is through testing his supposed "ultimate" convictions by his attitude to *thoroughly specific problems*, in which the issues are sharply accentuated.'[1] The present chapter will follow this approach, by looking at examples of Weber's writing on specific problems, as the best means to defining his general political standpoint and values. Three works will be discussed, each typical of a different period of his life. From the early period of the 1890s comes the Inaugural Address at Freiburg, 'Economic Policy and the Nation State,' which combines a summary of Weber's researches on the conditions of East Prussian agriculture with an expression of his nationalist conviction typical of this time. Second will be considered the two extended articles he wrote on the Russian revolution of 1905–6. These belong to the new phase of his writing after his illness, and are representative of the more universalist character of his outlook in this period, expressed in his concern with the problem of freedom in an increasingly rationalised world. Third is the most substantial example of his wartime polemics, 'Parliament and Government in a Reconstructed Germany,' which is again typical of its period in his return to a preoccupation with the problems of German politics, and in the greater emphasis given to the analysis of political institutions. After a brief summary of each of these works, their wider significance will be discussed. In this way it is hoped to provide a representative view of Weber's political values, as well as some idea of the development in his thinking.

ECONOMIC CHANGE AND THE NATIONAL INTEREST

The Freiburg Inaugural Address is the most important statement of

Weber's political ideas in his early period.[2] It begins with a brief summary of his main findings on agricultural conditions in East Prussia. Weber wrote numerous different accounts of these findings, all with slightly different emphases, but the situation he found was broadly as follows.[3] The recent intensification of international market competition had threatened the economy of the large estates in East Prussia, particularly those on poor soil, and accelerated the introduction of mechanisation and of crops such as sugar beet which could be cultivated intensively. Instead of a feudal patriarch the landowner became a capitalist entrepreneur.[4] The agricultural worker changed correspondingly from a tied cottager, who shared in the produce of the harvest and thus had a common interest with the landowner, to a 'potato-eating proletarian' whose interests were in direct conflict with those of his employer.[5] The introduction of capitalism brought not only class conflict, but also competition among the workers themselves. It was generally cheaper for the landowner to import Polish casual labourers for the summer season than to employ German workers who had to be paid all the year round. The result was a large-scale emigration of German workers to the towns or abroad, particularly of the more enterprising, who saw no chance of achieving economic independence under existing conditions. In some of his accounts, particularly to the Protestant Social Congress, Weber emphasised the more positive aspects of this process: the 'deep-felt' desire of the German worker for freedom from his traditional subservience.[6] In the Inaugural Address, however, it was the displacement of Germans by Polish immigrants that he concentrated on.[7] The competition among the workers, introduced by capitalism, favoured those whose standard of living and expectations were lower. The same was also true in the independent smallholdings, as well as on the large estates. The German small-holders, who produced for the market, were unable to make the best use of the land in the circumstances of increased competition, and were replaced by Polish peasants who operated a subsistence economy. In each case, that of labourers and of independent farmers, the process of economic development favoured the Poles precisely because their economic needs were lower than their German counterparts, because they represented a 'less developed cultural type'.[8]

From this situation Weber drew a number of general conclusions in his Inaugural Address. First was to question the assumption that economic development could serve as a self-evident goal for economic policy.[9] Economic development could produce the triumph of an inferior type of man. The Poles were able to survive, and drive out the Germans, because their standard of living, their economic and cultural demands, were lower than those of their German counterparts. What happened was the survival of the *un*fittest. This threatened the basis of German culture in the east, and the national security of the eastern frontier. Such a threat could only be overcome and the 'Slavic flood stemmed' by a policy of state support for the re-colonisation of German farmers, and by closing the eastern frontier.[10] However, it was not so much the specific remedy as the general lesson that Weber was concerned to develop in his Address. This was that the maximisation of production could never serve as the unquestioned goal for economic policy, but must be subordinate to national and cultural values. Weber poured scorn on the 'Endaimonisten', who believed that economic development would effortlessly produce a general increase in happiness. What such people overlooked was the universality of conflict and struggle, between groups and between nations, which economic development only intensified, as the situation on the eastern frontier showed. In such a context of struggle, the promotion of German national and cultural values was all-important. So, he concludes this section of the Address, the goal of German economic policy as well as the standards of German economic theory could only be national, German ones. 'The science of economic policy is a *political* science; it is the servant of politics . . . of the long-term great power interests of the nation.'[11]

If one consequence of the economic situation in the east was the threat to German culture and national interests, a second was the crisis of political leadership brought about by the economic decline of the Junkers, and the movement of the centre of economic power from the rural estates to the towns.[12] The Junkers were an economically declining class, and such a class could not provide strong national leadership since they were primarily concerned to use their political power to bolster up their declining economic position. 'They have performed their task,' said Weber, 'and now lie in an economic struggle to the death, from which no economic policy on the part of the state can restore them to their traditional social character.'[13] However, although economic power had passed to the towns, the bourgeoisie were politically immature and uneducated. One of the chief reasons for this was the dominance exercised by Bismarck. Bismarck had stifled all political talent, and the bourgeoisie had become accustomed to having a great man take the initiative. As a result they had had no chance to develop politically.[14] Germany was thus in the position where a declining class wielded political power in its own narrowly conceived interest, whereas the economically developing class was unfitted for wielding political power at all. Weber summarised the position succinctly:

> It is dangerous ... when an economically declining class holds political power. But it is even more dangerous when classes, to whom economic power and with it the expectation of political supremacy are passing, are politically too immature to take on the leadership of the state. Both these threaten Germany at the moment, and this is the key to our present dangers.[15]

The crucial question was how the bourgeoisie could become fit to rule. At least part of the answer lay, according to Weber, in political education; and what more worth-while task could there be for a national economist than that?

> For the immediate future one thing stands out: there is a huge task of *political* education to be accomplished. No more serious duty faces us than ... to play our part in the work of educating the nation *politically*, which must remain the final goal of our science.[16]

Weber's Inaugural Address has been dismissed by some critics as a youthful excess. It is true that some views were expressed here with a crudity not found later, and others came to be substantially modified, most notably Weber's assertion of the subordination of economic science to political goals.[17] Yet even on the question of value freedom there were seeds of his mature doctrine here in his repeated insistence that the mere fact of economic development could not provide any self-evident value or standard, whether for practical policy or for science; values could not be deduced from facts.[18] And in general the Address expresses attitudes which are repeated in Weber's mature works, and can be regarded as characteristic of his political thought. The most important of these will be considered briefly.

Most obviously typical of the attitudes expressed in the Address is its explicit affirmation of Germany's national interest as the decisive value for political and economic policy. This was affirmed repeatedly by Weber in his later life. In a speech in 1909 he said: 'Many of us take the view that the ultimate definitive value ... is the power position of a nation in the world.'[19] And again in 1916 he wrote that he had 'always viewed policy from a national stand-point alone.'[20] As will be explored in a later chapter, Weber's nationalism was more complex than has frequently been made out by critics. A central part of it was his commitment to the value of 'Kultur', the cultural uniqueness embodied in national communities in general and the German nation in particular, which could only be protected under modern conditions by means of the power state. At the same time there was an important economic element. The pressure on land and resources brought about by the growth of population and industrial development—the 'harsh gravity of the population problem', as he called it in the Address[21] —made the assertion of national economic self-interest paramount. Germany, in particular, now that national unification had set her firmly in the arena of the great powers, could not opt out of the international struggle. To do so, as he said in the Address, would be to make a mockery of German unification. It was the fate of his generation to live under the shadow of the great generation who had established the Reich, to be 'Epigoni', mere descendants of the great. At least they should see to it that the achievements of their predecessors did not mark the end of German history, but rather the beginning.[22] Thus the protection of German culture (particularly against the Slavs), the assertion of economic self-interest, the satisfaction of a new generation's honour and responsibility to the future, all formed part of the nationalism expressed in the Inaugural Address. Chapter 5 will show how far this mellowed, particularly after Weber's Russian studies had awakened him to the problem of national minorities. Nevertheless, nationalism in some form was to remain central among his political values.

A second theme of the Inaugural Address, equally typical, was its criticism of the absence in Germany of any political leadership which could give adequate expression to her national purpose and promote it effectively. Emphasis on the central importance of political leadership was a constant preoccupation of Weber's political writings, as much in his later as his earlier period. Throughout he was convinced that such leadership could only come from a strong economic class—the bourgeoisie. If, however, a strong economic class was a necessary condition for political leadership, it was not a sufficient one; it required also political capacity and political consciousness. 'We forget,' said Weber in the Address, 'that economic power and a calling for political leadership of the nation do not necessarily coincide'.[23] How to instill a political consciousness in the bourgeoisie and wean them from habits of political subservience remained a constant question of German politics for Weber. It was a question he answered differently in different periods. In his early writing the answer lay in calls for political education and in the development of a vigorous bourgeois democratic party as a means to this;[24] in the wartime period his attention concentrated on the reform of political institutions, particularly of the subordinate position of Parliament, to encourage qualities of political will and responsibility.[25] In each case the role of class remained indispensable in providing the social basis and support for political leadership.

If a commitment to national values and to the importance of political leadership form the main political themes of the Inaugural Address, the speech is also important for the explicitness with which it gives expression to certain more general assumptions central to Weber's conception of society. The most important of these is the theme that struggle and conflict form a central and permanent feature of social life—struggle between groups, classes, nations, as well as the conflict between differing values. Even where such a conflict is not apparent, it is still going on under the surface. 'There is no peace in the economic struggle for existence', says Weber in the Address, 'only . . . the illusion of peace'.[26] A similar statement from one of his last writings demonstrates the continuity of this theme: 'Conflict cannot be excluded from social life . . . "peace" is nothing more than a change in the character of conflict.'[27]

The Inaugural Address demonstrates clearly the conclusions Weber derived from this fact of struggle and conflict both for empirical analysis and for political values. As to the first, a central feature in the analysis of social structures became the question of what qualities, what types of individual were selected out by the particular character of the conflict taking place within these structures. How did they so shape the character of struggle that they brought certain qualities to supremacy at the expense of others? This concept of 'Auslese' (selection) reappears as a central feature in nearly all Weber's writings on contemporary society. Thus one theme of his studies on East Prussia was how the terms of economic conflict favoured a particular cultural type, the Polish seasonal worker, at the expense of the Germans.[28] The theme of the massive study he supervised for the Verein in 1907–9 on conditions in large-scale industry, indeed its explicit title, was what particular psycho-physical qualities and types of worker were 'selected' by the conditions and pressures of modern factory life.[29] The theme of two of the major projects he outlined to the first meeting of the German Sociological Society in 1910—systematic studies of voluntary associations and of elites—centred on the process whereby certain qualities came to be selected and reinforced by the character of the association or the requirements of the elite role.[30] In the political sphere, also, Weber was concerned with the qualities and types of politician selected by different kinds of political system.[31]

This emphasis on the process of selection through conflict and competition, whether open or concealed, not only provided a focus for empirical analysis; Weber also derived conclusions from it for the sphere of values, as the Inaugural Address shows. Recognition of the inevitability of conflict ruled out certain kinds of value position as untenable. If values themselves were in irreducible conflict, then those who believed that all good things could somehow coincide in some future Utopia and refused to admit the necessity for choices between them, were too naïve to be taken seriously. More specifically, the inevitability of conflict between groups and individuals ruled out that range of ideals for mankind in which peace and happiness formed a substantial part; such ideals could only be illusory, because they were based on a false conception of reality. 'For the dreamers of peace and happiness', said Weber, 'there stands written over the door of mankind's unknown future "surrender all hope".'[32]

However, in the process of seeking to shatter such illusions, Weber's position showed a subtle shift from regarding conflict as simply a fact of life against which the ideals and values of others should be tested for their realism, to regarding it as something to be positively welcomed, even encouraged. This is implicit in the tone of the Inaugural Address, but is made much more explicit in a speech Weber made to the Protestant Social Congress, also on the problems of East Prussia. Here he expanded on his proposed policy of re-colonisation, which he admitted could only promise German farmers at best a hard struggle to maintain their livelihood. Was this a brutal policy? he asked. They were not involved in 'Sozialpolitik' to increase human happiness:

> Our aim is . . . so to create conditions, not that men may feel happier, but that under the necessity of the unavoidable struggle for existence the best in them—those physical and spiritual characteristics which we want to preserve for the nation—will remain protected.[33]

Here conditions of struggle were to be welcomed because they fostered qualities of independence that Weber regarded as desirable. Indeed, for Weber the highest values could only be developed through conflict—conflict with other individuals, or with other values, or 'struggle against the difficulties which life presents'.[34]

It was partly in such terms that he justified the risk-taking activity
of the entrepreneur in a context of market competition, in contrast to the bureaucratic 'order' of a planned economy, and a social
policy which puts the emphasis on extending the effective rights
of trade unions to pursue improvements for themselves, in preference to a paternalist system of industrial relations and welfare
provision.[35]

It should be said that the concept of 'Kampf' was one of the
least specific of Weber's concepts, ranging from open conflict
between people to an unconscious process of selection within
social structures. In the section devoted to the term in *Economy
and Society*, written at the end of his life, Weber was much more
careful than in the Inaugural Address to distinguish between the
different types of 'Kampf', and their widely differing significance.[36]
Although he uses the concept more indiscriminately in his political
writings, it is mistaken to call his position a Social Darwinist one,
as is often done.[37] First, even in the Inaugural Address Weber
explicitly rejected as metaphysical any belief in the survival
of *superior* types in the process of historical development. It was
precisely the higher cultural types who might be least adapted to
new environmental circumstances and social arrangements.[38]
The concept of 'selection' provided Weber with a perspective and
a tool for analysis, rather than with a dogma. Secondly, his belief
in the value of struggle and competition was nowhere related to a
theory of the transmission of favourable characteristics through
heredity. The personal qualities developed by such conditions
were sufficient justification in themselves.

Thus a heightened awareness of 'selection' at work within social
processes, and a readiness to ascribe value to struggle and conflict
(albeit within limits not clearly defined) formed central aspects of
Weber's social outlook, and the Inaugural Address is typical of
these. This brings us to a final point about his political values for
which the Address provides evidence, and that is their non-
materialist character. For Weber it was non-material values that
were important, as opposed to 'bread and butter' questions. Not
that he underestimated the practical significance of the latter.
But such questions should not form the end of politics. Hence his
insistence on German cultural values in face of the assumption
that the maximisation of production formed a self-evident goal;
and his conviction that the end of 'Sozialpolitik' could never be
merely improving the material position of the working class,
but the 'development of those characteristics . . . which make for
human greatness'.[39] 'It is what seems to us valuable in man',

he told the Protestant Social Congress, 'that we seek to protect: personal responsibility, the deep aspiration for the moral and spiritual goods of mankind . . .'[40]—qualities whose possession Weber argued was in inverse proportion to 'a subjective feeling of happiness'. Politics for Weber was a sphere for the assertion and pursuit of non-material values. While the attainment of power and the satisfaction of material interests were necessary means for the politician, they should not form ends in themselves; the true politician was one who committed himself to a cause.[41] The problem of how such a conception of the politician could be realised in practice will be considered in later chapters. For the present we shall turn to look at a different order of values from those expressed in the Inaugural Address, that of freedom.

FREEDOM AND THE RUSSIAN REVOLUTION

The tone of all Weber's writings of the 1890s was one of self-confidence, of self-assertiveness. Although he set out to shatter illusions, and in this sense called himself a pessimist,[42] the illusions were not his own, but those of his fellow members of the Verein für Sozialpolitik and the Protestant Social Congress. In contrast, the character of the writings of the new phase after his illness is very different. Not only is the perspective more universal—it is not Germany that is the theme, but modern society in general; not capitalism as it affected Germany's political structure and standing as a world power, but capitalism as a universal institution—his outlook also is much less self-confident, more genuinely pessimistic. His own ideals had now come up against the limitations of empirical reality. This is particularly apparent in the theme which occurs in one form or another in most of his writings and speeches in the years 1904–10, that of the decline of human freedom in the face of the increasing rationalisation of life, and the bureaucratisation of economic and political structures. It would be wrong to suggest that all Weber's writing in this period was 'really' about this theme. But the fact that it occurs, even by way of digression, in works as diverse as those on the 'Protestant Ethic' and the 'Agricultural Conditions in the Ancient World' is evidence that it was a constant preoccupation.

The theme of freedom was dealt with most explicitly in Weber's writings on the Russian revolution of 1905–6. In her biography Marianne Weber describes the impact the revolution made on her husband. He learnt Russian so that he could read reports of

the happenings in the Russian newspapers, and he 'followed the
. . . drama for months on end in breathless excitement'.[43] The two
articles he wrote for the *Archiv für Sozialpolitik und Sozialwissenschaft*,[44] intended initially as a review of literature, developed into
his most substantial work on politics in this period. They contain
a great deal of detailed analysis of the Russian social structure and
the course of the political conflict, which will be discussed in a
later chapter in the context of Weber's theory of the relationship
between society and state. What is of interest here is their underlying theme, the question of what were the chances for freedom
in Russia, and in modern society more generally. Only the main
outline of Weber's answer will be sketched in here.

The question which forms the main theme of Weber's analysis,
particularly in his first article ('The Outlook for Bourgeois
Democracy in Russia'), was what social forces existed in Russia
which could act as a vehicle and support for the various liberal
programmes being put forward.[45] Weber's assumption was that
the ideological movement to establish personal and civil liberties
and constitutional government was insufficient to make headway on
its own, unless it could harness important social interests in its
cause. But what were these social interests? Weber's conclusion
was pessimistic. Of the 'historical' institutions of Russia, the
Church hierarchy formed one of the main social supports of
absolutism, despite the existence of liberal elements among the
clergy. Any threat to the Tsar was also a threat to its own hierarchy.[46] The other 'historical' force, the peasantry, was not interested in any reforms going beyond the redistribution of land.
It would support a revolution only to the point where its hunger for
land was satisfied, and no further.[47] Even this much, involving
a reform of the land system, could only be achieved with a measure
of dictatorial imposition, such was the conflict of interests among
the peasants themselves.[48] If the historical institutions of Russian
society thus promised little real support for liberalism, the outlook
from its more modern social forces was no brighter. Of these,
capitalism, having been 'superimposed in its most advanced
form' on top of an 'archaic peasant communism', received direct
encouragement from the state, and was able to satisfy its needs
through direct liaison with the Tsarist bureaucracy.[44] The urban
proletariat, on the other hand, had been recruited into a social
democratic movement of a particularly authoritarian temper;
they were drilled by their leaders 'into a spiritual parade march'
altogether foreign to liberal ideas or practice.[50] None of these
forces, therefore, offered any permanent support for liberalism

as such, whatever temporary alliance they might form in opposition to Tsarist repression.

This pessimistic analysis led Weber to reflect on the unique constellation of factors which had given rise to European liberalism, factors which were not present in Russia and which were no longer repeatable. This passage is worth quoting at some length:

> The historical development of modern 'freedom' presupposed a unique and unrepeatable constellation of factors, of which the following are the most important: first, overseas expansion ... secondly, the characteristic economic and social structure of the 'early capitalist' period in Western Europe; thirdly, the conquest of life through science ... finally, certain ideal conceptions which grew out of the concrete historical uniqueness of a particular religious viewpoint, and which, working together with numerous unique political circumstances and the material preconditions mentioned above, combined to fashion the 'ethical' and 'cultural' character of modern man. The question, whether any process of material development, in particular that of present-day advanced capitalism, could of itself maintain these unique historical circumstances in being or even create them anew, has only to be asked for the answer to be obvious.[51]

A central feature of Weber's analysis here was the observation that modern advanced capitalism was a completely different creature from the early capitalism described, for example, in *The Protestant Ethic and the Spirit of Capitalism*. It was increasingly subject to that outward rationalisation of life whose development it had helped initially to promote. Modern production was typically standardised, cartellised, bureaucratised production. Such a development left little scope for economic individualism, nor did it share any particular relationship with liberalism in the area of politics:

> All the *economic* weather signs point in the direction of increasing 'unfreedom'. It is ridiculous in the extreme to ascribe to modern high capitalism, as currently being imported into Russia ... any inner affinity with 'democracy' or even 'freedom' (in *any* sense of the word). The question is rather 'How are any of these at all possible in the long run under its domination?'[52]

Weber's conclusion about the chances for the freedom movement in Russia was thus a pessimistic one. A society which had not achieved a tradition of liberalism before the arrival of the modern rationalised form of capitalism, had only a slim chance of developing it then. In missing the moment in history when a unique series of factors combined to provide the impetus for liberal ideas, it had conceivably missed it for good. 'All the forms of development are excluded which in the West put the strong *economic* interests of the possessing classes in the service of the movement for bourgeois liberty . . . Never has a struggle for freedom been carried out under such difficult circumstances.'[53] Weber could only express his admiration for an attempt which seemed so doomed to failure.

Though the subject of Weber's articles was specifically Russia, with its peculiar social structure and history, yet he clearly regarded his analysis as having a wider significance for modern society in general. Even for societies which had an established tradition of liberalism, the increasing rationalisation of the external conditions of life was progressively eliminating the social structures and areas of independent action which could support that tradition. 'We are individualists *against* the stream of material constellations . . .' wrote Weber in his first article.[54] This sounds defiant, but it is also touched with pessimism, as many references in other works of this period show. At the end of *The Protestant Ethic and the Spirit of Capitalism* Weber turns aside from his main theme to contrast the free spirit of the early capitalists with the 'iron cage' of modern industrial life, in which material goods have 'achieved an inexorable power over the lives of men'.[55] In his studies on 'Agriculture in the Ancient World' (somewhat misleadingly titled), the total bureaucratisation of life which was a central feature of ancient Egypt and the late Roman Empire is used as an explicit paradigm for the unfreedom progressively developing in the modern world, 'only on a technically more perfect basis'. Such unfreedom would be at its extreme in a society in which all independent sources of economic activity were removed through the expropriation of private capitalism by the state.[56] This is also the theme of Weber's speech to the Verein meeting in 1909, in which he depicts a time not far distant when every worker would be simply a small cog in the vast bureaucratic machinery, his only interest being how to become a bigger cog. 'The central question', said Weber, 'is what we can *oppose* to this machinery, so as to keep a portion of humanity free from this parcelling out of the soul'.[57] This concern with the diminution of freedom in face of the rationalisation of life was thus a constant preoccupation in this period, and the conclusions he drew were largely pessimistic.

We need to be clear, however, about precisely what Weber meant by 'freedom'. At least three different concepts can be distinguished in his writings. First, there is economic individualism: the possession of an independent sphere of activity, guaranteed by private property, over which the individual is master.[58] Secondly, there are civil and political freedoms: guaranteed rights for the individual and the constitutional rule of law.[59] Thirdly, there is a more internal concept of personal autonomy or responsibility, the capacity not to 'let life run on as a natural event' but to treat it 'as a series of ultimate decisions in which the soul . . . chooses the meaning of its own existence'.[60] Of the three, it was particularly the first that Weber saw as being progressively eliminated in modern society, with the expropriation of the small producer. Of course he exaggerated even this; he himself was well aware of the scope which still remained within industry, and even more within agriculture, for individualism of the old kind. It was one of his frequent assertions that the desire for economic independence on the part of the German peasant and small farmer made him unavailable for socialism, and that most socialists failed to perceive the difference in mentality between the urban and the rural worker.[61] Equally there remained a scope for entrepreneurial skills and the exercise of individual responsibility in even the largest economic concerns. Nevertheless the trend against economic individualism was clearly established, and its analysis is a characteristic Weberian theme.

The diminution of one kind of freedom, however, did not necessarily rule out all others as well. Though historically connected with economic individualism, other kinds of freedom might still survive, if with difficulty, under the progressive rationalisation of the outward circumstances of life. In respect to Weber's concept of personal autonomy, Karl Löwith has shown how Weber believed it possible to preserve individual freedom and responsibility, 'amid and in spite of the inescapably compartmentalised humanity' of modern life, by insisting on a tension 'between man and specialized man'—the difference between the routine performance of a role, and the capacity to affirm oneself in it while also recognising its limitations.[62] How far, though, Weber believed such a consciousness to be available to the average official in a bureaucratic organisation, is open to question. In his 'Rundschreiben' on social policy he argued that their conditions of work threatened their 'personal development' even more than those of the manual worker, and created a stratum of men 'altogether lacking in spiritual independence'.[63]

. As to the political freedoms, which concern us more here, Weber believed that to establish them initially without the support of a strongly individualist society, as the Russian example showed, was more difficult than to sustain them once firmly established. Political freedoms were still possible in modern society, and Weber was clear about what was necessary to sustain them: strong Parliamentary institutions and the existence of competing sources of power within society, particularly as between bureaucracies of the state and private industry.[64] While the process of bureaucratisation itself, in politics as in industry, spelt an end to individualism, to maintain a tension between a number of bureaucracies was a necessary condition for civil and political freedom. Although, as we shall see, Weber provides evidence to question whether this condition was in fact a sufficient one, it is mistaken to interpret him as saying that, because individualism was in decline, all forms of freedom must vanish with it. The situation, as he himself analysed it, was more complex than this.

In his writings on the Russian revolution Weber demonstrated a similar capacity to that shown in his writing on East Prussian agriculture, of bringing out the general significance of a particular phenomenon by setting it in a wider context and showing its relationship to a clearly articulated set of values. Weber penetrated beneath the conditions of agricultural labourers in East Prussia to reveal a political crisis facing the nation, and beneath the Russian revolution to demonstrate the dilemma of liberalism in modern society. In this sense he was always a strongly theoretical writer, even when dealing with apparently localised phenomena. What is important to emphasise here, however, is that, while showing a similar theoretical depth, the works from the two different periods embody different values and concerns. In the earlier period it was an exclusively German problem that concerned Weber and it was viewed from a strongly nationalist perspective. In the later period it was the more universal problem of freedom in a rationalised society. This is not to say that the question of freedom did not appear in Weber's earlier writings. It is a matter of emphasis. The writings on Russia are typical of a widened perspective, and of a range of concerns that is easy to underestimate, if one seeks to give an account of Weber's political values from a narrow concentration on his German writings alone. It is to these latter, however, that we shall turn for the last example discussed in this chapter.

BUREAUCRACY AND POLITICAL LEADERSHIP IN WARTIME GERMANY

Weber's wartime writings mark a return to the mood of the 1890s and the Inaugural Address. They contain a similar vigorous affirmation of national values, and express a similar sense of urgency at the absence of political leadership and the resulting damage to the nation in the arena of international conflict. However, the problem is now analysed differently, with much greater emphasis on the obstacles to leadership presented by defective political institutions. This emphasis on institutions in fact dates back to 1907, when Weber insisted in correspondence with Friedrich Naumann that it was not persons but institutions that were responsible for the erratic course of German policy.[65] Yet the theme was only fully developed in his wartime writings. In these he showed his attitude to political institutions to be a purely instrumental one; forms of constitution held no intrinsic value in themselves, but were to be judged solely for their effectiveness in serving ends external to them.[66] Indeed, Weber expressed some regret at having to spend time discussing 'technical' questions of constitutional reform, instead of the great cultural issues confronting the nation.[67] But the history of the previous forty years had shown that the main obstacle to the effective promotion of Germany's national and cultural goals had been her defective system of government. The analysis of political institutions therefore took on an urgency and significance it did not normally merit. Once having committed himself to their analysis, Weber did so with his usual thoroughness and with a typically theoretical emphasis. The writings of this period develop what amounts to a theory of political institutions, in particular of their effect on the character of political activity and leadership. The most substantial of these writings is the series of articles Weber wrote for the *Frankfurter Zeitung* in 1917, later reworked and published as a single pamphlet in 1918, under the title 'Parliament and Government in a Reconstructed Germany'.[68] Its main themes will be briefly summarised here.

The main theme of this work is that modern government is inevitably government by means of a bureaucracy; administration is in the hands of an expert, salaried, career officialdom. But without the *political* leadership capable of controlling this administration, all political decision making falls into their hands; it becomes government *by*, and not merely *through*, bureaucracy. This had happened to Germany. Although Germany was in theory a monarchical system, in practice the monarch was merely a dilettante in face of the expertise of modern officialdom, and could not be otherwise. A properly political leadership could only exist where there were the appropriate institutions, most important of which was a strong Parliament. Through lack of such institutions Germany suffered from government by bureaucracy, with pernicious results particularly for her international position and for the vigour and consistency of her foreign policy.

As in the Inaugural Address, the source of the trouble was traced back to Bismarck.[69] But now it was not merely that the dominating influence of the great man had encouraged habits of subservience. The political structure he left behind perpetuated this lack of political leadership. The crux of the problem was the weak constitutional position of Parliament.[70] Under the German Constitution the government was neither chosen from the Reichstag nor responsible to it. There was the additional disability that if a party leader was appointed to a ministry, he had to surrender his seat in the Reichstag, and so cut himself off from his political power base in the support of the electorate. When there was added to this a general preference for appointing civil servants to ministerial positions, the result was a government of bureaucratic complexion through and through, lacking in political responsibility and political will. This created its own vicious circle: because Parliament had no real power, it did not attract men of calibre or capacity for leadership; those who wanted a field in which to exercise responsibility went elsewhere, for example into business. 'Our so-called monarchical government', wrote Weber, 'when divested of all its fine phrases, means nothing else than a kind of *negative selection*, which diverts all major talents for leadership into the service of capitalist industry.'[71]

Essential to understanding Weber's critique of the German system of government is the distinction he drew between the roles of civil servant and politician, and the different character of their activities and the different qualities required of each.[72] Where the civil servant was typically responsible to a superior, and operated within an ordered hierarchy of command and obedience, the politician or political leader had to take responsibility on himself, and operated within a system of voluntary recruitment of support in conflict with other groups and other points of view. 'The struggle for personal power and the individual responsibility which flows from this power—this is the life-blood of the politician.'[73] The two roles required, and encouraged, quite different qualities. In particular the task of an administrator working to set rules within an ordered hierarchy offered little opportunity for the development of the qualities necessary for political leadership and responsibility, which could only be developed in the political arena of open struggle against opponents. Hence the incapacity for political leadership repeatedly demonstrated by Germany's bureaucratic leaders, which was responsible for, among other things, the catstrophic course of Germany's prewar foreign policy.[74] 'We should have had politicians in control', wrote Weber, 'who would have had to take responsibility before Parliament for their foreign policy, not bureaucrats, who repudiated in private what they declared in public',[75]

The solution required more than merely political education, which is what Weber had advocated in the 1890s; it needed a reform of the whole system of government, so as to encourage the development of leaders capable of exercising political responsibility and of restricting the administrators to their proper role. Such a reform meant in the first instance strengthening the position of Parliament, so that the government became recruited from, and directly answerable to, Parliament.[76] Weber recognised that under conditions of universal suffrage, the position of Prime Minister increasingly resembled that of a President; democracy was evolving in a plebiscitary direction, with the relationship between leader and mass becoming all-important. However, a strong Parliament was necessary as a recruiting ground for such leaders, and to train them in the political skills necessary for office. Only such a reform could render Germany politically capable of pursuing her national aims effectively and conducting an appropriate role in world affairs.

The concluding paragraphs of the work are worth summarising more fully. It was idle to imagine, argued Weber, that changing some clauses of the constitution would suddenly produce political leaders overnight. But it was a prerequisite for this, in removing major obstacles to such leadership. 'A nation which could only produce competent administrators . . . and allowed itself to become subordinate to the uncontrolled rule of officials would be no "Herrenvolk" and would do much better to get on with its everyday affairs than foster pretensions to concerning itself with the fate of the world'.[77] Without internal reform, the war, which was in part a contest to secure Germany's right to have a say in the future of the world along with others, would be rendered senseless. Without it, all Germany would be good for in future was a purely defensive policy, never for 'tasks of world stature'.[78]

The topics covered in 'Parliament and Government' are too many to do justice to in so short a summary. However, enough should have been said to show the continuity between Weber's wartime writings and the early period of the Inaugural Address, as well as the different emphasis in the later work on the reform of

Parliamentary institutions. This later concentration on the institutional basis for the political leader has led some to see a major development in Weber's political theory, away from the earlier concentration on class to an emphasis on individual leadership. Although, as will be discussed below,[79] there are problems about the relationship between class and political leadership in Weber's work, this way of presenting it is an oversimplification. To the end Weber insisted on analysing contemporary politics in class terms. Institutions and individual leaders alike depended upon a social basis of support, which under modern conditions meant class support. Thus a central feature of his analysis of German politics remained the control exercised by the Junkers over the institutions of government, in association with large-scale capitalism.[80] Whatever the historical origins of the weak Parliamentary system it persisted because it served the interests of major social groups. Any strategy for change could therefore not simply be institutional, but was a question of how to detach the 'broad strata of the bourgeoisie'[81] from their acquiescence in the existing structure. Equally, the viability of a different system depended upon the character of their support for it. How central this was in Weber's thinking can be judged from the following typical passage, written in November 1918 in an article in which Weber reviewed a variety of possible constitutional schemes for the future German state:

> Unfortunately, constitutional questions are not unimportant, but naturally they are not the most important thing for politics. Far more decisive for the future of Germany is the question: whether the bourgeoisie as a whole will develop a new readiness for political responsibility and a more self-conscious *political spirit*.[82]

The difference of emphasis thus lies within an underlying continuity. But what of the theme of freedom, which had been so central to the prewar writings? This had become submerged, though not entirely so. In 'Parliament and Government' Weber also justifies a strong Parliament as a guarantor of individual rights and liberties.[83] And the work contains a number of passages reminiscent of prewar themes, for example where he describes bureaucracy as a living machine 'fabricating the cage of bondage which men may one day be forced to inhabit, as powerless as the fellahin of ancient Egypt'.[84] Although this problem was less immediately pressing than the reform of institutions to encourage political leadership, it still remained at the back of Weber's mind, as is shown explicitly in a series of questions he asks at a central point in the work.[85] The onward march of bureaucratisation, he writes, poses a number of questions for political organisation. First of these is, 'How is it . . . possible at all, to preserve *any* element of "individualism" and freedom in face of this powerful onset of bureaucracy?' However, he goes on, this question won't concern us on this occasion, but rather two others: what forces exist capable of exercising some effective control over the bureaucratic machine? and what are the inner limitations of this machine, what is it *not* capable of achieving? Although under the pressures of war the problem of freedom had thus become displaced by more urgent questions, it nevertheless remained firmly on the agenda of inquiry, representing a quite different order of values and concerns.

Thus, though 'Parliament and Government' may appear simply as a return to the concerns of the 1890s, it also contains evidence for a duality of values in Weber's political standpoint, which is one of the themes of this chapter. This duality has led to very different interpretations of Weber, according to which aspect is emphasised. On the one hand there is Weber as presented, for example, by Wolfgang Mommsen's book—the vigorous exponent of German nationalism, eager for the rise of a political leadership capable of extending her power, and ready to subordinate institutional arrangements and even all other values to this end. At its most extreme, this view traces a direct line of descent from Weber to national socialism.[86] On the other hand there is the view put forward by, among others, Christoph Steding, of Weber as the pessimistic liberal, as an exponent of individualism in an increasingly hostile environment, only too conscious of himself as an 'Epigone', a survivor from a previous era, swimming against the current of his times.[87] Put at its extreme, as in Steding's later work,[88] this view sees Weber as a typical representative of the decadent civilisation that national socialism set out to replace.

There is truth in both these views, though Steding ignores the subtlety of Weber's liberalism. More often, in fact, the interpretation of Weber as a liberal is offered as a mark of approval by those who seek to defend him against what they regard as the excesses of Mommsen's approach.[89] Yet on their own these remain only partial accounts, as the material presented in this chapter should make evident. Any account which is to do justice to the complexity of Weber's political standpoint must recognise alike his commitment to German cultural values, his emphasis on leadership in society and his concern for liberty in an increasingly bureaucratised age. These values stood in some tension to one another. Such tension, however, was not unique to Weber, nor to the context of German politics, but was a characteristic feature of a bourgeois political standpoint in the circumstances of capitalist development of his time. This brings us to a central theme of this work: that it is not simply as a propagandist and commentator on German politics, with its unique configuration of problems, that Weber should be understood, but also as having a wider significance as a theorist of bourgeois politics. The final section of the chapter will consider what this means.

WEBER AS A THEORIST OF BOURGEOIS POLITICS

To call Weber in the context of his political writings a bourgeois theorist, a theorist of bourgeois politics, is both to characterise a political position, and to define a problem. Weber was, as he himself frequently asserted, a 'self-conscious' or 'class-conscious' bourgeois.[90] 'I am a member of the bourgeois classes', he said in the Inaugural Address: 'I feel myself as such, and have been brought up in their opinions and ideals'.[91] The values already considered—national, liberal, elitist—were, in the character of their emphasis, bourgeois values, and form an obvious contrast to the collectivist, egalitarian ideals of socialism to which Weber remained opposed throughout his life. At the same time, however, his standpoint did not involve any simple acceptance of capitalism in all its features, much less an identification with the attitudes of the bourgeoisie at any given moment. The problem, therefore, is to clarify what is to be understood by the term 'bourgeois', and what its relationship is to capitalism, particularly to the form of capitalism that was developing in Weber's own time.

The appropriate place to start in considering what is meant by the concept 'bourgeois' is with Weber's own definition. This is to be found most clearly in his writings of the period 1904–6. His works on *The Protestant Ethic* and the Russian revolution respectively defined two different elements in the bourgeois outlook. First of these was the distinctive attitude to work characteristic of the 'spirit of capitalism', and the variety of qualities associated with successful business activity: on the one hand devotion to work as a 'calling', as an end in itself, and an ascetic outlook which imposed its own limitation on material consumption; on the other hand the possession of qualities such as reliability, shrewdness, readiness to take calculated risks, qualities developed in the 'hard school of life' and the struggle of the market.[92] The second set of features which could be defined as distinctively 'bourgeois' were those associated with the concept of individualism: the ideal of an independent sphere of activity for each individual as a means to distinctive personal development, and its expression in the political sphere in the demand for individual civil and political rights. In Russia this ideal stood in opposition both to traditional patriarchalism and also to the communism of the peasantry whose commitment to the 'ethical equalisation of opportunities', Weber wrote, 'could only hamper the development in that country of an individualistic culture of a Western European kind'.[93]

Both sets of 'bourgeois' values were strongly affirmed by Weber himself. On the one hand the ascetic attitude to work and the associated qualities described in *The Protestant Ethic* defined his own personal ideal, in contrast to the easy-going approach to life of the 'natural' man.[94] His affirmation of struggle in the hard school of life and his opposition to materialist values, described earlier in the chapter, typified this outlook. Alongside this went a preoccupation with securing 'freedom of movement' for the individual. Whatever his sympathies with the working class, his wife wrote, he could never become a member of a socialist party, because 'in the substance of his being he remained an individualist'.[95] In both respects Weber's political standpoint was an embodiment of bourgeois values, as he himself defined them.

Both sets of qualities were historically linked to the ownership of private property and the conditions characteristic of early capitalism. But how far could they be preserved under the circumstances of a more developed stage of capitalism? Weber himself argued that, as a result of the operation of these very qualities, capitalism had come to take a form which put their continuance in question. Capitalism was the 'pacemaker' for the process of bureaucratisation in both industry and state which threatened to stifle all individualism.[96] It also encouraged the pursuit of material goods as a major end of human life, rather than as a by-product of 'hard work in one's calling'.[97] Both these developments Weber described, somewhat dramatically, as the 'iron cage' of modern life.[98] At the same time the growth of class conflict had destroyed for ever the 'belief in the natural harmony of free individuals',[99] while the internationalisation of economic activity was intensifying national conflicts and making more necessary the assertion of a national cultural identity.[100] None of these developments were consonant with the distinctive 'bourgeois' values, as defined above. Indeed the dilemma, to which Weber's writing gave typical expression, was that the system of private property was becoming divorced from the values which provided its main justification.

This is not to say that Weber believed these values to belong entirely to a past age. He wished to appeal to them as a still valid justification for capitalism as an economic system against two different forms of threat, both apparent in German society. One of these was the threat to capitalism from within: that the bourgeoisie would go 'soft'; that its members would seek a respite from the hard calling of the entrepreneur in the quiet comfort of a rentier existence, or alternatively in the easy profits to be made from a state-oriented form of capitalism.[101] In this context the bourgeois ethic provided a standard from which the German bourgeoisie could be shown to be in danger of deviating.[102] The other threat came from socialism, which sought to replace the dynamic process of market competition by a system of bureaucratic 'order', and the distinctive qualities of the entrepreneur by state officials whose ambition, in many cases, was confined to securing a progressive income appropriate to their status, lasting if possible to the grave.[103] Such an 'order' would also remove the tension between the bureaucracies of capitalism and the state, on which political freedom, even for the masses, depended. Thus Weber could write, in the first of his Russian articles, that whatever measure of personal freedom was not won for the masses in the course of the next generations, while the 'much abused "anarchy" of production' remained, might well be lost to them for good.[104]

The characteristic 'bourgeois' values, therefore, as Weber himself defined them, were not simply a feature of the past, but also served as a justification, and set a standard, for capitalist activity in the present. At the same time, however, the developments generated in society by a more advanced stage of capitalism, mentioned above, called for a political standpoint which went beyond these values. The bureaucratisation of social and political structures led Weber to give a major emphasis to the role of the individual leader who stood at the head of such organisations. The intensification of international competition and conflict led to a strenuous assertion of national cultural values, as well as a commitment to an expansive capitalism as a necessary means to provide for mass needs and the population problem. In these positions elements of the other values can readily be discerned. Thus Weber's nationalism embodied an appeal to his society to accept the challenge and responsibility of world tasks, as a historical 'calling', in contrast to the 'peace and quiet' of smaller nations.

On the other side, his conception of leadership was defined primarily in individualistic terms. In a sense, these are the familiar bourgeois values writ large. The process of enlargement, however, produced its characteristic tensions; the expression of individual personality on the part of a leader, for example, involved a corresponding suppression of individuality on the part of his following, and the dominance of a great figure threatened the independence of society at large. The values of nation, leadership and freedom thus rested uneasily together. This tension was not unique to Weber alone, but represents a point at which bourgeois political values were themselves undergoing change, in response to the changes capitalism was producing in the character of modern society.

It should be clear from the preceding discussion that to describe Weber's political theory as 'bourgeois' is not to offer a situational critique, in which conclusions drawn from his social position are then imposed *ab extra* on the character of his thought. It is rather to accept his own characterisation of his political values, and to show how these provided the focus for the empirical analysis of his political writings. Among other features of this analysis, Weber gave a major emphasis to the phenomenon of class. Class conflict, he told the Protestant Social Congress amid protests, was 'an integral part of the present social order'; it was time the church recognised this, and in recognising it, thereby *legalised* it.[105] Here also Weber was truly 'class-conscious'. This was so, not only in his recognition of the particular dilemma confronting the German bourgeoisie as a result of Germany's retarded development—caught between the Junker class clinging to political power above them and the working class demanding it from below. It was also in part the prevalence of class and economic interests in modern society that led Weber to insist so strongly on a political dimension which went beyond them. Thus in the Inaugural Address, he insisted on the goal of social unity for the nation, because modern economic development had 'burst it asunder', and on the necessity for the political education of society, because modern economic development threatened to 'destroy men's natural political instincts'.[106] Weber at once both recognised the significance of class and economic interests, and sought to emphasise a political dimension which would transcend them.

This interaction between the economic and the political is an important feature in Weber's perception of his contemporary society, as expressed in his political writings. It is also reflected in the structure of this book. Chapters 3 to 5 will concern themselves with the more exclusively political aspects of Weber's account of modern politics: his account and critique of bureaucracy; his account of democracy and mass politics; his conception of the nation and nation state. These are considered largely in abstraction from his theory of society. Chapters 6 and 7 will then discuss the relationship between class and political structure in his accounts of Germany and Russia respectively. This will in turn be completed in Chapter 8 by considering the account of political leadership in his later writings, as seen in the context of his theory of society. The individual chapters are thus not intended to be read in isolation, but as parts of an interrelated whole.

As already mentioned, these different features of Weber's empirical analysis will be treated within the framework of values discussed in this chapter. By characterising these values as 'bourgeois', it is not intended to reduce everything Weber wrote to a crude bourgeois perspective, but rather to identify the most general assumptions within which the analysis contained in his political writings was set. The rest of the book will look systematically at his analysis of the nature and problems of modern politics, as seen from this standpoint.

REFERENCES

1 GPS, 1st edn, p 474.
2 GPS, pp 1–25.
3 The account here is drawn mainly from the Inaugural Address, but is also supplemented from two other writings, especially *Schfriften des Vereins für Sozialpolitik*, vol 55, pp 774–804, and GASW, pp 444–507.
4 GPS, pp 7–8; SVS, pp 774–5; GASW, pp 474–6.
5 SVS, pp 777–81; GASW, pp 449–50, 499–500.
6 *Mitteilungen des Evangelisch-sozialen Kongresses*, pp 1–5.
7 As also in his verbal report to the Verein meeting, GASW, pp 451–6.
8 GPS, pp 8–9; cf GASW, p 452.
9 GPS, pp 11–15.
10 GPS, p 10; cf GASW, pp 456–67, 505–7.
11 GPS, p 14.
12 GPS, pp 18–25.
13 GPS, p 19.
14 GPS, pp 21–2.
15 GPS, p 19.
16 GPS, p 24.
17 This point is discussed in Arnold Bergstraesser, 'Max Weber's Antrittsvorlesung in zeitgeschichtlicher Perspektive', *Vierteljahrshefte für Zeitgeschichte*, vol 5 (1957), pp 209–19, especially p 213.
18 GPS, p 16.
19 GASS, p 416.
20 GPS, p 152.

21 GPS, p 12.
22 GPS, pp 21, 23.
23 GPS, p 18.
24 GPS, p 28.
25 See pages 50–53.
26 GPS, p 12.
27 GAW, p 503; MSS, pp 26–7.
28 'It thus appears to be a *process of selection* that we see taking place;
    ... that [sc. national group] is victorious, which possesses the greater
    adaptability to the existing economic and social conditions.' GPS, p 8.
29 GASS, p 1.
30 GASS, pp 443–4, 447–8.
31 See Chapter 4.
32 GPS, p 12.
33 *Verhandlungen des 5. Evangelisch-sozialen Kongresses* (1894), pp 80–1.
    In a speech to the Congress three years later Weber even used the phrase
    'the gospel of struggle' ('das Evangelium des Kampfes'). *Verhandlungen*
    (1897), p 113.
34 GAW, p 152; MSS, p 55.
35 See page 168.
36 WG, pp 10–11.
37 R Aron in O Stammer, ed, op cit (English edition), pp 92–3.
38 GPS, p 9. In a note on the same page Weber questions the value of apply-
    ing the Darwinist theory of selection to the sphere of economics, particu-
    larly when used in support of an ideological position: 'the mistake of most
    of the attempts made from the side of the natural sciences to illuminate
    the questions of our discipline lies in their misguided ambition to "refute"
    socialism at all costs'.
39 GPS, pp 12–13.
40 *Verhandlungen* (1894), p 80.
41 GPS, p 532; GM, p 115.
42 *Verhandlungen des 5. Evangelisch-sozialen Kongresses* (1894), p 80.
43 *Lebensbild*, p 342.
44 *Archiv*, vol 22 (1906), Beiheft, pp 234–353; vol 23 (1906), Beiheft, pp
    165–401, hereafter cited as *Archiv*, 22B and 23B.
45 The problem is posed most explicitly at *Archiv*, 22B, pp 280–1, 346–9;
    23B, p 398; GPS, pp 39–40, 59–62, 107.
46 *Archiv*, 22B, pp 273–80; 23B, pp 199–200.
47 *Archiv*, 22B, pp 317–8, 321–2, 332–6; GPS, pp 45–51.
48 *Archiv*, 23B, pp 311–4; GPS, pp 90–1.
49 *Archiv*, 22B, pp 292–3, 347–9; 23B, pp 231–2, 372–3, 398; GPS, pp 40–1,
    60–2, 79, 107.
50 *Archiv*, 22B, pp 284, 291–2, 349; GPS, pp 40, 62.
51 *Archiv*, 22B, pp 348–9; GPS, 61–2.
52 ibid.
53 *Archiv*, 23B, p 398; GPS, p 107.
54 *Archiv*, 22B, ibid.
55 GARS, vol 1, pp 203–4; PE, p 181.
56 GASW, pp 277–8.
57 GASS, p 414.
58 It was individualism in this sense that the Russian peasants would reject,
    in Weber's view. GPS, pp 45, 51.

59 These formed the main political demands of the liberal movement in Russia, GPS, p 40.
60 GAW, pp 493–4; MSS, p 18.
61 *Mitteilungen des Evangelisch-sozialen Kongresses*, 6 (1892), p 2; GASS, p 516.
62 Löwith, op cit, pp 96–9; Wrong, ed, op cit, pp 119–22.
63 'Rundschrieben', p 3. This could happen, even though they formed a socially and economically *privileged* stratum.
64 GPS, pp 242, 320, 383; GASS, p 504.
65 GPS, 1st edn, pp 457–8; Baumgarten, op cit, p 488.
66 'Forms of constitution are for me technical questions, like any other machinery.' GPS, 1st edn, p 470; cf GPS, pp 296–7.
67 GPS, p 298.
68 GPS, pp 294–431.
69 GPS, pp 299–308.
70 GPS, pp 327–31, 339–53.
71 GPS, p 334.
72 GPS, pp 322–3, 335, 339–42, 365, 411–2.
73 'As also of the entrepreneur.' GPS, p 323.
74 GPS, pp 357–70.
75 GPS, p 365.
76 GPS, pp 327–31, 339–42, 366–70, 426–31.
77 GPS, p 430. By 'Herrenvolk' Weber means a people who have the capacity to play a role in world politics, a minimum qualification for which is the capacity for *internal* self-government.
78 GPS, p 431.
79 This point is discussed further in Chapter 8.
80 See Chapter 6.
81 The phrase is quoted in W J Mommsen, op cit, p 109.
82 GPS, pp 441–2.
83 GPS, p 383.
84 GPS, p 320.
85 GPS, pp 321–2.
86 W J Mommsen, op cit, ch. 10, especially p 410.
87 C Steding, op cit, ch. 1.
88 C Steding, *Das Reich und die Krankheit der europäischen Kultur* (Hamburg, 1938).
89 e.g. P Honigsheim, 'Max Weber und die deutsche Politik', *Kölner Zeitschrift für Soziologie und Sozialpsychologie*, 13 (1961), pp 263–74; E Nolte, 'Max Weber vor dem Faschismus,' *Der Staat*, 2 (1963), pp 1–24.
90 e.g. *Verhandlungen des 5. Evangelisch-sozialen Kongresses* (1894), p 77; *Christliche Welt*, vol 8 (1894), col 477; letter to R Michels (6.11.07), quoted in W J Mommsen, op cit, p 123.
91 GPS, p 20.
92 GARS, vol 1, pp 30–62; PE, pp 47–78, passim.
93 GPS, p 51.
94 This was one ground for Weber's hostility to his father's way of life. See A Mitzman, op cit, pp 47–50.
95 *Lebensbild*, p 642.
96 GASW, pp 277–8; WG, pp 129, 562.
97 GARS, vol 1, pp 203–4; PE, p 181.
98 ibid; cf GPS, p 242.

99 GPS, p 40.
100 GPS, pp 13–14.
101 See page 159.
102 This is particularly clearly expressed in an article Weber wrote at the same time as *The Protestant Ethic:* 'Agrarstatistische und sozial-politische Betrachtungen zur Fideikommissfrage in Preussen', GASS, pp 323–93.
103 See page 81.
104 GPS, p 62.
105 *Verhandlungen des 5. Evangelisch-sozialen Kongresses* (1894), p 73.
106 GPS, pp 23–4.

Chapter 3

The Limits of Bureaucratic Rationality

Of all the features which Weber regarded as definitive of the modern state and its politics, his account of bureaucracy is the most familiar.[1] Most students of sociology and government can recite the various characteristics—salaried, hierarchical, rule-governed, etc—that constitute his bureaucratic model, and are aware of his claim that it was technically superior to all other forms of administration. Yet the account of bureaucracy in *Economy and Society* forms only one of three different aspects or theories of bureaucracy to be found in Weber's writing. Even the significance of this account for Weber's contemporaries has not been fully grasped, because the controversy within the Verein für Sozialpolitik, which provides its context, has been ignored.[2] All three of Weber's theories were conceived in opposition to the view of bureaucracy accepted by the 'conservative' wing of the Verein. It is appropriate, therefore, to take this view as the starting point for a consideration of Weber's own account.

The conception of bureaucracy held by the 'conservative' wing of the Verein was typified by Gustav Schmoller, the historian of Prussian administration. Schmoller's view was that bureaucracy stood, alongside the monarchy, as a neutral force above the competing particular interests of party and class, embodying the universal interest of society as a whole, and endowed with a special political wisdom.[3] This conception was a recurring one in German thought, its best known exponent being the philosopher Hegel. Dieter Lindenlaub argues that Schmoller's view was not in fact taken from Hegel, but derived directly from his own historical researches, and his 'personal experience and observation over forty years of public life'.[4] Whatever the source, his conclusions were similar. While Schmoller did not regard the bureaucracy as perfect—there was too much 'mandarin scheming and red tape'—

yet there was nothing about it that could not be put right by a few simple administrative reforms.[5] Essentially, bureaucracy was conceived as an independent political force, endowed with the qualities of wisdom and disinterestedness, and hence supremely fitted to direct the affairs of society. Among the older generation of the Verein, the magnificent achievements of the German and Austrian bureaucracies formed a constant refrain.[6] Their opposition to political democratisation lay in the fear that the independent government of monarch and bureaucracy would be replaced by government based upon the particular interests of party and class.

The three different aspects of Weber's theory of bureaucracy were all opposed to this 'conservative' view. First was his familiar conception of bureaucracy as a technically efficient instrument of administration, 'technically the most perfectly adapted for achieving the highest level of performance'.[7] Almost all commentators have seized upon the claim to technical superiority as the key point in this account, but also significant in the light of the conservative view was Weber's insistence that bureaucracy was *only* a technical instrument, and nothing more. This point was emphasized clearly by his brother Alfred at the meeting of the Verein in 1909, which became notorious for the attack on bureaucracy by the Weber brothers:

> I do not speak for the older generation, who insist on endowing the bureaucratic apparatus with values which belong to the community at large, with the result that the civil servant and the bureaucracy as a whole become surrounded with an aura of emotional approval. . . . I speak rather for those . . . who regard bureaucracy as a technical instrument alone, and the civil servant as much a technical official as the private industrialist with an apparat at his disposal, those, in other words, for whom the public service is divested of all emotional value.[8]

Divesting bureaucracy of its 'sacred halo' was an important feature of Max Weber's theory also. The state apparatus was to be viewed simply as a technical instrument, and considered on the same level with others as merely one example of a type of administration increasingly prevalent throughout all spheres of modern life. Far from this involving an idealisation of Prussian bureaucracy, as some critics claim, it effectively dethroned it. Thus when Max Weber in the same Verein debate emphasised the character of bureaucracy as 'precise, soulless and machine-like', this was greeted with shouts of 'ridiculous', since it denied the state apparat that superior status, that emotional mystique, which was its distinctive feature in conservative eyes.[3]

To say that Weber regarded the state administration as entirely on a level with others would be misleading. He recognised the special characteristics of the civil service, which stemmed from the unique position of the state as possessing a monopoly of the means of coercion; it was therefore concerned with power in a special sense.[10] In his writing the concept of bureaucracy carries a dual meaning. It can refer either to any system of administration which approximates to the 'rational' model, including that of the state, or to the latter alone; it can designate either the total body of officials who work in offices, in whatever sector of activity, or the specific group of men who comprise the civil service.[11] This designation of a specifically political concept of bureaucracy, however, formed part of a wider conception, which stressed the common characteristics of bureaucracy as an administrative instrument. It was this stress on its instrumental function that distinguished Weber's theory from that of the 'conservative' school. Indeed, freeing bureaucracy from the latter's adulation was a necessary starting point for appreciating its proper value, which lay in its purely technical superiority in the performance of administrative tasks.

The recognition that bureaucracy for Weber, though a supremely effective technical instrument, was nevertheless *only* an instrument, is necessary to appreciate the significance of the second aspect of his theory. This was that bureaucracy had an inherent tendency to exceed its instrumental function, and to become a separate force within society, capable of influencing the goals and character of that society.[12] It constituted a separate power group within the state, a separate status stratum within society at large. Thus in the political sphere Weber recognised as an empirical phenomenon the ability of bureaucracy to become a separate force, which was central to the conservative view. But far from this being the essence of bureaucracy, as they believed, Weber criticised it as an aberration, since it involved usurping the goal-setting function which properly belonged to the politician. Not only did this role belong to the politician, it was also one for which the civil servant was by training unsuited. Central to this second conception of bureaucracy, therefore, was an account of its inherent limitations, 'what it *cannot* achieve'.[13] Where the emphasis in *Economy and Society* was on the technical superiority of bureaucracy, Weber's political writings were concentrated explicitly on its negative side, on what it could *not* achieve.

The third aspect of Weber's theory of bureaucracy, like the second, is to be found only in his political writings. It involved a conception of bureaucracy as reflecting the class structure of society. Far from embodying the universal and disinterested outlook ascribed to it by conservative mythology, in practice it was unable to free itself from the outlook of the social classes from which it was recruited and to which it was allied. This conception was an important feature in Weber's analysis of German politics.[14] The claim of the Prussian bureaucracy to be above party was so much 'cant'; in practice it operated as an instrument for the preservation of Junker dominance.[15] By permeating the bureaucracy and army with its attitudes, this class determined the main features of German policy.[16] The class outlook of bureaucracy was equally evident in Russia, where 'the higher echelons of the civil service, as well as the officer corps, are recruited mainly from the propertied classes, just as they are everywhere else'.[17] This view of bureaucracy as grounded in the class structure of society was held in common by the younger generation of the Verein.[18] It was given characteristic expression by Alfred Weber in the same debate already mentioned:

> It is a fundamental error to imagine that bureaucracy has the characteristic of being independent of any social basis. It finds its social basis in those power groups which control the organisation of society.[19]

The shouts of approval and disagreement which greeted these remarks bears witness to the contentiousness of the subject within the Verein. Max Weber was, with his brother Alfred, a leading exponent of an alternative conception of bureaucracy to that of the conservative wing. Where the latter applauded the Prussian bureaucracy for its political achievements, and looked to it as a model of independence above party and class, Max Weber insisted that bureaucracy was essentially a technical instrument; that its admitted capacity to assume a directing role in society was an aberration from its proper function; that, far from it being independent, it was unable to free itself from the class structure of society. At the same time, these different aspects of Weber's theory also modified each other. In particular, his political writings offer a modification of the conception of bureaucracy to be found in *Economy and Society*. In the latter, central place is given to the development of a model or 'ideal type' of bureaucracy: to an account of the criteria a system of administration must satisfy if it is to count as bureaucratic, and of the typical preconditions and consequences of its doing so. The political writings show that in practice bureaucracy does not fulfil these criteria. It has an inherent tendency to exceed its administrative function; the official does not act entirely *sine ira et studio*, but his outlook is affected by the presuppositions of social class. These deviations from the 'ideal type' are not accidental, but systematic. Bureaucracy is not merely a technical instrument; it is also a social force with interests and values of its own, and as such has social consequences over and above its instrumental achievements. As a power group it has the capacity to influence the goals of the political system; as a status stratum it has a more unconscious effect upon the values of society at large. At the same time it is not independent of other social forces, particularly that of class. These are the chief features of Weber's account of bureaucratic operation in practice, and they constitute an important qualification of his 'ideal type'.

Of the three aspects of Weber's theory of bureaucracy outlined here, the class context of bureaucracy will be left to later chapters, which deal with his account of the relation between society and state. The present chapter will begin with a brief summary of the most familiar aspect of his theory: his account of bureaucracy as a technical instrument, and of its irresistible advance in modern society. This will provide the context for his critique of bureaucracy and its tendency to exceed its instrumental function, which forms the main theme of this chapter.

THE IRRESISTIBLE ADVANCE OF BUREAUCRATIC ADMINISTRATION

'The degree of advance towards a bureaucratic ... officialdom', Weber wrote, 'provides the decisive yardstick for the modernisation of the state'.[20] The theory of bureaucracy forms a central part of his account of modernisation, involving an explicit contrast with traditional systems of administration. Bureaucracy is itself defined in opposition to traditional types; it is the 'counter-image of patrimonialism transposed into rationality'.[21] For Weber, a chief characteristic of modern society as well as the state was the replacement of patriarchal and patrimonial systems of administration by the bureaucratic, of traditional authority by authority which he called 'rational' or 'legal'. This process, once begun, was irreversible.

Although the terms 'rational-legal', used to characterise bureaucracy, are generally run together by translators, these were two separate, if overlapping, concepts in Weber's writing. The concept of 'legality' defined the characteristic basis of authority in modern institutions, which lay in procedural correctness. According to Weber, those subject to authority, whether of a law or a person, accept it as legitimate if it is constituted according to the correct procedures.[22] Hence the two characteristics which most distinguish modern from traditional authority: where the latter is personal, involving allegiance to the person of the ruler, 'legal' authority is impersonal, involving allegiance to rules and written procedures.[23] Secondly, where under the traditional authority, resting as it does on a belief in the sanctity of the past, scope for positive enactment, for the creation of new law, is limited; under legal authority there is in principle free scope for new enactment, provided only the formal procedures are observed.[24] Both qualities are central to bureaucratic administration. Allegiance to impersonal rules and procedural correctness is the hallmark of the official: he is disciplined to treat like cases alike, irrespective of the personal status of the individual, and to apply rules consistently, even though he may disagree with their content. At the same time bureaucracy forms part of a total structure of authority, which has the capacity to change law at will according to a change in circumstance or in the personnel occupying positions of power; the administration as a whole is conditioned to obey political masters with widely different policies and ideals, provided they proceed in a manner that is formally correct.[25]

This emphasis on procedural correctness as the criterion of legitimacy is consonant with the generally instrumental character that Weber ascribed to modern institutions. Here we come to the second concept that he used to characterise bureaucracy, that of 'rationality'. When Weber spoke of the 'rationalisation' of modern life, he did this in a number of different senses.[26] One was that of purpose, or means–end, rationality. Modern life was distinguished by systems of purpose-rational action, involving the explicit definition of goals and the increasingly precise calculation of the most effective means to achieve them, in contrast to action arising from habit or from traditionalism as a principle. Overlapping with this was a conception of rationality as embodying certain qualities implicit in the exercise of reason as such, whether it involved a means–end schema or not. A pattern of activity was 'rationalised' to that extent that it was governed by explicitly formulated rules, that its scope was precisely delimited and involved the application of specialised concepts and knowledge, and that it was systematised into a coherent whole. These were characteristics which could apply to a pattern of religious belief or conduct, to law or ethics, as well as to systems of action that were specifically instrumental, such as administration or economic management. When applied to the latter, these characteristics ensured maximum precision and calculability of operation. Bureaucracy exemplified 'rationality' in all these different senses. Thus Weber called it specifically 'rational' because it involved control on the basis of knowledge, in particular specialised knowledge; because of its clearly defined spheres of competence; because it operated according to intellectually analysable rules; because of the calculability of its operation; finally, because technically it was capable of the highest level of achievement.[27]

These 'rational' characteristics of bureaucracy guaranteed it a superiority in technical performance over all other forms of administration, as great as the machine over non-mechanical forms of production. This was particularly true of what Weber called the 'monocratic' type, where the administration came to an apex under a single chief or head, which marked the culmination of bureaucratic development. In comparison with all historically known forms of administration—by personal retainers, unpaid amateurs, elected officials, collegial bodies, etc—monocratic bureaucracy was superior in the technical qualities of 'precision, speed, continuity . . . reduction of friction and of personal and administrative costs'.[28] It was the only type capable of coping with the complexity and scale of modern administrative tasks, particularly those generated by the requirements of a capitalist market economy. Hence its progress was irresistible and irreversible:

> In comparison with other historical bearers of the modern rational order of life, bureaucracy is distinguished by its much greater *inescapability*. There is no historical example known of where it once achieved supreme dominance—China, Egypt, in a less thoroughgoing form in the late Roman empire and Byzantium—that it disappeared without the complete downfall of the whole culture that it carried. And these were relatively irrational forms of bureaucracy—'patrimonial bureaucracies'.[29]

Two examples of the spread of monocratic bureaucracy in the political sphere, which particularly impressed Weber, are evidence of his conviction that the process was irresistible—one from the USA, the other from Russia. In the USA Weber remarked how, despite the strong material and ideological factors supporting the *election* of officials, this was inexorably giving ground to the bureaucratisation of administration through civil service reform.[30] A system of election of officials proved wasteful and corrupt. The criterion for selection of candidates was more a question of services rendered to the party than of any qualifications for the particular office, and the system of election destroyed the basis of administrative discipline and subordination of the official to his superiors. The corruption and waste involved could only be tolerated by a country with unlimited economic opportunities, and this was possible no longer. 'The time has naturally long since come, when even in America administration can no longer be carried out by dilettantes. Specialised officialdom is expanding rapidly'.[31] In Russia it was a question of the replacement of a quasi-collegial system of administration by a monocratic bureaucracy.[32] The traditional pattern of administration, Weber observed, was by ministries which operated independently of one another, each reporting separately to the Tzar. Such a system involved the separate departments in an infinite amount of time trying to outwit or reach compromises with one another. Again the result was a great waste of time and resources, although one unintentional by-product was a certain freedom for the governed in the conflict between the ministries. The unification of these disparate elements into a monocratic bureaucracy was the only permanent result on an institutional level of the 1905 revolution. In theory, at least, it marked the end of traditionalism in administration, and the 'definitive establishment of the centralised authority of a modern bureaucracy'.[33]

Both examples, from the USA and Russia, demonstrated the replacement of competing sources of authority by a single source, that is, a concentration of power. Such concentration was a typical feature of bureaucracy and the increasing rationalisation of administration. It formed the basis for Weber's critique of those democratic and socialist ideals which held out the possibility of minimising or dispersing the exercise of authority in modern society.[34] The only possible room for democracy in the mass state lay in the election of a political head for the bureaucracy to serve; a bureaucratic system could be *controlled* from above by a democratically elected politician, but could not be *replaced* by election from below.[35] Even mobilisation of the vote itself required the bureaucratisation of political parties, and this brought a concentration of power in the hands of those who controlled the organisation.[36] If in the political sphere the possibility of control from below was increasingly Utopian, this was equally true at the work place.[37] The separation of the worker from the means of production that socialist theory attributed to capitalism was in fact a feature of bureaucratic operation itself; with the increasing sophistication of technology and the spread of bureaucratic administration within industry, this 'separation' was an increasingly prevalent condition, irrespective of private ownership:

> Everywhere it is the same. The means of operation within the factory, the state, the army, the university, are, through the mediation of a bureaucratically structured apparat, concentrated in the hands of those who control this apparat.[38]

It was therefore unrealistic to envisage a dispersal of authority in modern society. 'It is the dictatorship of the official, not of the worker, that is—for the present at least—on the advance'.[39]

The bureaucratic type of administration, then, according to Weber, was advancing irresistibly because of its technical superiority. Weber recognised a clearly positive side to this. Like the industrial machine, so the 'human machine' brought an extension of human capacities; it increased man's capacity to achieve his ends in an increasingly complex society. At the same time—and here Weber echoes Marx's concept of alienation—bureaucracy was a social force with powers and values of its own, and its development increased the forces to which man was subject. Karl Löwith was one of the first to recognise the 'ambivalence of rationality' as a central theme in Weber's writing, in his articles on Marx and Weber in 1932. For Weber, he writes, the process of rationalisation 'combines at once the specific achievement of the modern world and the whole questionability of this achievement'.[40] Where through the rationalisation of life men sought to bring their external circumstances more under their control and so increase their freedom, at the same time this also increased the powers to which they were subject. The rest of the present chapter will discuss this critique of bureaucracy to be found in Weber's political writings. Where the theme of *Economy and Society* is the superiority of bureaucracy as an instrument for mastering complex administrative tasks, the theme of the political writings is its tendency to become an independent social and political force with distinct values of its own and a capacity to affect the ends and culture of society. This theme is similar to that pursued by Robert Michels in the sphere of party organisation,[41] but Weber applied it to the societal level as a whole. Two different aspects of the theme will be distinguished, corresponding to the two different meanings of the term 'bureaucracy' adopted by Weber: the particular one, which denotes the specifically political administration of the state; and the more general one, which denotes a 'rational' type of administration wherever it occurs in society. Though the distinction is not always clear-cut in Weber's writing, it provides a useful demarcation for two different kinds of problem he discusses. The first is a specifically political issue of the power and independence of the state bureaucracy, and the problem of how it can be controlled; the second concerns the cultural effects of the development of bureaucratic administration throughout society, and the problem of the type of individual and the kind of society it encourages. The latter will lead on to a discussion of Weber's critique of socialism.

BUREAUCRACY AS A POWER GROUP

The bureaucracies which Weber analysed in Germany and Russia were to some extent a special case, in that they had been allowed to achieve a dominant position within the process of government, and were not subject to effective political control. It is clear, however, that Weber regarded them as chronic cases of what was a general phenomenon. Though in theory only an impersonal apparatus, a bureaucracy formed at the same time a separate group within the state, with its own special interests, values and power basis.[42] Its separate interests lay in the maintenance and extension of administrative positions and power; its distinctive outlook lay in a belief in its own superior objectivity in interpreting the national interest free from party bias; its power lay in its knowledge and experience and in the cloak of secrecy with which it concealed its operations. While these features were important to its effectiveness as a technical instrument, they also helped mould a bureaucracy into a special group within the state, with its own separate interests. The examples of Russia and Germany showed how far this process would go, if it was not subject to a strong counteracting power.

The phrases, the 'interests', the 'prestige interests', the 'power interests', of the bureaucracy occur repeatedly throughout Weber's political writings. Contemporary Russian and German history showed a variety of such interests at work: their interest in minimising the power and importance of Parliament; in by-passing Parliament and co-operating directly with interest groups; in centralising the activities of local government; in maximising the secrecy of governmental operation; in monopolising positions in government as posts for bureaucratic advancement; in extending the influence and power of the state externally. All these were interests which the bureaucracy was able to pursue successfully.[43] They all involved an interest in power, not merely as a means to improve administrative performance, but as an end in itself. Hence the explanation for the rapid development of bureaucracy in modern society and state lay not simply in its technical superiority, but also in the pressure exerted by officials in pursuit of their own special interests as a group.

In pursuit of these interests state officialdom was sustained by a set of beliefs and values which constituted what Weber called its 'Amtsehre' or 'code of honour'. Besides a sense of duty to their office, this typically comprised a belief in the superiority of their own qualifications and competence, as compared with others who did not possess these, MPs in particular. They saw Parliament as a 'talking shop for vain individuals, to whom every competent official felt far superior in the command he possessed of his department'.[44] Combined with this attitude went a pride in being impartial, 'above party', true interpreters of the national interest.[45] These different aspects of the 'Amtsehre' appear together in a typical passage where Weber describes the outlook of the Russian bureaucracy:

> Quite in keeping with its character, it looked down scornfully on the 'bungling' and impractical 'pigheadedness' of the intelligentsia and the various organs of self-government— their 'defence of special interests', their 'stupidity' and egoism, their Utopian dreams—all of which constituted in its view a perpetual obstacle to the welfare and happiness of the people which it was striving to promote from above, and undermined the appropriate respect for authority that 'reasons of state' demanded.[46]

The claim to be 'above party' needed to be viewed with scepticism, as Weber realised. His own Prussian bureaucracy, in particular, was recruited almost exclusively from conservative social groups whose interests in turn it supported. Their definition of state interests was thus invariably conservative.[47] At the same time the administration had interests and values of its own over and above those of the class from which it was recruited, which it concealed under the conveniently vague term 'Staatsraison'. 'In the canonisation of this abstract idea are inseparably woven the sure instincts of the bureaucracy for the conditions which preserve its *own* power in the state'.[48] These various attitudes embraced by the concept of 'Amtsehre'—belief in their own superiority and impartiality, canonisation of the 'national interest', etc—certainly contributed to the morale and technical functioning of the apparatus; but they also reinforced the separateness and exclusiveness of the bureaucracy as a group.

If the bureaucracy had distinctive interests and outlook, its most crucial feature was the power with which it could promote these. Its distinctive source of power lay in knowledge—both technical expertise, and the more general knowledge which came from experience and the possession of files:

> The power position of all officials rests . . . on *knowledge*, which is of two kinds: first, specialised knowledge gained through specialised training, which can be called 'technical' in the widest sense . . . secondly, official knowledge, that is concrete information relevant to his performance, which is available only to the official through means of the administrative apparat.[49]

A typical instance given by Weber of the use the apparatus made of such knowledge for its own particular ends was in the question of suffrage reform, an issue raised frequently in this period both in Prussia and Russia.[50] The bureaucracy's monopoly of census statistics put it in an impregnable position for producing reform proposals which would achieve the right result in terms of its own standpoint, but which 'could be presented as the result of objective, scientific calculation'.[51] The Prussian statistical bureau in particular achieved great sophistication in this 'science' of voting arithmetic, which it used to ensure that 'not too many of the centre party and left liberals, and for God's sake no social democrats, should find their way into the Prussian Parliament'.[52] Similarly, in the equally disputed issue of trade policy, the administration's monopoly of production statistics gave it an immense advantage. Such knowledge was of no use unless protected by secrecy. Secrecy was its essential concomitant:

> . . . the most decisive means of power for officialdom is the transposition of official knowledge into secret knowledge, by means of the notorious concept of the 'official secret'. This is simply a way of securing the administration against external control.[53]

This attitude was particularly apparent in its relations with Parliament. An administration had a vested interest in keeping Parliament ill-informed, and tended to resist attempts by delegates—for example, through committees of inquiry—to improve their access to information. The secrecy inherent in bureaucracy conflicted directly with the openness necessary to the activity of a Parliament.[54]

It was knowledge, then, protected by secrecy, which made bureaucracy not only an effective administrative instrument, but also a potent force in the promotion of its own interests and outlook. The possession of such knowledge, in particular, made it difficult for officials to be controlled by their political masters, unless the latter had their own source of expertise.[55] There was thus an inevitable tendency for the apparatus to exceed its advisory and executive functions and come to control the determination of policy as well. This was particularly true in the kind of monarchical system, typical of Russia and Germany, where the monarch, through ignorance or inexperience, was powerless in the face of his bureaucratic 'advisers'.[56] Weber believed that the monarch in modern circumstances could only be a dilettante, not a specialist, except conceivably in the military field. He would be at a loss in face of specialists, who would 'spoon-feed' him with the relevant decisions. Even when he sought to exert his power, it could either be ignored by the apparatus, or, where not, it would operate in an unsystematic and arbitrary manner.[57] Such bursts of assertion might give the outward appearance of power and satisfy the monarch's vanity, but in reality it was the bureaucracy who ruled. 'The monarch imagines it is he who is ruling, when in fact what he is doing is providing a screen, behind which the apparatus can enjoy the privilege of power without control or responsibility'.[58]

Thus Germany and Russia, though in outward form monarchies, were in reality examples of what Weber called 'Beamtenherrschaft' or government by officials. Weber talks about the 'rule of officials' in two quite different senses which need to be distinguished. One is the general sense in which all modern government can be said to be ruled by officials, in that it is officials to whom people are immediately subject in their day-to-day activities.[59] In this sense the rule of bureaucracy is coextensive with the development of bureaucratic administration. Weber calls this 'Herrschaft der Bürokratie' or 'Herrschaft des Beamtentum'.[60] The second is a particular or technical sense, which we are concerned with here ('Beamtenherrschaft' or 'pure Beamtenherrschaft'). Weber defines this as being where the bureaucracy occupy the leading posts in the state,[61] which can happen either formally, when civil servants are appointed to be heads of ministries, or informally, when through weakness of the political head the officials in effect assume the function of determining policy. This will happen wherever the system of government is incapable of producing the political leadership capable of controlling the apparatus.[62]

'Beamtenherrschaft', it could be said, formed the ultimate aim of bureaucracy as a separate group within the state. It was an example of the 'irrationality of rationalisation', of the means becoming an end in themselves. In 'Beamtenherrschaft', so Weber argued, the apparatus was usurping a political function for which it was not equipped, it was exceeding the limitations inherent in its character as an administrative instrument, with damaging consequences for the course of government.[63] Here we come to a central theme in Weber's theory of bureaucracy—its inherent limitations—which he developed in his frequently repeated distinction between the official and the politician.[64] The distinction is not a totally simplistic one. Weber dismissed as naïve the view that the official had merely the simple routine tasks to perform while his political superior had all the interesting and demanding work which required qualities of judgement.[65] However, there were important differences, the main features of which can be drawn from Weber's various statements on the subject.

First, in respect of his responsibility, the official is responsible to a superior for the quality of his advice and administration of policy; he does not carry any personal responsibility for the policies themselves. He may express disagreement, and in important matters he should do so, but once a policy is decided upon, his duty is to carry it out regardless of his own views. Without this 'discipline' and 'self-denial' the whole apparatus would fall apart.[66] The politician's responsibility, in contrast, is to be personally accountable for the policies he pursues. 'It is the struggle for personal power and the resulting personal responsibility which is the life-blood of the politician'.[67] In the course of this struggle he will have to make compromises, to sacrifice the less to the more important. But if he is unable to win support for, or to carry through, policies to which he is essentially committed, then his duty is to resign. If he does not, he is a 'clinger' and no true politician. It is this assumption of personal responsibility that characterises the politician, in contrast to the official's disciplined performance of the duties of his office.[68]

Not only is their responsibility different, but also the whole character of their activities. The civil servant works within a compulsory organisation which functions, usually in secret, by the issuing and obeying of instructions and the correct following of rules ('nach Reglement und Befehl').[69] The politician's arena, in contrast, is the open struggle to win a *voluntary* following in conflict with other groups and other points of view. 'The nature of all politics is struggle, the recruitment of allies and of a voluntary following'.[70] These activities are carried on according to very different criteria. The official judges a situation by reference to rules and technical expertise; the politician by an assessment of how much support he can get for his policies. An illustration of this is Weber's reference to the difference between German and British treatment of workers on strike in wartime. The German officials typically defined the issue in bureaucratic terms, and responded with an authoritative enunciation of the rules: if the rules said 'don't negotiate with striking workers' then no negotiation must take place, however much this might alienate support. The British government in contrast perceived it in political terms—how to maintain the allegiance of the workers to the war effort—and therefore looked for some compromise.[71] It was precisely this failure to distinguish between an administrative and a political problem or situation that in Weber's view typified the German bureaucratic system of government.[72]

These differences between the official and the politician, in the nature of their activity and responsibility, serve to define the different qualities necessary for their respective spheres. For instance, Weber points out, though language is an essential instrument for both, their use of it is different.[73] The civil servant uses language in a precise 'objective' manner, suitable for an official memo or issuing an instruction; the politician uses language in order to win supporters in face of opposing viewpoints. His trade is to 'fight with the spoken word'. Hence advocates make good politicians, where officials do not.[74] Above all, the politician differs from the official in the qualities of decisive leadership which are developed by the need for taking a personal responsibility for policies and staking his career on his success or failure in winning public support for them. These are qualities which the official has no opportunity to develop in the regular course of ordered administration and advancement in a career, however good he may be at his job.

> The position of the modern administrative official is totally unfavourable to the development of political self-assurance. . . . The arena of the modern politician is struggle in Parliament and country and there is no substitute for this—least of all the orderly competition for career advancement.[75]

While Weber's emphasis here on the limitations of bureaucracy

may not appear consistent with his account of its capacity to
extend its own power successfully, the point about the latter was
that it was essentially a secret operation, never the product of
open struggle in which the individual had to take public responsibility for his actions.

As a decisive illustration of the inadequacy of officials when
usurping a political role Weber repeatedly cited the conduct of
German foreign policy in the decades before the war. Discussion of
this forms an important part of his articles on 'Parliament and
Government',[76] though Weber remarks that he could find just as
many glaring examples from the sphere of internal policy.[77]
Here Weber analyses the disastrous series of public interventions
by Kaiser Wilhelm from the Kruger telegram to the *Daily Tele-
graph* interview which 'helped to build up a world coalition against
Germany'.[78] These interventions were tolerated, even instigated,
by members of the German government, yet they never took the
appropriate responsibility for them. The question at issue was not
whether the monarch should issue public statements. Rather it was
that, since they irrevocably committed the nation's prestige to a
course of action, they should have been carefully weighed and
responsibility for them accepted by the individuals concerned. If
they misfired, they should then have accepted responsibility and
resigned. This never happened; instead those concerned simply
congratulated themselves that at least Germany did not have a
'shadow monarch'.[79] The result was that Germany was compelled
to use its military machine in war to recover from the mistakes
made by its system of government in peace. The reason for these
errors lay in the mistaken political system, 'which promotes men
with the outlook of officials to positions where independent
political responsibility is needed'.[80] This criticism was not only a
feature of Weber's wartime writings, though it was most insistent
then. It had also appeared earlier—for example, in his 1909 speech
to the Verein für Sozialpolitik, in which he contrasted the achievements of German foreign policy with those of America, France and
Britain, and argued that the latter had been much more successful
albeit with a 'partly corrupt' officialdom than had Germany, which
was run by a 'morally impeccable bureaucratic machine'.[81]

However perfect an instrument bureaucracy might be, it ceased
to be so once it stepped outside its limits. This is the nub of Weber's
critique; this is where he saw the ambivalence of bureaucratic
rationality. The very qualities which made it such a technically
effective form of administration—knowledge and expertise protected by secrecy, the confidence in its own superior competence

and impartiality—also gave it the means and the impetus to wield power beyond its inherent limitations. This was not an accidental phenomenon, but integral to its nature. The central political problem posed by bureaucracy, therefore, was how to restrict it to its proper function, how to ensure that the official's concern with administrative effectiveness, and hence with power, was properly subordinate to the politician's function of defining the ends that power was to serve and taking responsibility for them. The next chapter will consider the kind of answer Weber gave to this problem. For the present we shall turn to the second aspect of Weber's critique of bureaucracy—its cultural impact on society at large.

BUREAUCRACY AS A STATUS STRATUM

As already mentioned, the term 'bureaucracy' in Weber indicated not only the state apparatus, but also the type of 'rational' administration predominant in all areas of modern life, involuntary associations and private businesses, as well as the state. The development of bureaucracy had not only specific consequences for politics, but wider consequences for society as well, in its capacity as a 'status stratum'. Here also, bureaucracy could be seen to exceed its instrumental function. Just as in the political sphere bureaucracy became more than an instrument of administration, so in general it came to exercise a significant effect on the culture and values of society, on the ends that men thought worth pursuing. The starting point here will be Weber's analysis of the effect of bureaucracy on social stratification.

Weber distinguished two different consequences of the growth of bureaucracy for social stratification. On the one hand it resulted in a process of social levelling and the destruction of privilege, particularly that based upon birth.[82] Not only did it grow up historically in association with demands for equality before the law, but the principles of 'rational' administration themselves, based on specialist knowledge and the employment of experts, demanded the broadest possible social base for recruitment. Bureaucracy was thus an agent for social democratisation and the levelling of social differences. At the same time the development of bureaucratic administration throughout society created a new status stratum of officials, separated off by the new social barrier of the educational qualification. Where in the past the proof of personal superiority lay in one's pedigree, this was now replaced by the educational certificate:

Differences of education, in contrast to the *class*-forming elements of property and economic function, are nowadays undoubtedly the most important factor in the creation of *status* difference. It is essentially the social prestige of education . . . that the modern official owes his position to in society. Whether one likes it or not, education is one of the strongest social barriers. . . .[83]

Weber traced a close link between bureaucracy and the growth of higher education. The administrative official, whether the public civil servant or the technical officer in private industry, was recruited on the basis of his educational qualifications. The spread of bureaucracy created a huge demand for these qualifications and for the schools which would supply them. This 'irresistible demand for certificates' had nothing to do with a thirst for education as such, but rather for the tangible advantages which the certificate could guarantee: a salaried and pensionable position, and the social prestige of being a 'cultivated' man.[84] The new stratum of the 'certificated' was thus largely co-terminous with officialdom.

Weber's identification of officialdom as a status stratum was important for the cultural conclusions he drew from their attitudes and outlook. In his well-known distinction between a class and a status stratum ('Stand'),[85] the latter is identified as a social stratum whose cohesion and significance stem not from the common economic position and interests of its members, but from the prestige of the life-style which distinguishes them. A 'Stand' is typically a stratum whose attitudes and ideals are normative for the rest of society; they are the 'specific bearers of all conventions'. Such strata might overlap or coincide with economic classes. Indeed, in his contemporary society, Weber recognised that they largely did, because the sons of the wealthy were advantageously placed to acquire the education necessary for status-group membership.[87] But this overlap between status stratum and class did not make them identical. The 'Stand' was identified by the common attitudes derived from the education process itself, and it was these that Weber believed to be increasingly influential for the culture of society.

What were these attitudes? Their typical characteristic was what Weber called 'Pfründenhunger', hunger for salaried posts, which would provide a salary commensurate with the social prestige of the educated man, continuing if possible to the grave. Their highest ideal was security: a position from which they could not be dismissed, and the certainty of advancement in predictable stages.[88] These were the typical attitudes of the 'Diplom-mensch',[89] and with the extension of bureaucracy and higher education they were becoming a dominant ideal of modern society:

> The present war means the triumph of this form of life over the whole world. It was well advanced before. Universities, technical and trade colleges, business schools, military academies, specialist institutions of every conceivable kind, directed their daily activities to the same goals: the specialist examination as the prerequisite for any worth-while and above all 'secure' post, private or public; the educational certificate as a basic qualification for acceptance in 'society'. . . . the secure pensionable salary, commensurate with one's social prestige and providing where possible increments and advancement to old age.[90]

Status, security, order, were the chief elements of this ideal. With the further impetus given to bureaucratic development by the war, the world was well on the way to the kind of society Weber had envisaged in a famous passage at the Verein meeting in 1909, a society dominated by men

> . . . who need 'order' and nothing but order, who are so totally adjusted to it that they become nervous and cowardly if this order falters for a moment, and quite lost if they are torn away from it. That the world should know nothing but these men of order—this is the development in which we are caught up, and the central question is not, how we may still further promote and accelerate it, but what we can oppose to this machinery, in order to keep a portion of humanity free from this parcelling out of the soul, from this total dominance of the bureaucratic ideal of life.[91]

It would be mistaken to regard Weber's view of bureaucratic values as completely negative. Here he was reacting sharply to the adulatory attitudes common within the Verein. At the end of the war, in face of sharp criticism of the social prestige of officialdom, especially from socialists, he found it necessary to insist on the indispensability of their 'code of honour' in securing the qualities of integrity, sense of duty, etc, necessary to the technical performance of their office. Without this, the level of technical performance would suffer, and corruption would predominate.[92] 'Let not the new democracy imagine,' he wrote, 'that an officialdom *without* "*Amtsehre*" would be capable of maintaining the high integrity and specialist competence of German administration in the past. . . .'[93] What is important, however, is Weber's observation that the preservation of 'Amtsehre', necessary to the internal functioning of the administration, was inextricably bound up with a status position within the wider society. 'In the interests of integrity', he wrote, 'officialdom possesses a highly developed status honour' ('ständische *Ehre*').[94] Similarly, the education necessary to administrative functioning could not be divorced from the prestige of education in society at large, or, to use Weber's terms, the attainment of specialist qualifications ('Qualifikation von *Fach*wissen') be separated from the prestige of general culture ('allgemeine *Bildung*').[95] Thus officialdom, for Weber, had not merely an instrumental significance, but, in its development as a 'Stand', a wider consequence for social values at large. However much the education and outlook of the 'Diplommensch' and the 'Ordnungsmensch', and the 'Amtsehre' of the official, were necessary to the technical functioning of the administration, he could only judge these attitudes negatively in terms of their wider social consequences.

SOCIALISM, STAGNATION AND SLAVERY

Weber's image of a future society dominated completely by a bureaucratic power structure and bureaucratic ideals provided one of his chief arguments for capitalism against socialism. The preservation of the capitalist system and an entrepreneurial class could stem the development towards this kind of society in two important ways. First, by preserving a very different human ideal from the 'man of order'. The role of the entrepreneur was opposed to that of the official in the same way that the politician was.[96] Much of what Weber wrote in contrasting the politician with the official applied, *pari passu*, to the entrepreneur also. He was engaged in 'the free struggle for economic existence', whereas the official sought a 'secure pensionable income appropriate to his status'.[97] In this struggle with others, the entrepreneur's continued existence depended on his capacity to innovate and take risks, and on his determination in fighting to win a market for his goods. Just as the politician in the political sphere, so the entrepreneur in the economic sphere had to exercise an *individual* responsibility,[98] whereas a state official engaged in economic activity could always shuffle off the risk on to the bottomless coffers of the public treasury.[99] The maintenance of any dynamism whether in economic or social life depended on the continuation of this entrepreneurial class.[100]

Weber recognised that the German bourgeoisie did not altogether measure up to this ideal.[101] He deplored their desire for a secure existence and their aspirations to the status of country gentry. He also recognised that the scope for entrepreneurial qualities was being reduced as small businesses continued to be incorporated into larger concerns. Nevertheless he was explicitly opposed to the view that the entrepreneur at the head of the organisation could simply be replaced by an official. It was not only a question of expertise, but also of the dynamism he believed inherent in a free market system. 'It was with good reason', he wrote, 'that the *Communist Manifesto* emphasised the *economically revolutionary* character of the work of the bourgeois capitalist entrepreneurs. No trade union, much less a state-socialist official, can perform this role for us in their place'.[102] A form of socialism which ruled out the entrepreneur, or unduly restricted his scope for making profit where he saw fit, would, Weber believed, result in economic and social stagnation.

The preservation of a separate entrepreneurial class was important to Weber, secondly, in providing a counter-bureaucracy to that of the state. Private industry was a significant factor in promoting the spread of officialdom, in its need for clerical staff and technical experts of all kinds.[103] But it was an officialdom separate from the state, providing an independent source of knowledge and expertise, and counterbalancing the power of the state. Weber saw the tension between the two as an important element in the preservation of individual freedom. Socialism threatened to remove this tension between the bureaucracies of industry and government by unifying them into one massive hierarchy. If one of Weber's horror images of the future was that society 'would know only the bureaucratic ideal' of security and order, the other was that it would be dominated by a single bureaucratic hierarchy which would destroy all possibility of freedom.

> If private capitalism were abolished, the state bureaucracy would rule *alone*. Where now the bureaucracies of government and private industry can at least in principle counterbalance each other and hold the other in check, they would then be forged together into a single hierarchy.[104]

The result would not be any greater freedom for the worker, but less. The state as employer would be forced to adopt the typical employer's point of view, of keeping wages down and the workers submissive.[105] Only now the whole apparatus of the state would stand directly behind the employer. The worker would find no one within the spheres of law and administration who would have an interest in taking his side against his employer, now the state itself.[106] Weber's frequently repeated example of this was from the Prussian state-owned coalmines, where strikes were impossible and conditions, from the point of view of social policy, were 'the worst anywhere'.[107] Weber recorded how, on one occasion, an employee was called to give evidence in a dispute before a local court. Could he have an assurance, he asked, that he would not be laid off if he told the truth? The director of mines, who was present in court, refused to answer.[108] Although this kind of situation was not intended by socialists, yet a massive increase in the scope and integration of bureaucracy would be a necessary consequence of any policy which sought to end the so-called 'anarchy of production' under capitalism, and meet the welfare needs of society on the basis of public ownership. Since Weber himself gave only a low priority to the values of social justice and equality of welfare provision, he could only judge socialism in a negative light, for the loss of freedom he believed it would entail. Freedom, as well as social dynamism, was tied to the maintenance of a capitalist system.

Weber's horror images of the future—of a society impregnated with the bureaucratic values of order and security as its sole ideal and dominated by a single all-embracing hierarchy—struck many of his contemporaries as far-fetched. He particularly came in for criticism at the 1909 meeting of the Verein, which became notorious for the fact that the Weber brothers had 'preached' against bureaucracy, as one of their critics afterwards complained, and had 'turned a scientific gathering into a public spectacle'.[109] The actual subject of debate at the meeting was the economic activities of local government.[110] All the contributors to the debate before the Webers had been eulogistic of municipal enterprise. A particularly notable contribution in this vein was a speech by the Mayor of Oderburg (in upper Austria), who expressed great pride in his town's achievements in running services as profitably as under capitalism, and outlined the various methods they adopted for boosting revenue, such as offering cut-price tickets on the municipal tram service for those who also used the public baths.[111] The Webers threw a douche of cold water on this universal enthusiasm with their attacks on the belief that nationalisation or municipalisation would provide a simple solution to the 'social question'.[112] Although their names were linked in this debate, Alfred was in fact less out of line with the general direction of the Verein than his brother Max. As he admitted in a second contribution at the end of the debate, he remained on balance a supporter of municipalisation; it was only that his youthful enthusiasm had become tempered by scepticism.[113] Yet together their attacks on the 'metaphysic of bureaucracy' caused equal offence.

The Weber brothers did not have it all their own way in the debate, however. Paul Kompert, of Vienna, subjected their contributions to a particularly sharp analysis, arguing that their criticism of municipalisation depended upon a conception of bureaucracy which was unique to Prussian experience alone.[114] Though bureaucracy might be necessary, it was not everywhere identical. There were a number of distinctive features about the Prussian bureaucracy which could not be generalised. One was the excessive centralisation of the Prussian state, such that if a local community wanted, for instance, to lay on a water supply, it had to approach the state officials for permission first. Another was the aura of infallibility, the mystique, that surrounded the Prussian bureaucracy. It was mistaken to base a general critique of bureaucracy, much less of socialism, on features which were unique to Prussia. 'What really underlies your complaint', he concluded, 'is the exaggerated respect paid to officialdom in Prussia, not the principle of state ownership itself'. This was a local, not a general problem. The Webers should address their remarks to the Prussian people, not to a gathering discussing socialism.

As a critique of Max Weber's position, this has some validity. Weber was not always careful to distinguish those aspects of Prussian experience which could be universalised, and those which could not. An important aspect of his own critique of Prussian officialdom, whether in industry or state, was that it was impregnated by attitudes typical of the Junker class, which were uniquely authoritarian.[115] It was hardly fair, therefore, to take the experience of employees in the Prussian coalmines as evidence for a socialist future. However, his version of a bureaucratised society was also extrapolated from factors which he saw as integral to bureaucratic functioning as such. In this context, the Prussian administration had a universal significance, as simply the most developed example of a general type which existed elsewhere in more embryonic form:

> Just as the Italians and after them the English developed the modern form of capitalist organisation, so . . . have the Germans shown great virtuosity in the development of the

rational . . . bureaucratic organisation over the whole field of human associations, from the factory to the army and the state.[116]

In the same way that the Lancashire cotton industry had served Marx as a model for capitalism, so Prussian administration served Weber as a model for bureaucracy and for the possibilities of its future development.

At the same time, Weber's analysis of the likely character of a totally bureaucratised society was not based on contemporary evidence alone, but also depended largely on historical analogies, particularly those of ancient Egypt and the Roman Empire. Here were examples of societies dominated by an all-embracing bureaucratic state, albeit with large elements of patrimonial, non-rational features. These historical examples not only provided general evidence for the inescapability of bureaucracy, for the fact that once it had developed it 'disappeared only with the decay of the total surrounding culture'.[117] They also offered more precise analogies to give substance to Weber's image of the future in a socialist society. Rome provided an example of the stifling of capitalism by the state, with consequent economic stagnation and cultural decline, where Egypt offered an image of a society living without freedom under a single bureaucratic hierarchy.

The relevance of Roman experience to the present was suggested at various points in Weber's study on 'Agricultural Conditions in Ancient Times' (1909) and his later *General Economic History*. The latter singled out the Roman *equites* as the only capitalist class of pre-modern times which could be compared with the modern in terms of its degree of 'rationality', and argued that the throttling of this class through the takeover of its functions by the imperial bureaucracy was a major cause of Rome's decline, however much this may have increased the material welfare of her subjects in the short term.[118] This stifling of the one source of vigour in Roman society was also emphasised in the earlier 'Agrarverhältnisse',[119] and from it Weber in his conclusion drew a direct parallel with the present:

The bureaucratic order destroyed every economic as well as political initiative of its subjects. . . . The stifling of private economic initiative by the bureaucracy is nothing specific to antiquity. *Every* bureaucracy has the *tendency* to achieve the same results as it develops; our own is no exception.

Imagine, Weber goes on, that all major industries were nationalised or their production controlled through bureaucratic regulation:

> ... then we would have reached the position of late imperial times, only on a technically more perfect basis. ... The bureaucratisation of society will in all probability at some time or other come to master capitalism with us as much as it did in antiquity. Then we shall also experience, in place of the 'anarchy of production', a similar kind of 'order' to that which distinguished Imperial Rome and, still more, the 'new kingdom' in Egypt and the rule of the Ptolemies.[120]

Where Rome provided a model of the economic and cultural stagnation of bureaucratised society, Egypt offered an example of the total unfreedom of a society in which bureaucratic provision of needs was universal. The source of dominance of the bureaucracy in Egypt was the River Nile and the need to provide for its regulation. Every inhabitant was bound to a specific function within the social hierarchy, and had to be registered in a district where he could be requisitioned for compulsory labour. All private property was held at the service of the Pharaoh. In principle everyone was unfree; there were privileged, but no free, classes. Egypt thus formed an image of what society *could* be like under state socialism and universal welfare provision, of which it formed an early example. The number of times Weber refers to Egypt when discussing contemporary bureaucracy shows how much its example of a servile society overshadowed his thinking.[121]

Weber's evidence for the possible future in a totally bureaucratised society was thus drawn as much from the ancient world as from existing trends within the Prussian state, and was an example of his characteristically historical cast of mind. The justification for drawing these historical analogies is given in a very rough kind of way at the end of 'Agrarverhältnisse'. History, he says, can be conceived partly as developmental, partly as cyclical. Some social forms of antiquity form the basis for later developments, and thus lie along a unique sequence. Others are repeated again, albeit at different levels of development:

> The development of central European culture has known up to now neither closed 'cycles' nor a single unambiguous 'linear' development. From time to time social forms of the ancient world, long since buried, have re-emerged in an alien world. On the other hand, forms such as the cities and patterns of rural landholding of late antiquity were necessary steps on the way to the Middle Ages.[122]

The bureaucratic state was one of those structures that died with antiquity, only to re-emerge in a much more rationalised and technically developed form in the contemporary world. The history of its previous incarnation could thus provide evidence for its possible future development.

Weber's conception of life in a future socialist order has been hailed as prophetic. But it also depended upon an appeal to historical analogies which was itself uncritical. The assumption that a society in which economic provision was subject to public ownership and state planning would reproduce the stagnation of Imperial Rome or the unfreedom of ancient Egypt ignored the important differences of technological innovation and cultural values in modern society. The use of the term 'socialist' to describe ancient Egypt was itself tendentious.[123] Weber invariably insisted on taking the worst of all possible futures as the basis for a judgement of socialism, whether it be his assertion that there could be no efficient allocation of resources under a planned economy, or the conclusion that it would be impossible for the actions of a state administration to be conducted according to liberal or humane values.

Such conclusions depended upon characteristically pessimistic assumptions about the present. In the economic sphere Weber believed that technological development was not open-ended, but had a fixed limit, and that once this was reached, society would be condemned to providing for an increasing population out of a static national product. This at least was his belief in the early period, when he wrote that he did not share the optimism in the 'unlimited future of technical progress', but that the 'present age of technical evolution will come to an end'.[124] Even if he came to modify this view later, he still believed that economic development was something fragile, and that the stagnating forces of a rentier class on the one side and bureaucracy on the other could only be kept at bay within a capitalist economy where reward was vigorously geared to results: that is, private profit for the entrepreneur and a piece-work system for the workers. Only 'the maximum rationalisation of economic activity', he wrote in 1917, 'that is, the adjustment of economic reward to the rational ordering of production', could secure even a tolerable existence for the nation after the war.[125]

In the political sphere, Weber's assumption about the lack of freedom in a socialist society was conditioned, if not by Prussian experience, then at least by the conception of bureaucracy which he himself opposed to the 'conservative' view. His answer to the conservative 'metaphysic' of bureaucracy, with its essentially authoritarian conception of an administration standing above the forces of society, was to insist on the strictly instrumental function of bureaucracy and to give an account of it in purely instrumental terms, rather than oppose to the conservative view a conception of an administration operating within a democratic society and itself imbued with liberal and democratic values.[126] It is true that Weber was a proponent of political democratisation, but this meant a system in which the bureaucracy was kept in place by a political leader, not one in which the officials themselves were imbued with the values of the wider society in which they were placed. Such a view was inconceivable in Weber's terms; it would erode the all-important distinction between the official and the politician, which allowed the former no room for responsibility except to his superior. The only values which were appropriate for the official were those which made for a consistently functioning administration: instrumental, hierarchical, oriented towards order. It was these values that would prevail in the totally bureaucratised society that Weber envisaged socialism to entail. That men might conduct their administration in the spirit of other values, that they might even choose a reduction in the technical efficiency implicit in a bureaucratic solution to administrative problems for the sake of these values, he never considered. Thus an inflexible conception of bureaucracy produced a deterministic conclusion about future possibilities.[127]

Socialism itself Weber did not consider to be inevitable, at least in the foreseeable future. If it came, he believed, it would not bring a transformation in the human condition, but merely accentuate the worst features of existing developments. He therefore remained committed to capitalism, on both economic and cultural grounds. Even within the capitalist system however, bureaucracy retained its problems, the most important being how to keep it subject to political control. How Weber sought to resolve this will form the subject of the next chapter.

REFERENCES

1 WG, ES, vol 1, III, 2; vol 2, IX, 2; GM, pp 196–244.
2 The issue came up in one form or another in all three meetings: 1905, 1907, 1909.
3 This view is a recurrent one in Schmoller's writings. See D Lindenlaub, op cit, pp 240–50.
4 ibid, p 240. The quote is from Schmoller himself: SVS, vol 116 (1906), p 427.

5 D Lindenlaub, op cit, p 246.

6 A typical example is the speech by Adolf Wagner at the Verein meeting in 1909, in which he contrasted the achievements of German bureaucracy with the corruption of private capitalism in the USA. SVS, vol 132 (1910), pp 253–62.

7 WG, p 128; ES, p 223.

8 SVS, vol 132 (1910), p 239.

9 ibid, p 283.

10 See, for example, his distinction between a bureaucratic 'Behörde' and 'Betrieb' (public authority and private management), WG, p 551; ES, p 956.

11 In WG it usually carries the wider sense, in GPS the narrower, though here it is occasionally specified by the prefix 'staatliche'. Even within the political sphere Weber used the term 'die Bürokratie' in more than one sense: e.g. 'die Bürokratie' as a 'rational' form of administration contrasted with an elected officialdom or a traditional type of administration (GPS, p 171, and passim); 'die Bürokratie' as the body of civil servants as a group (GPS, p 230, and passim). In this latter sense the term is used interchangeably with 'das Beamtentum' (officialdom).

12 See the rest of this chapter for an elaboration of this aspect of Weber's theory.

13 GPS, p 322. 'The most important [sc question] of all arises from a consideration of what the bureaucracy *cannot* achieve. It is an easy matter to establish that its powers of operation . . . have a fixed internal limitation.'

14 See Chapter 6.

15 GPS, p 351; GASS, pp 381, 389.

16 GM, p 373.

17 GPS, p 194.

18 It was also held by 'liberals' among the older generation, especially Brentano and Herkner. According to the latter, the Prussian and Austrian experience demonstrated that the bureaucracy 'in the overwhelming majority of cases, consciously or unconsciously serves the interests of the social strata from which it is recruited'. Quoted in D Lindenlaub, op cit, p 258.

19 SVS, vol 132 (1910), p 243.

20 GPS, p 308.

21 WG, p 654; ES, p 1111. None of Weber's 'ideal types' are defined absolutely but only in terms of a contrast with others; it is part of their logic.

22 'Today the most usual basis of legitimacy is the belief in *legality*: the readiness to conform with rules which have been enacted according to the *formally* correct and accepted procedure.' WG, p 19; ES, p 37. Of all the many different accounts of the threefold typology in Weber's work, his article 'Die drei reinen Typen der legitimen Herrschaft' is distinctive for barely mentioning the concept of 'rationality' when discussing the modern, legal type. It is published in J Winckelmann, ed, *Staatssoziologie* (Berlin, 1956), pp 99–110.

23 The contrast is a frequent one, e.g. WG, p 130; ES, p 227.

24 'The basic principle [sc of legal authority] is that any law can be created or altered at discretion through formally correct enactment.' J Winckelmann, ed, op cit, p 99.

25 Weber also speaks of the official's loyalty to the impersonal function of

his office, which will lead him to continue operating even after a formal break in legitimacy. WG, pp 128, 570–1; ES, pp 224, 987–9.

26 The following summary has been distilled from sources in Weber too numerous to mention. The most complete account of Weber's concept of 'rationalisation' is in J Dieckmann, *Max Webers Begriff des 'modernen okzidentalen Rationalismus'* (Düsseldorf, 1961). Dieckmann singles out the concept of 'calculability' ('Berechenbarkeit') as its most central feature, and the belief 'that all things can be mastered through calculation' (GAW, p 578) as its metaphysical presupposition.

27 WG, pp 126, 128, 129, 132, 141, 563; ES, pp 220, 223–5, 244, 973–4. Weber called these characteristics 'formally' rational, as opposed to the *content* of the rules or administrative performance, which could only be judged as 'rational' or 'irrational' from particular substantive points of view, e.g. the welfare of the governed. WG, p 130; ES, p 226, and passim.

28 WG, pp 561–2; ES, p 973. Martin Allbrow, in his book on bureaucracy, denies that Weber was concerned with 'efficiency' in his bureaucratic model, though this seems as good a shorthand term as any to summarise these characteristics. M Allbrow, *Bureaucracy* (London, 1970), pp 62–6.

29 GPS, pp 318–9; cf WG, p 128; ES, p 223.

30 GPS, pp 279, 385–6, 388, 466; GASS, pp 495–7.

31 GASS, p 496.

32 GPS, pp 72–80.

33 GPS, p 75.

34 See particularly his lecture on 'Socialism', GASS, pp 492–518.

35 'Modern democracy is everywhere . . . a bureaucratised democracy.' GASS, p 497; GPS, pp 386–7, 466.

36 GPS, pp 316–7, 520–3.

37 GASS, pp 498–501.

38 GASS, p 501.

39 GASS, p 508.

40 K Löwith, 'Max Weber und Karl Marx', *Archiv für Sozialwissenschaft und Sozialpolitik*, 67 (1932), p 88.

41 R Michels, *Political Parties* (London, 1915). It first appeared as articles in the *Archiv* in 1905–8.

42 Though this conception of bureaucracy is only developed at length in GPS, it also appears in WG, pp 572–4; ES, pp 990–4.

43 GPS, pp 32–3, 82–3, 140–1, 194, 276, 340, 349, 370, 403–6, 412, 506.

44 GPS, p 198.

45 GPS, p 339.

46 GPS, p 32.

47 GPS, p 351.

48 WG, p 565; ES, p 979.

49 GPS, p 340.

50 GPS, pp 34, 83–5, 189, 253.

51 *Archiv*, 23B, p 267.

52 GASS, p 407.

53 GPS, p 341; cf GASS, p 407; WG, pp 572–3.

54 GPS, pp 352–3.

55 'Only the person who can procure this factual information independently of the good will of the officials, is able to control the administration effectively in the individual case.' GPS, p 340.

56 GPS, pp 76, 277, 325–7.
57 GPS, pp 198–9.
58 GPS, p 326.
59 'In a modern state the effective "Herrschaft". . . necessarily and unavoidably lies in the hands of the officials.' GPS, p 308.
60 GPS, pp 256, 327, 531.
61 GPS, p 513; cf pp 213, 276, 367, 416, etc.
62 'It is politicians who must provide a counterweight to the rule of officials. But against this is set the power interests of the leading civil servants. . . .' GPS, p 340.
63 'The rule of officials has completely failed when it has taken on *political* questions.' GPS, p 339.
64 The main places for this are: GPS, pp 198–9, 249–50, 322–3, 339–40, 365–6, 410, 512–13. GPS, 3rd edn, pp 224–5.
65 GPS, pp 322–3.
66 GPS, p 512, and passim.
67 GPS, p 323.
68 It is noticeable that, when contrasting the politician with the official, Weber sets out a strong thesis about his duty to resign: he should take his leave on any major issue where the decision runs counter to his political convictions (GPS, 3rd edn, p 224). This needs complementing by his distinction between the ethic of conviction and the ethic of responsibility; according to the latter, the politician must take responsibility for what happens if, by resigning, he is no longer able to influence events (GPS, pp 539ff).
69 GPS, pp 249–50.
70 GPS, p 335.
71 GPS, p 286.
72 'With us, the responsibility of the statesman is always being confused with that of the official. Both types are quite different, and each is appropriate in its place, but *only* there.' GPS, 3rd edn, p 224.
73 GPS, pp 249–50, 162, 342–3.
74 GPS, pp 352, 512.
75 GPS, p 335.
76 'Die Beamtenherrschaft in der auswärtigen Politik', GPS, pp 357–70.
77 GPS, p 363.
78 GPS, p 367; cf pp 357, 365.
79 GPS, p 359.
80 GPS, p 365; cf 359.
81 GASS, p 416; cf GPS, p 198: 'Germany has the best and most reliable officialdom in the world . . . but the dreadful failures of German policy have also shown what *cannot* be accomplished by such an instrument.'
82 GPS, pp 256, 279. WG, pp 567–9; ES, pp 983–7.
83 GPS, pp 235–6.
84 WG, p 577; ES, p 1000.
85 WG, pp 180, 531–9; ES, pp 306–7, 926–39.
86 WG, p 537; ES, p 935–6.
87 WG, p 577. Education was also a market resource and thus in itself a class-forming element. Weber talks of officialdom as a 'class' as well as a 'Stand'. E.g. 'Rundschreiben', p 3; WG, pp 179–80; ES, p 306.
88 GPS, pp 235–7, 318. '. . . men who cling to some minor position and strive only for a bigger one—an attitude increasingly common among

modern officialdom and especially among its new recruits, our present-day students.' GASS, p 414.

89 GPS, pp 273, 429.
90 GPS, p 315.
91 GASS, p 414.
92 GPS, pp 504–5.
93 GPS, p 466.
94 GPS, p 504; cf WG, p 553; ES, pp 959–60.
95 GPS, p 236.
96 'The directing spirit, of the entrepreneur on the one side and the politician on the other, is quite different from that of the official.' GPS, p 322.
97 GPS, p 236.
98 GPS, pp 323, 448, 474.
99 GPS, p 448.
100 Weber's most explicit justifications for bourgeois capitalism on economic grounds are to be found in the first part of his article on 'Wahlrecht und Demokratie', where he was arguing mainly against a rentier and a 'booty-capitalist' society; and in his writings and speeches after the end of the war, when socialism was the main target.
101 See Chapter 6.
102 GPS, p 448.
103 'Capitalism today is the pacemaker for the bureaucratisation of economic activity.' GASW, p 277.
104 GPS, p 320; cf p 242.
105 GASS, pp 414–15. 'It is always the officials, even in private industry, who are more popish than the Pope.'
106 GPS, pp 242, 320.
107 ibid GASS, p 415.
108 GASS, pp 403–4.
109 Correspondence by G F Knapp, quoted in F Boese, op cit, p 135.
110 SVS, vol 132 (1910), pp 175–325.
111 ibid, pp 230–8. They had to prove complete immersion! (p 235).
112 Max Weber's contribution is reprinted in GASS, pp 412–16. Its substance has been largely included in the previous discussion.
113 SVS, op cit, pp 309–14, and again pp 621–3.
114 ibid, pp 297–305.
115 See Chapter 6.
116 GPS, pp 317–18.
117 GPS, p 319.
118 S Hellmann and M Palyi, eds *Wirtschaftsgeschichte* (Tübingen, 1923), pp 286–7.
119 GASW, pp 1–288, especially pp 271–8.
120 GASW, pp 277–8. But, he adds, 'these perspectives do not belong here'!
121 GPS, pp 319–20, 384; GASS, pp 413–4. Weber's main account of Egypt is in GASW, pp 62–83; cf WG, pp 607–8; ES, pp 1044–7.
122 GASW, p 278.
123 GARS, vol 1, p 9; WG, p 645; ES, p 1102.
124 *Christliche Welt*, 8 (1894), col 477.
125 GPS, p 239.
126 This was more the approach of his brother Alfred, who argued that, the more extensive the bureaucratic machine, the more important it was to

insist that its operation should be imbued with liberal values. SVS, vol. 132 (1910), p 247.

127 In a different context, the critique of Weber's model of bureaucracy for its inflexibility has been a frequent theme of modern theories of administration and management. For useful summaries of the literature, see M Allbrow, *Bureaucracy* (London, 1970) and P M Blau, *Bureaucracy in Modern Society* (New York, 1956).

Chapter 4

Parliament and Democracy

The ambivalent character Weber ascribed to bureaucracy—its indispensability for handling the complex tasks of modern society on the one hand, its tendency to exceed its function as an administrative instrument on the other—defined for him one of the main problems of modern politics: how to keep the bureaucracy subject to political control. The answer lay in the kind of politician who would be able to subordinate the apparat to political direction, and in the conditions necessary to his development. As shown in the previous chapter, opposite to Weber's account of the typical official stood a conception of the 'model' politician, who was capable of taking personal responsibility for a policy and its consequences. In 'Politics as a Vocation' Weber defined the qualities necessary to this type as being a combination of passion with 'Sachlichkeit': the determination to fight for a cause he believed in, combined with a very practical and down-to-earth knowledge of the means by which it could be attained.[1] Control over the bureaucracy required the development of politicians with these capacities. Though this was partly a question of cultural and personal factors, development of such qualities also depended on the political structure. Central in this was the constitutional position of Parliament. Weber drew a basic distinction between, on the one hand, what he called 'token' constitutionalism or Parliamentarism, exemplified by Russia and Germany, where a Parliament of weak powers could produce neither the personnel nor the training for political leadership, and the strong Parliament of the British type on the other hand, to which the government was constitutionally answerable, and membership of which formed the normal avenue to governmental office.

This contrast between the two types of Parliamentary system formed part of Weber's theory of democracy and of his justification for democratising the German constitution. In this he again shared a view common to the younger generation of the Verein für Sozialpolitik, who advocated the introduction of universal suffrage in Prussia, and strengthening the powers of Parliament in the states and the Reich itself.[2] Yet here Weber was distinctive in regarding democratisation not so much as a means to giving more power to the people, but rather as a means to providing more effective political direction of the state apparat. Although he only produced a fully developed theory of political institutions in his wartime writings, first evidence of it occurs much earlier, in his articles on Russia. One of the conclusions which he reached in his analysis of Russian politics, that monarchy as a system was incapable of providing consistent leadership in the face of modern bureaucracy,[3] had a clear bearing on the German situation. In a letter to Friedrich Naumann in 1908 he repeated the point, made in the Russian articles, that a legitimate ruler could only be a dilettante, and argued that, without the removal of the 'personal regime' of the Kaiser, Germany would be incapable of producing a foreign policy of any consequence.[4] In a further letter from the same period he urged Naumann not to exaggerate the significance of the Kaiser's personal failings; it was the *institutions* that were at fault.[5] Germany had desperate need for organisational change, and Weber went on to advocate an end to token constitutionalism by making the 'Bundesrat' into a fully-fledged Parliament. This account broadly anticipated the theme of his wartime writings, and needed only to be completed by the more explicit emphasis on the function of a strong Parliament as a recruiting and training ground for political leadership, that followed from his closer acquaintance with the British system of government.[6] While the account which follows is drawn from Weber's wartime writings, therefore, its main features were established earlier.

PARLIAMENT AS A TRAINING GROUND FOR POLITICAL LEADERSHIP

The difference between 'token' and strong Parliamentary institutions forms a central theme of Weber's articles on 'Parliament and Government in a Reconstructed Germany'.[7] His starting point was with the common function of Parliaments everywhere in expressing the consent of the governed to their government:

> A certain minimum of consent, at least of the socially important classes among the governed, is a precondition for the permanence of even the best organised systems of rule. Parliaments

are nowadays the means for giving outward expression to this minimum of consent.[8]

However, it was the differences in the constitutional position of Parliaments that were significant. On this depended the whole character of politics as well as the development of political leadership. If a Parliament was limited to the role of refusing financial or legislative approval to the government, or of presenting petitions on behalf of the subjects, that is to token constitutionalism, it could not participate positively in the work of government. Its members could only carry on 'negative' politics: could only 'stand over against the government as a hostile power, be fed by it with the absolute minimum of information, be treated as an obstacle . . .'[9] It was different with a Parliament where the government was either directly chosen from its members, or had to maintain the support of the majority to remain in office, and hence be responsible to Parliament for the conduct and approval policy. This was Parliamentary government in the true sense. 'In this case the leaders of the dominant parties are necessarily positive sharers in state power. Parliament is then a factor of *positive* politics . . .'[10]

The characteristic type of politics fostered by weak Parliamentary institutions was what Weber called in the passage above and in his other writings of the period 'negative politics'. According to this, political parties and their leaders, excluded from sharing in real power, were confined to complaint and protest, and to the negative role of reacting to proposals initiated elsewhere.[11] 'Negative politics' had two distinct manifestations. One was that the energy of politicians was largely directed towards securing minor administrative posts for party members. Politics always involved a striving for personal power; but where the system excluded elected representatives from positions of real power, their attention became absorbed in minor office. 'Everything revolves round the patronage of minor subordinate positions'.[12] These were the sops with which the bureaucracy reconciled them to the system of bureaucratic rule. The height of endeavour became 'to alter a few paragraphs of the budget in the interests of a party's electorate, and to ensure a handful of sinecures for the protégés of the party bigwigs'.[13] The other feature of a weak Parliament was that it encouraged politics of an extreme ideological tone, in which the consequences of politics were never adequately considered. The unrealistic posturing of politicians was a consequence both of their lack of power and of their being denied access to information on which realistic policies could be based. 'Either ignorant demagogy or routinised impotence . . . hold the stage'.[14] Thus, for example, the 'unpolitical brotherhood ethic of class comradeship' that already held elements of the SPD in its grip, in their determination to have nothing to do with the capitalist system, was reinforced by a Parliamentary system which encouraged opposition for its own sake, since representatives were never in the position to have to take responsibility for the consequences of what they proposed.[15]

'Negative politics' could be said to be a type of politics in the purely neutral sense in which Weber defined it, of striving to influence the exercise of leadership and the distribution of power. It could have some influences on the course of policy even if only through the exercise of a kind of veto. But in terms of politics as defined in the 'ideal type' of politician—one who pursues power in order to exercise personal responsibility—it was not real politics at all, since the power to make that responsibility a reality was lacking.[16] Further, just as the position of Parliament determined the character of politics, so it encouraged the types who would be suited to this kind of activity: placemen who sought office without the responsibility of power, and demagogues who did not have to weigh the consequences of their speeches. These were the antithesis of the true politician. Such men won supremacy under a system of negative politics, which operated a kind of 'negative selection', diverting all major talents into other fields of activity.[17] Thus on the rare occasions when a weak Parliament had the opportunity to assert itself positively, as the German Reichstag in the Chancellor crisis of 1917, it could do so only in a haphazard and disorganised manner, 'like an uprising of slaves', since it lacked the leaders to give direction to its newfound upsurge of political will.[18]

If 'negative' politics was the typical form of politics in weak Parliaments, 'positive' politics, involving the exercise of political responsibility, was typical of strong Parliamentary systems, in which the government was recruited from Parliament and was directly answerable to it. In such a system the chief function of Parliament was as a recruiting and training ground ('Auslesestätte') for future political leaders.[19] Weber regarded this as the most impressive feature of the British Parliament. By a process of selection from its ranks politicians had come to the fore who had succeeded in subordinating a quarter of mankind to the rule of a tiny minority—'and voluntarily at that!'[20] A strong Parliamentary system attracted men with the capacity for leadership ('Führernaturen'), because Parliament was recognised as the normal route to office with its exercise of personal responsibility.

In emphasising the function of a strong Parliament as a recruiting ground for leadership, Weber sought to defend it from challenges from both the Right and the Left. Both argued from a common dislike of the pettiness and place-seeking of German Parliamentary life, but drew different conclusions from this. The Right argued that a Parliamentary system was essentially un-German, or else that the Germans were not yet ready for it; the Left advocated a system of direct democracy, without the mediation of Parliament. Against the former view that the nation was either unique or constitutionally unsuited to Parliamentary institutions, Weber insisted that the low level of political ability in Germany was a consequence of the institutional weakness of the Reichstag, and could not be laid at the door of Parliamentarism as such.[21] Up till that time, said Weber at the end of 'Parliament and Government', there had been no room for men of leadership qualities in the German Parliaments. It was therefore unfair to deduce that the nation was unripe for Parliamentary government: 'It is the height of political dishonesty to complain of the "negative" politics of the Parliaments, and at the same time to block the way for men of leadership capacity to play a positive part and exercise responsible power with the backing of a Parliamentary following'.[22] The low level of political ability in Germany was thus a consequence, not a cause—a consequence of institutions which had been designed at least partly to prevent men of calibre from emerging through the process of Parliamentary politics.[23]

From the Left the inadequacy of Parliament was also criticised, though not in the name of authoritarianism but of direct democracy and government by referendum. The 'democrats' objected not only to the careerism of Parliamentary politics but also to its voluntary character, in that it involved a distinction between a few 'active' and the majority of 'passive' participants. Weber answered them in his other major polemic of the wartime period, 'Suffrage and Democracy in Germany'. 'There are', he said, 'many upright and even fanatical "democrats", who see in Parliamentarism a system for careerists and spongers, leading to the perversion of democracy and the rule of cliques'.[24] For these, only 'true' democracy could provide an administration which would serve the needs of the broad masses of the nation. But there were two questions they must answer:

First, if the power of Parliament is removed, what organ is left

to democracy to control the administration of officials?...
Secondly, what does it put in place of the rule of Parliamentary
cliques? The rule of even more inaccessible... cliques. The
system of so-called direct democracy is technically only possible
in small states or cantons. In every mass state democracy leads
to bureaucratic administration, and, without the introduction of
a strong Parliament, to bureaucratic *rule*.[25]

For Weber, leadership recruited and developed in Parliament
provided the only means of controlling the administration. This
was the only viable form that democracy could take under modern
conditions.

Besides serving as a recruiting ground for political leaders, a
strong Parliament also provided the means for training them.
Here again Britain provided the model. An essential instrument in
this training was the system of inquiry by committees, armed with
the right to probe the administration and scrutinise relevant docu-
ments.[26] Such a system ensured the accountability of the administration to Parliament and provided a direct check on the civil
service. Since knowledge formed the major source of bureaucratic
power, the opportunity to share in their knowledge and expertise
was necessary to controlling them effectively. Taking part in
committee work was therefore the best form of training for
a future political leader, as the British system indicated:

> It is only this school of intensive work in the realities of
> administration . . . that equips an assembly to be a selecting
> ground, not for mere demagogues, but for effective politicians
> with a grasp of reality, of which the English Parliament is the
> supreme example. Only this kind of relationship between
> officials and professional politicians guarantees the continuous
> control of the administration, and through this the political
> education of both leaders and led.[27]

Naturally such scrutiny was resented by the officials, since it conflicted with their norm of official secrecy, but it was a necessary
condition for the development of political leadership, as opposed
to demagogy and dilettantism.[28]

Weber's answer to bureaucratic control was thus based on a
contrast between two kinds of Parliamentary system—the weak or
'token' Parliament typified by Germany, the strong by England—
and the typical consequences of each for the style of politics and
the character of political leadership. His concern to change the
character of German politics and its politicians likewise depended

on institutional reform, in particular of those paragraphs of the constitution that limited the role of Parliament, such as the notorious Article 9, section 2, which debarred a member of the Reichstag from holding governmental office and cut him off from his political base if he accepted it.[29] Weber was not so simple as to believe that similar political institutions produced similar consequences in all countries. France enjoyed Parliamentary government in the full sense, yet its parties were chronically fragmented and incapable of producing the kind of political leadership Weber expected from a Parliamentary system. But this was a consequence of her particular social structure. 'France is not the country', Weber argued, 'where the *typical* consequences of democracy for Parliamentarism can be studied'.[30] Nor did he believe that the alteration of a few clauses of the German Constitution would produce political leadership overnight. The habits of mind, the 'will to powerlessness', inculcated over generations could not be changed easily. Yet institutional reform was a *necessary* condition, in that it would remove the obstacles to the development of leadership:

> No one should imagine that a paragraph of this kind, which linked the appointment and dismissal of the Reichskanzler to a Parliamentary vote, could suddenly conjure up 'leaders' out of the ground, when these have been excluded from Parliament for decades because of its powerlessness. But the essential prerequisites for this can be institutionally created, and everything now depends on this being done.[31]

It should be said that the contrast between the British and German systems of government was a commonplace of German political analysis, and that the British Parliament was an accepted model for those who advocated democratic reform. In this sense there was nothing particularly original about Weber's typology. However, Weber had his own way of setting the commonplace in a new light by approaching it from a different perspective. Here, the distinctive feature of Parliamentary government emphasised by Weber was not so much that it was more 'democratic', but that it developed the kind of leadership capable of controlling a modern bureaucracy. It is true that he spoke of the process of giving power to Parliament as 'democratisation', and that his strong Parliamentary type included distinctively democratic features, such as the power to subject the activity of government to public scrutiny. But his theory of Parliamentary government cannot be called a *democratic* theory, since it did not seek to justify such government in terms of recognisably democratic values, such as increasing the influence of the people on the policies pursued by those who governed. The peculiarity of Weber's position consisted in his belief that under modern conditions formally democratic institutions provide the best guarantee of vigorous political leadership. Thus, although he could align himself with radical democrats, his commitment to the institutions of democracy was only a contingent one, not a matter of principle. How far this was so, was shown in a letter to Professor Ehrenberg in 1917:

> Forms of constitution are for me technical means like any other machinery. I'd be just as happy to take the side of the monarch against Parliament, if only he were a *politician* or showed signs of becoming one.[32]

This remark is no doubt an exaggeration, since the whole point of Weber's opposition to the monarch was to the *system*, and not to the person; an exceptional monarch might provide political leadership, but the monarchy as such could not guarantee continuity of political direction in the way that a Parliament could. Further, as will be discussed later in the chapter, Weber saw important advantages in a Parliamentary system as a guarantee of political liberty. Nevertheless, the letter is a clear indication of the priority he gave to political leadership in his theory.

Weber's discussion of Parliamentary institutions demonstrates his characteristic emphasis on the process of selection, on the way in which different institutional and social structures encouraged and selected different types and qualities of person. Whereas a weak Parliamentary system drove men of leadership quality away from politics, and encouraged 'mere demagogues' and those concerned with petty patronage, a strong Parliament brought a very different type of politician to dominance. Underlying this distinction was the more general assumption that what mattered in politics, as elsewhere, was the few people at the top; indeed, that oligarchy was inevitable, and that therefore the quality and character of the oligarchy was of the first importance. The empirical side to this assumption—the inevitability of oligarchy—will be examined more explicitly in the context of Weber's account of mass politics and universal suffrage, which forms the second aspect to his theory of democracy.

MASS DEMOCRACY AND ELITES

If part of Weber's theory of democracy consisted in his account of Parliamentary institutions, the other part lay in his justification for universal suffrage and his account of mass democracy. Here again, Weber's theory was distinctive, both in the character of his justification for universal suffrage and also in his insistence that its introduction did not alter, but only reinforce, what he called 'the law of the small number', the law that politics was controlled by small groups from above.[33] As with other so-called 'elite theorists',[34] the involvement of the mass in politics was not regarded by Weber as modifying the fact of oligarchy, but rather the methods by which the few were selected, the type of person who reached the top and the qualities necessary for the effective exercise of power. The advent of democracy changed the rules of selection, but not the process of selection itself.

Weber's discussion of mass democracy introduces a further feature which he regarded as typical of modern politics alongside bureaucracy: its mass character. As well as being typified by bureaucratic administration, the modern state is also the mass state, in the sense that the mass cannot be ignored in the political process, whatever the type of constitution. The term 'mass' was used in his political writings in rather different senses. Sometimes it indicated merely an aggregation of large numbers, as in the term 'Massenstaat', which indicated a major power, or when he spoke of 'the mass as such, whatever social classes compose it in any particular instance'.[35] At the same time, the term usually also indicated something about the character of such aggregations and the society of which they were a part. The 'mass' was the product of the process of social levelling, which had dissolved the traditional distinctions of birth and status, and destroyed the relationships of traditional society.[36] The existence of the 'mass' was thus itself an indication of democratisation, in one sense of that term. Weber drew a familiar distinction between the social and the political aspects of democracy, between the levelling of social distinctions on the one hand, and the introduction of universal suffrage and Parliamentary government on the other. Social democratisation was already far advanced, and was being reinforced by the growth of mass literacy and the popular press. It was these factors that made the 'mass' significant for politics, irrespective of the type of constitution, and even where there was no political democracy. The appeal to the mass by propaganda and demagogy was as much a feature of monarchies and dictatorships as of political democracies. It was a standard feature of German government, particularly as a weapon in the internal struggle between contending departments or governmental

factions.[37] Mass demagogy was also a typical instrument of the
military dictatorships which, Weber argued, to a greater or lesser
degree came to dominate all the contending nations in the World
War.[38] The appeal to the masses was thus not confined to political
democracies.

What differed, however, was the manner in which the mass
became involved. It could be activated in a spasmodic and 'irrational' manner, as in the 'politics of the streets' or the appeal of a
dictator.[39] Weber regarded the U-boat agitation in wartime Germany as a typical example of the damaging effects of such mass
involvement in issues which required careful strategic calculation.
Alternatively, the mass could be activated in a regular and disciplined way through constitutional means in a political democracy.
What distinguished political democracy was not the fact of mass
involvement, but the manner of it: the use of demagogy was linked
to the regular exercise of the vote for choosing a leader, and to the
organisation of the mass by political parties.

> Demagogy . . . is independent of the type of constitution . . .
> Monarchies have also trod the road of demagogy in their own
> way. Speeches, telegrams, all the possible means of propaganda
> are mobilised to protect their prestige, and no one can maintain
> that this form of political propaganda has proved any less
> prejudicial to state interests than electoral demagogy, even of
> the most violent conceivable kind. In fact just the opposite.
> And now in wartime we have experienced the phenomenon,
> novel even for us, of demagogy by the admiral. . . . So one
> cannot conclude that demagogy is a peculiarity of political
> democracies. . . . In Germany we have demagogy and mob in-
> fluence without democracy—or rather *because* of the lack of an
> ordered democracy.[40]

Weber's justification for political democracy here was thus not so
much that it would give the masses an influence they would not
otherwise enjoy,[41] but that their involvement in politics would be
orderly and regular rather than spasmodic and 'irrational'.[42]
There were other reasons also why he favoured universal suffrage,
and these are set out most coherently in his article 'Wahlrecht
und Demokratie'. Here he argued that anything short of universal
suffrage was incompatible with the character of modern institutions. A basic presupposition of these institutions—capitalism,
bureaucracy, the state itself—was that men shared a formal
equality of status, and that there were no special privileges
recognised or guaranteed by law. Equal suffrage was merely an

extension of this principle. 'It is no accident', he wrote, 'that the demand for universal suffrage is with us. This equality corresponds in its mechanical character with the nature of the modern state. It is only with the modern state that the concept of "state citizen" comes into being.'[43] He went on to link this concept to citizenship with the obligation to take part in military service, and the equality between men in the face of death. This was a consideration particularly prominent in wartime. Weber continually denounced the Prussian three-class suffrage, and the anomaly of allowing political rights to those who stayed at home which were denied to soldiers at the front. But there was a more general historical point. Citizenship and political rights were historically associated with differences in men's capacity to provide their own military equipment. Such differences no longer existed, since, in the army as in other modern institutions, men no longer owned the equipment they used:

> All men are equal in the face of death. . . . All inequalities of political rights in the past stemmed ultimately from the economically related inequalities of *military* qualification, which no longer have any place in the bureaucratised state and army.[44]

Thus universal suffrage and mass democracy followed on from, and were made necessary by, the prior process of social democratisation that was already far advanced. Given the nature of modern society, there was no basis for any suffrage short of universal. In his various writings Weber showed himself to have thoroughly mastered the intricacies of 'suffrage politics'—the multifarious schemes to keep the masses disenfranchised based upon property, occupation, education and what not. In 'Wahlrecht und Demokratie' he examined each of these in turn, and showed that none had any viable basis in the character of society.[45] Once the agitation for an extension of the vote had begun, the only end possible was universal suffrage; people might as well recognise this at once, and save their energy for other issues.[46] Political democracy, then, for Weber, followed from the formal equality presupposed by the institutions of modern society, and was necessary if the masses were to be involved in an orderly way in the political process rather than by spasmodic and 'irrational' interventions.

If universal suffrage was in the long run unavoidable for modern states, its introduction did not alter, but only reinforce, what Weber called the 'law of the small number', the universal principle that politics is dominated by small groups. 'Everywhere the principle of the small number—that is, the superior political manoeuvrability of small *leading* groups—determines political activity.'[47] The assertion of this principle forms one of the common links between *Economy and Society* and Weber's political writings, where it is insisted on equally.[48] Policy is always determined by a few, who then involve others only to the extent that their support is judged necessary, a principle which is as true of democracies as any other form of government. The mass only becomes involved as a result of initiatives from above, never from below; their role is limited to that of response.

> It is not a question of the politically passive 'mass' throwing up a leader of itself, but rather of the political leader recruiting a following and winning the mass by demogogic appeal. This is true even in the most democratic constitutions.[49]

The 'law of the small number' did not mean that leaders could dispense with a following, or that the following might not need to be large and enthusiastic, as for example in wartime. It meant that the initiatives always lay with the 'small leading groups', whose command of a 'staff' and ability to plan a strategy in secret ensured them the advantage. At most, a following might enjoy an occasional veto power.

Weber was less than explicit about how far the 'law of the small number' applied to the direct democracies of ancient Athens, and the Swiss cantons. Although they might have their 'Caesarist' demagogues or their traditional aristocracies, he insisted on drawing a sharp distinction between these types of democracy, based upon neighbourhood and personal relationships, and the modern mass democracies.[50] Though it might be possible to produce a definition of the term 'democracy' that included both (for example, that democracy is where 'no formal inequality of political rights exists between the social classes'),[51] this was too general to be useful; modern mass democracy could be called 'democratic' in only a derivative sense. When compared with the oligarchies it had replaced, the advent of universal suffrage had not made politics any more democratic in the sense of any greater diffusion of power; if anything power was more concentrated. The term 'democratisation' could thus be misleading, Weber wrote, since the *demos* could never rule, only be ruled. What had changed was the manner in which the small number was selected, the qualities required of it, the chance for a different type of person to reach the top.[52]

Weber's account of mass democracy is thus an account of the new elite roles brought about by the advent of universal suffrage, and the qualities required for these. The classical analysis of the effect of the mass vote on the character of political activity was Ostrogorski's study of Britain and the USA, and Weber borrowed freely from this.[53] Ostrogorski's theme was the development of the extra-Parliamentary caucus, the permanent party organisation, as an instrument for mobilising the mass vote. Weber, in his accounts in 'Parliament and Government' and in 'Politics as a Vocation', emphasised two particular consequences of this development.[54] One was the decline in the importance of local notables (*Honoratiores*) who had previously played a major part in the selection of candidates and the organisation of elections, replacement by the party boss, the paid election agent or party official, whose professional job was to mobilise the vote whether on an entrepreneurial basis or through a bureaucratic party organisation. 'Every extension of the suffrage . . . signifies the extension of the strict inter-local bureaucratic organisation of parties, and thereby the increasing dominance of the party bureaucracy and its discipline at the expense of the association of local notables.'[55] The struggle between the *Honoratiores* and the party official might be longer or shorter, but in the end the latter was bound to prevail.

The other significant consequence was the increasing importance of the political leader who stood at the head of the party machine, at the expense of the individual MP. Where MPs were now dependent upon the support of the machine for their election, both in turn depended on the personality of the party leader and his ability to capture the mass vote in the demagogic content of the election campaign. Where previously MPs may have acted more as individuals, they were now aggregated into a 'following' behind a personality, dependent on his success for their own. 'Nowadays the members of Parliament, with the exception of a few cabinet ministers (and a few eccentrics) are normally nothing better than well-disciplined lobby fodder.'[56] Weber followed Ostrogorski in regarding contemporary British democracy as a plebiscitary type, with the Prime Minister similar in fact if not in form to the American President. Leaders such as Gladstone and Lloyd George had successfully appealed over the heads of Parliament and party directly to the masses in the country. With such leaders, members of Parliament were 'merely political spoilsmen enrolled in their following.'[57]

Weber's attitude to these developments was different from Ostrogorski's, in that he regarded them as irreversible. Ostrogorski had criticised the dominance of the party organisation and the plebiscitary leader as a perversion of democracy, which could only be restored by the abolition of permanent party structures with their insidious pressures on individuals. In their place he favoured a system of *ad hoc* coalitions for specific and temporary ends, as being the only way in which the popular will could be adequately represented. Here the MP would be individually responsible to his constituents, and the cabinet minister to the 'popular will' as this expressed itself from time to time.[58] Weber regarded all such proposals as doomed from the start, in that they failed to recognise the indispensability of party organisations in the era of the mass vote, and the permanence of the change which the latter had brought. 'All attempts to subordinate the representative to the will of the voters have in the long run only one effect: they reinforce the ascendancy of the party organisation over him, since it is the party organisation alone that can mobilise the people.'[59]

Weber thus emphasised the two major roles which had been brought to the fore by the extension of the suffrage, as permanent features of modern politics. On the one hand was the full-time party agent, whether a political entrepreneur like the American boss, or a paid official within a bureaucratic structure as in England and Germany. In each case his power rested on the control of the machinery of vote-getting. Where the *Honoratiores* had wielded influence by virtue of their status in the locality, the party agent was a person totally devoid of status, who typically sought power for its own sake. 'He does not seek social honour; the "professional" is despised in "respectable society". He seeks power alone . . .'[60] On the other hand was the plebiscitary leader, the grand demagogue, the 'dictator of the electoral battlefield', selected by his ability to command a mass vote in the electoral contest.[61] In addition to these two major roles, Weber pointed to others which had become important with the extension of the suffrage, such as the party 'Maecenas' who paid for the machine, or the journalist, 'that most important representative of the demagogic species', whether he worked inside a party or outside it. What was characteristic of all these new roles, except possibly for the Maecenas,[62] was that recruitment to them did not depend upon birth or even education, which Weber insisted had nothing to do with political skill. The qualities 'selected' by the new circumstances of universal suffrage were those which led to success in mobilising the vote—skills of organisation and propaganda, qualities of mass leadership, the ability to contribute finance to the party machine.

Political democracy, according to Weber, thus did not bring any diminution or diffusion of power, but rather a shift in its location from the local notables and individual MPs to a new set of roles which demanded different qualities and a different pattern of recruitment. The law of the small number still operated as before, only now power was concentrated in the hands of the full-time professionals who operated the machine and the leader who stood at its head. The most succinct expression of the law of the small number at work in mass democracy is Weber's thumbnail sketch of political parties at the end of Part 1 of *Economy and Society*. The chief elements in party activities, he says, are the following:

1 Party leaders and their staffs, who control the operation.
2 Active party members, who for the most part merely have the function of acclamation of their leaders, though in certain circumstances they may also act as a check, participate in discussion, voice complaints, submit resolutions.
3 The inactive masses of electors, who are merely objects whose votes are sought at election time . . .
4 Contributors to party funds, who usually, though not always, remain behind the scenes.[63]

Weber's account here sounds more oligarchical than it in fact is, since in these passages quoted, particularly from *Economy and Society* and 'Politics as a Vocation', he is referring exclusively to the formal structures of power.[64] It needs to be kept in mind throughout that Weber saw the political process as operating within a class context. Thus the advent of universal suffrage not only brought a change in the machinery of politics, but meant giving some acknowledgement to the working class and the issues which concerned them.[65] In the German context, in particular, it meant striking at one of the roots of Junker power in the class-based Prussian suffrage.[66] Weber also held that the relationship between leader and following presupposed a basis of class interests. Political leaders were the product not only of the political structure, but also of class. Weber's archetype of a political leader, Bismarck, was not an isolated phenomenon, but 'the last and greatest of the Junkers';[67] though his outlook may have transcended that of his class, his achievements would have been impossible without its support. As Weber wrote explicitly in 1917, 'Any policy of great consequence [grosse Politik] is always made by small groups of men, but decisive for its success . . . is the *willing* support of a sufficiently broad and powerful social class.'[68]

The interests of a class, and its level of political awareness, set limits to what a political leader could achieve. Hence Weber's insistence that, whatever changes were made in the political structure after the war, they would have little effect unless the bourgeoisie developed 'a more self-conscious political spirit'.[69] Weber's elite emphasis was thus set within, or at least alongside, a class analysis, and was not an alternative to it. The present discussion must therefore be regarded as provisional, until Weber's theory of society has been considered.

Despite this limiting assumption about the social context within which political structures were set, it remained true that political initiatives stemmed from the top, and therefore the character of the leader or leading group was crucial. Hence Weber's emphasis on elite roles, and his presentation of the differences between political structures as differences in the types and qualities 'selected' to predominate within them. If political structures could not be distinguished from one another by being more democratic in any meaningful sense, then all the more significance attached to the character and quality of the elite or oligarchy they threw up. The evaluative implications of this are stated explicitly in a passage in Weber's 1917 article on 'The Meaning of Value Freedom':

> Every type of social order, without exception, must, if one wishes to *evaluate* it, be assessed according to *which type of man* it gives the opportunity to rise to a position of superiority through the operation of the various objective and subjective selective factors.[70]

As with the strong Parliamentary system itself, so also the electoral contest in a mass democracy encouraged the rise of men with very different qualities from those 'selected' in the process of bureaucratic administration, and ones much more suited to the political struggle:

> Only those characters are fitted for political leadership who have been selected in the political struggle, since all politics is in its essence 'Kampf'. The much abused 'work of the demagogue' provides this training on average better than the administrator's office.[71]

The distinctive features of modern political democracy, then, according to Weber, were a strong Parliament, which ensured the selection of men equipped to exercise political responsibility; and universal suffrage, which ensured that the involvement of the mass in the political process would take place in an orderly fashion, and which at the same time changed the character of elite roles, giving supremacy to the party machine and the individual who stood at its head. This is a theory remarkably similar to that later popularised by Joseph Schumpeter, whose conception of democracy as a technique for producing political leaders continues to enjoy wide currency.[72] Schumpeter's account clearly owes a good deal to Weber, not least in its thoroughgoing critique of classical democratic theory for attributing to the electorate an 'altogether unrealistic' degree of initiative.[73] The crusading zeal with which Schumpeter demolishes the illusions of popular sovereignty matches that of Weber himself, as typically expressed by the latter in correspondence with Robert Michels:

> Ah! How much disillusion you still have to endure! Concepts such as 'the will of the people', the true will of the people, have long since lost any meaning for me; they are fictions.[74]

In the case of Weber and Schumpeter alike, the apparently tough realism with which they assert the inevitability of oligarchy conceals a prescriptive premise. Their view that initiatives in politics stem from a few at the top is coloured by their fear of what will happen if they do not. The law of the small number, the fictional character of the popular will, has to be asserted as the truth, so that it should become if possible more firmly established.

Underlying this ambiguous position can be discerned the ambivalent attitude towards the 'mass' that is typical of most elite theorists. On the one hand the mass is seen as a passive object, incapable of any independent action and initiative, easily led by the nose. On the other hand it is a disturbing phenomenon, potentially dangerous, needing to be kept subject to 'order'. These two faces of the mass are given extreme expression in the influential work by Gustav le Bon on the crowd, where the crowd is at once 'a servile flock that is incapable of ever doing without a master' and also possessed of 'savage and destructive instincts left dormant by previous ages'.[75] This double image of the mass produced in the elite theorists the simultaneous assertion of two mutually inconsistent principles: on the one hand a law, 'oligarchy is inevitable'; on the other a principle, 'a few heads are sounder'.[76]

Both propositions are to be found in Weber's political writings, though not in so sharp a form. Thus he writes, as in the passage quoted above,[77] that there is no question of the 'politically passive mass' throwing up a leader of itself, even in the most democratic system. They can only wait to be won by a leader, and it is he who controls the initiative. Then a few pages later we learn that the mass as such 'thinks only of the morrow'; it is always subject to emotional and irrational influences. Realistic and responsible policies require that matters should be left in the hands of a few:

> A cool and clear head—and successful politics, no less success-ful democratic politics, can only be made with the head—is more likely to prevail . . . the smaller the number of those taking part in the deliberations.[78]

This ambivalence between a descriptive and a prescriptive account of the 'mass' finds its parallel in Weber's account of individual leadership. The importance of the individual leader to Weber lay not only in what he could achieve historically, in his empirical exploits, but also in the intrinsic value which lay in individual as opposed to collective action. This is shown clearly by a passage in Weber's account of the 1905 revolution in Russia, which he con-trasted with previous European revolutions for its lack of 'great leaders'. Everything, he wrote, was simply a 'collective product'. This was in part explained by the character of modern revolution and the tactics necessary to fight a police state. So much effort had to be devoted to tactics that 'it was difficult for "great leading personalities" to play any role. Against vermin it is impossible for "great" deeds to be accomplished.'[79] It is clear that it is the quality of the revolution that Weber is questioning here, not the extent of its possible consequences. Only an individual could perform 'great' deeds, not a collective. The 'mass' for Weber, as an undifferentiated collective, had a largely negative signifi-cance. While being an inescapable feature of modern politics, its only useful role lay in providing an ordered response to a leader's initiative.

What is distinctive about this account of democracy, like that of Schumpeter subsequently, is that it makes no reference to demo-cratic *values*, much less regards them as worth striving for.[80] A strong Parliamentary system was justified because it provided a training ground for leadership; the advantage of mass democracy lay in the opportunities it provided for the rise of outstanding individuals. However, if Weber gave little room in his theory to democratic values, what of liberal ones? Schumpeter certainly regarded his own conception of democracy as a means to preserv-ing political liberties. How far Weber did so is a matter of some debate, and the chapter will conclude with an examination of this question.

PARLIAMENT IS A PROTECTOR OF LIBERTY

According to Wolfgang Mommsen, the *only* functions assigned to Parliament in Weber's theory were those of developing a political leadership and scrutinising the administration:

> The purpose of parliamentary democracy in Weber's conception reduced itself essentially to two functions: the selection of politicians with the capacity for leadership and the control of ... the administrative apparat.[81]

In Mommsen's view, Weber's account of modern democracy involved the abandonment of the ideas of liberal constitutionalism, and this for a number of reasons.[82] One was his rejection of natural law theory, which had previously provided the philosophical basis for human rights, as being no longer valid or acceptable to modern man. A second reason lay in the rise of the organised party machine, which diminished the significance of Parliament as a forum for the free expression of individual opinion. Such developments 'destroyed the ideological basis . . . of liberal constitutionalism'.[83] Here Mommsen overstates his case, as well as ignoring the distinction in Weber between individualism and civil or constitutional rights. Because deputies were organised into a party following, it did not follow that Parliament could no longer be an effective guarantor of political liberties. Because civil rights were no longer underpinned by natural law beliefs, it did not follow that they could not be protected by institutional structures which enjoyed a backing of social support. Mommsen writes almost as if he himself believed that there could be no constitutional structures which enjoyed a backing of social support. Mommsen writes almost as if he himself believed that there could be no constitutional liberalism except on a natural law basis.[84]

In fact, there is ample evidence that, besides its other functions, Weber also regarded a strong Parliament as a protector of civil rights and liberties, and valued it for this reason. This is most clearly emphasised in his writings on the 1905 Russian revolution, in which he linked the possible attainment of civil rights and Parliamentary government together. In the event, as he showed, the various freedoms announced in the October manifesto— freedoms of expression, of conscience, of association, of assembly, of the person—remained only token, and could only continue to be so in the absence of an effective Parliament. The Duma was itself a token assembly, lacking the power to subject the administration to scrutiny, and because of this the system of administrative arbitrariness was able to proceed unchecked. Even the deputies themselves enjoyed a degree of immunity far inferior to normal European practice. A strong Parliament and the guarantee of civil rights belonged together.[85]

Weber made the same point explicitly in his wartime articles on 'Parliament and Government', significantly enough in the context of his discussion of the plebiscitary leader. The position of Lloyd George, he argued, though in theory dependent on Parliament, in practice had a plebiscitary basis: it owed its support to the masses in the country and the army at the front. Yet this did not make the existence of Parliament valueless. In face of the 'Caesarist leader who enjoyed the confidence of the masses' Parliament provided a check on his power, a guarantee of civil rights and a peaceful means of removing him when he lost popular confidence.[86] As Weber frequently observed, the Parliamentary and plebiscitary principles stood in some tension to one another. While it was possible for a plebiscitary leader to emerge within a Parliamentary system, at the same time the context of Parliamentary responsibility was important in keeping his powers in check. Thus, far from the advent of the party machine marking the end of constitutional liberalism, it made more necessary the function of a strong Parliament in protecting individual liberties in face of power of the plebiscitary leader; and this remained an important feature of Weber's theory at least until the postwar period.

As was pointed out in Chapter 2, a characteristic of Weber's political standpoint was his commitment to the values of strong leadership and political liberty at the same time. The significance of his theory of Parliament was that it was an attempt to hold them together, and combine both functions in the same institution. The fact that he did not devote much space to the liberal dimension of Parliament in his wartime writings does not mean that it was not important to him. As he wrote earlier in the same series of articles, it was a gross illusion to imagine that life would be at all worth living 'without the achievements bequeathed by the age of the "rights of man"'.[87] Because such rights were taken for granted did not make them any the less significant. Though Mommsen is right to insist that, in contrast with the liberal tradition, the weight of emphasis in Weber's writings on Germany is on the function of Parliament as a selector of leaders, he is mistaken to overlook its function as a protector of liberties as he does. Weber's conception of Parliament included both. This makes all the more significant the change of view which led him to advocate downgrading the position of Parliament in the postwar constitution.[88]

One writer who recognises the liberal features in Weber's political theory is Gustav Schmidt in his book *Deutscher Historismus und der Übergang zur parlamentarischen Demokratie*.[89] Schmidt is representative of the opposite tendency to Mommsen, of those who claim to find a much more liberal, even democratic, element in Weber's work. The aim of his book is to show how a number of German thinkers, contemporary with Weber, attempted to adapt the British theory of Parliamentary government to the uniqueness of the German historical tradition. According to Schmidt, a central feature of English constitutional theory, then as now, was that the—in theory—limitless power of the government was in practice restricted by the norms or 'operative ideals' of society, which constituted its real source of legitimacy. This concept of society, he argues, embodying a particular 'moral standard', was taken over by Weber to provide a missing element in his political theory: an account of the source of the political leader's legitimacy. In contrast to the 'legality' involved in bureaucratic authority, the *legitimacy* of the political leader lay for Weber in his conformity to the 'moral standard' or 'operative ideals' of society. Where the former element was implicit in the German historical tradition, the latter derived from the constitutional theory of Britain.[90]

Schmidt's interpretation is mistaken in this respect, that he makes Weber out, in his theory of legitimacy, to be engaged in a philosophical rather than a sociological enterprise. Weber was nowhere concerned to give the kind of philosophical account of legitimacy that Schmidt portrays, and that is characteristic of the English sources that he cites (notably Lindsay). Weber certainly wished to prescribe certain types of institution and political leadership as preferable to others, but he nowhere suggested that such institutions or leaders could only be *legitimate* if they accorded with a particular constitutional principle. This was wholly foreign to his conviction that constitutional principles were simply means, and had no value in themselves.

Nevertheless, Schmidt does identify an important element in Weber's political theory, and that is its dependence on a concept of society, though this should be seen more in sociological than philosophical terms. Weber's political theory was never merely institutional. While looking to Parliament for the institutional protection of liberties, he did not imagine that it could perform this function on its own, any more than it could guarantee political leadership, without a strong basis in society. This was worked out most fully in his articles on Russia, which went beyond an examination of the particular proposals for a liberal constitutional system to consider what basis of social support existed for Parliamentary government in the major classes and their conditions of life. In respect of German politics Weber was equally explicit that, without a politically self-confident bourgeoisie, the freest institutions would be 'a mere shadow'.[91] His conception of Parliament thus rested on a theory of society. The relationship was, however, sociological rather than philosophical. That is to say, Weber was more concerned with the question: what kind of social support is necessary to make political institutions effective? than the question: what kind of support is necessary to make them legitimate?

Weber's theory of society and its relation to politics forms the main subject of Chapters 6 to 8. Before turning to this, however, there is one further aspect of his political theory to be considered: his account of the nation and his justification for nationalism as a principle. This will form the subject of the following chapter.

REFERENCES

1 GPS, pp 533–4; GM, pp 115–6.
2 D Lindenlaub, op cit, pp 261–3, 393–9.
3 GPS, pp 76–8.
4 GPS, 1st edn, pp 455–7.
5 ibid, pp 457–8.
6 Two works on British government which were widely read in this period were Sidney Low, *Die Regierung Englands*, and A L Lowell, *Die englische Verfassung*, translated in 1908 and 1913 respectively.
7 Especially GPS, pp 327–57.
8 GPS, p 327.
9 GPS, pp 327–8.
10 ibid.
11 GPS, pp 213, 459.
12 GPS, pp 329, 354–5.
13 GPS, p 336.
14 GPS, p 343.
15 GPS, pp 353–4. In turn their oppositional attitude itself formed an obstacle to the introduction of Parliamentary government, ibid. See Chapter 6.
16 GPS, pp 336–7.
17 GPS, pp 334, 379.
18 GPS, pp 213, 348.
19 GPS, pp 331, 342, 391.
20 GPS, p 343.
21 GPS, pp 333–4.
22 GPS, p 428.
23 Designed by Bismarck and sustained by the power interests of the bureaucracy. See the articles, 'Bismarcks Erbe in der Reichsverfassung' and 'Die Erbschaft Bismarcks', GPS, pp 229–32, 299–308. For bureaucratic power interests, see GPS, passim.

24 GPS, p 276.
25 GPS, p 277. Weber also justifies a Parliamentary system here against government by referendum on the grounds that it allows for the 'relatively best' solution by means of compromise.
26 GPS, pp 214, 341–3, 353, 428.
27 GPS, p 343.
28 GPS, pp 352–3.
29 GPS, pp 330–1, 350, 412, 423, 426. See also the article 'Die Abänderung des Artikel 9 der Reichsverfassung', GPS, 3rd edn, pp 222–5.
30 GPS, pp 371–2, 317.
31 GPS, p 412.
32 GPS, 1st edn, p 470.
33 GPS, pp 197, 227, 336, 344, 368, etc.
34 The best account of the elite thesis is in G B Parry, *Political Elites* (London, 1969).
35 GPS, p 392.
36 GPS, p 279; WG, p 567; ES, p 983.
37 GPS, pp 292, 381.
38 GPS, p 278.
39 GPS, pp 274, 293.
40 GPS, p 381; cf 287, 423.
41 For a qualification of this, see page 109.
42 In a similar way he supported the trade unions in wartime as 'the only elements of mass discipline'. GPS, p 293.
43 GPS, p 254.
44 GPS, p 256.
45 GPS, pp 235–41.
46 cf GPS, p 394.
47 GPS, p 336.
48 e.g. WG, p 548; ES, p 952.
49 GPS, p 389.
50 WG, p 548; ES, p 952.
51 GASS, pp 494–5.
52 WG, p 568; ES, p 985.
53 M Ostrogorski, *Democracy and the Organisation of Political Parties* (London, 1902).
54 GPS, pp 371–6, 521–5; GM, pp 101–7.
55 WG, p 548; ES, p 952.
56 GPS, p 524.
57 ibid.
58 M Ostrogorski, op. cit.
59 WG, p 666.
60 GPS, p 527.
61 GPS, p 523. Weber was not alone in using the terms 'dictator' and 'Caesar' of the British prime minister; such terms were a commonplace of contemporary analysis. S Low, op cit, pp 150–1. F Tönnies, *Der englische Staat und der deutsche Staat* (Berlin, 1917), pp 50ff.
62 Herr A Thyssen, the Maecenas of the Catholic Centre party, claimed 'the social status of an archbishop'. GPS, pp 374–5.
63 WG, p 167; ES, p 285.
64 It is with this formal political dimension that the present chapter is concerned.

65 One of the arguments for universal suffrage in 'Wahlrecht und Demo-kratie' was that it was necessary if consumer interests were to have any influence against the otherwise dominant interests of industrialists. GPS, pp 255–6.
66 See Chapter 6.
67 GPS, p 19; SVS, 55 (1892), pp 803–4.
68 GPS, p 197.
69 GPS, pp 441–2.
70 GAW, p 503; MSS, p 27.
71 GPS, p 380.
72 J Schumpeter, *Capitalism, Socialism and Democracy*, 2nd edn (London, 1947), especially chapters 20–3.
73 ibid, ch 21. Schumpeter was one of the academic generation following Weber, who owed much to his influence.
74 4.8.08. Quoted in W J Mommsen, op cit, pp 392–3.
75 G le Bon, *The Crowd* (London, 1896), pp 43, 118, and passim.
76 While it may not be inconsistent to desire the inevitable, the second of the two principles is usually put forward as a prescription for restricting the influence of the many.
77 See p 106.
78 GPS, p 392.
79 GPS, pp 105–6.
80 For a critique of this kind of theory see C Pateman, *Participation and Democratic Theory* (Cambridge, 1970), and the literature cited there.
81 W J Mommsen, op cit, p 394.
82 ibid, pp 390–6.
83 ibid.
84 ibid, p 407.
85 *Archiv* 23B, pp 181–250. Weber's discussion of the token character of the different freedoms is at pp 181–224, and his analysis of the weak constitutional position of the Duma itself, pp 233–50.
86 GPS, pp 382–3.
87 GPS, p 321. It is significant that Weber appears most clearly as a proponent of liberal values when writing about the country, Russia, where they were most decisively denied.
88 See Chapter 8.
89 Lübeck and Hamburg, 1964.
90 ibid, pp 276–88, 316–21.
91 GPS, p 442.

Chapter 5

Nationalism and the Nation State

In discussing Weber's justification for Parliamentary democracy, it was argued that a major consideration was the political leadership it would encourage. This was not only leadership for its own sake, however, but leadership in relation to particular ends, which Weber defined in national terms. A frequent refrain of his writing was that forms of constitution only held their validity in relation to the tasks confronting society.[1] Germany was now a major power, and required a system of government commensurate to its position, and the opportunities this presented. One consequence of this strongly instrumental standpoint was that Weber could address his argument for democracy even to the extreme Right, who had no more love of democratic ideals than he had. In embracing a great power role for Germany, he could argue, while at the same time rejecting Parliamentary democracy, they were being inconsistent:

> The only *national* politician is one who considers internal politics from the standpoint of its necessary compatibility with our external goals. Whoever does not like the 'democratic' consequences which follow from this, must *renounce* the great power role, which makes them unavoidable.[2]

It is as part of a wider nationalist outlook, therefore, that Weber's justification for Parliamentary democracy must also be seen. The present chapter will examine the character of this outlook.

Few aspects of Weber's political theory have aroused as much controversy as the question of his nationalist convictions. The thesis of Wolfgang Mommsen's book, that nationalism was the driving force of his political activity, and that Parliamentary democracy was for him simply a means to providing leadership for national ends, was greeted with a hostile reaction when it appeared, and has continued to arouse controversy since. Such debate on the question as there has been, however, has tended to take the form of assertions for or against rather than an attempt properly to elucidate the character of Weber's nationalist commitment. Weber himself accepted that such commitments were ultimately a matter of faith, and could not be *proved* by scientific argument.[3] Many critics have, however, wrongly concluded that his nationalism must therefore have been wholly irrational. Hans Maier argues in an extreme form a familiar thesis, that once Weber had divorced science from values, the latter became excluded altogether from the realm of reason, and were reduced to emotional utterances.[4] Raymond Aron calls Weber's choice of the power of the nation state as the ultimate value a 'free and *arbitrary*' choice.[5] Arthur Mitzman regards Weber's nationalism as further evidence for his psycho-pathological condition: the assertion of German independence against the Russian and Anglo-Saxon powers was 'a respectable ideological screen for the age-old struggle of sons against paternal despots'.[6]

Such assertions fail to give proper weight to the role which Weber himself assigned to reason in the value sphere. He argued for a reciprocal relationship between rational and non-rational elements. If the impetus for ideas came from an emotional root, this was in turn shaped by the activity of reason. 'At the present time,' he wrote in the introduction to his studies on world religions, 'it is widely held that emotional content is primary, while thoughts are simply its secondary expression; naturally, this view is to a large extent justified.'[7] But he went on to say that ideas could develop an autonomy of their own, typically under the influence of the intellectual strata, and that this in turn shaped emotion and the manner in which it was expressed.[8] The phenomenon of nationalism provides an example of this. Weber regarded its emotional root to lie both in the psychology of the masses and (more continuously) in the prestige sentiments of the ruling political strata. Both became transformed under the influence of intellectual groups into the idea of the nation, which in turn influenced the shape and direction which the expression of emotion took.

In the Inaugural Address Weber wrote that 'the nation state rests on a basic psychological foundation which is shared even by the broad strata of the economically subordinate classes, and is by no means merely a "superstructure" created by the economically ruling classes'.[9] In the unfinished section on the nation in *Economy and Society* he equally distinguished between an emotional and a calculating, economically oriented, element in nationalism, though here he identified this emotional element in the first instance with the 'prestige sentiments' of the political strata—the bureaucracy, army, etc.[10] These sentiments, however, came to be modified under the influence of those strata responsible for the *culture* of a society into a specifically 'national' consciousness:

> The naked prestige of 'power' is unavoidably transformed under the influence of these groups into other specific forms, in particular into the idea of the 'nation'.[11]

As will be shown below, this process of modifying prestige sentiments into the intellectual idea of the nation not only provided a justification for the power of the state, in Weber's view, but also shaped the manner of its exercise and prescribed limits to its use. It was not merely a rationalisation of emotion, but could also be an effective principle which directed the use of power as well as setting limits to its exercise.

Most accounts of Weber's nationalism are thus too simplistic. His own analysis of nationalism as an empirical phenomenon showed it to be a highly complex affair, embracing economic, political, ideological, communal elements, some of which involved society as a whole, others touching only those groups with particular interests in it. Likewise his own commitment to German nationalism as a value was equally complex. The present chapter will therefore approach it from a number of different angles. The first part will draw on his academic as well as his political writings to show what he understood by the concept of the nation, and what kind of justification he gave for nationalism as a principle. This will be an abstract or 'ideal-typical' account only. The second part will consider Weber's nationalism in practice, to see how far it can be understood in terms of the principles outlined. A brief concluding section will anticipate subsequent chapters by considering his nationalism in relation to the internal divisions of class.

THE CONCEPT OF THE NATION

Besides being characterised by bureaucratic administration and a mass public, the modern state, according to Weber's account, is also typically the nation state. But what is a nation? The concept is notoriously difficult to define. Weber sets out an account in two different places in the older part of *Economy and Society*, and this is paralleled by his contribution to discussions on the subject at meetings of the German Sociological Association in 1910 and 1912.[12] According to these accounts, Weber regarded the nation as essentially a political concept, which could only be defined in relation to the state, though it was not identical with it. A nation is a 'community of sentiment, which would find its adequate expression only in a state of its own, and which thus normally strives to create one'.[13] It is also a subjective phenomenon—that is, a nation exists where people believe themselves to be one, or to put it in a less circular manner, where people have a sense of belonging to a community which demands or finds its expression in an autonomous state. The existence of a nation means that 'a specific feeling of solidarity can be expected from certain groups of people in the face of others'.[14] This sense of solidarity is not totally subjective, however. It is rooted in objective factors, such as a common race, language, religion, customs or political experience, any of which can promote national sentiment. Weber insisted that no single one of these factors was common to all examples of a nation.[15] Even community of language ('Sprachgemeinschaft'), which he regarded as the most common objective basis, was not a universal feature of all states, as in Switzerland, Canada, etc. Nor did the existence of such objective factors on their own make a nation; they merely created a potential for solidarity, and it depended on political factors whether this potential found expression in a national consciousness or not. Speaking of China, Weber remarked that it was doubtful whether at the turn of the century China constituted a nation; fifteen years later, observers judged very differently. 'It seems, therefore, that a group of people may under certain circumstances attain the quality of a nation through specific behaviour, or may lay claim to this attainment, and within quite short periods of time.'[16]

Three different elements can thus be distinguished in Weber's concept of a nation. A nation exists where, first, there is some objective common factor between people, which distinguishes them from others; secondly, where this common factor is regarded as a source of value and thus produces a feeling of solidarity against outsiders; thirdly, where this solidarity finds expression in autonomous political institutions, co-extensive with the community, or at least generates the demand for these. In so far as nationhood depended on a feeling of superiority in the face of others, it formed a kind of status group, unique, according to Weber, in that it was the only form of status superiority available to the masses at large.[17]

Of all the objective factors that could contribute to a sense of national identity, Weber regarded race as the least important. If it appeared important, this was because men assigned to observable hereditary differences a subjective significance which was empirically unwarranted, and which was usually based upon differences of custom and culture.[18] This had not always been Weber's view. In his Freiburg Address he had spoken of physical and psychical *racial* differences between the Poles and Germans, and had used this to explain their different adaptation to the social and economic environment of East Prussia.[19] Racial assumptions of this kind occur frequently in his early writings; but after this period he became increasingly sceptical of such explanations, on the grounds of their vagueness and untestability. 'With racial theories,' he said at a meeting of the German Sociological Association held to discuss the subject, 'it is possible to prove or refute whatever you like.'[20]

If common racial origin was the least important objective factor making for national consciousness, Weber regarded possession of a common language as among the most important. 'Today community of language is the normal basis for the state,'[21] he wrote, and elsewhere he speaks of the nation as a 'community of language and literature'.[22] While he attributed the intensity of nationalism in his own time, particularly in its expansive form of imperialism, in large measure to economic conflict,[23] it was also due to the democratisation of literary culture and its spread among the mass. 'With the democratisation of culture,' he wrote at the end of 1916, 'belief in the exclusiveness of their language community seizes the masses as well, and national conflicts become necessarily sharper, bound up as they are with the ideal and economic interests of mass communication in the individual languages.'[24] Weber cites examples of this intensification from the Russian and Austrian empires. Once separate Polish and Latvian newspapers existed, the language struggle conducted by governments composed of people from a different language community was hopeless, because 'reasons of state are powerless against such forces'.[25] For the same reason Weber castigated Prussian policy towards the Poles in her territory; restrictions on the Polish language brought the masses for the first time into hostility with Germany.[26] All experience showed that once a language community had its own press, opposition to such measures could never be overcome, such was the intensity of feeling generated.

If, however, with the democratisation of literary culture, language played an increasingly important part in national sentiment, possession of a common language was not itself everywhere paramount.[27] People who shared a common language could be differentiated by other factors which were more significant, as the Irish from the English by religion. Similarly, people without a common language could form a nation, like the Swiss, the French Canadians, the German speakers of Alsace. What bound these peoples together were factors present in all nations, but particularly noticeable here in the absence of a linguistic community: namely, common customs, social structures, ways of thinking, shared values. The Germans of Alsace were bound to France by common customs and patterns of thought which derived from the historical role of France in freeing them from feudalism, and which were symbolised for example in the military relics from the revolutionary period on display in the museum at Colmar—the 'pride of the museum keeper'. The Swiss were unified by a distinctive social structure and political tradition, self-consciously separated off from the politico-military structures of the great powers, with the consequences these carried for the internal character of the political community. The French Canadians' loyalty to the English community was conditioned by deep antipathy towards the economic and social structures and customs of the United States, in the face of which their own individuality was guaranteed by the Canadian state.

These common factors of custom, tradition and social structure were present in all nations, but were particularly crucial in the examples mentioned, though Weber never regarded them as being as strong a source of national consciousness as the possession of a common language. Together they made up what was commonly called a 'Volksgeist' or 'Volkscharakter', though Weber viewed these terms with as much suspicion as the concept of 'race' because of their ambiguity. In his earliest methodological writings, he criticised both Roscher and Knies and the national economists in general, for using the term 'Volk' as if it were a metaphysical entity from which all the empirical characteristics of a people sprang, rather than as itself constituted by these characteristics. 'This concept "Volksgeist" [national spirit] is treated . . . not as the *result* of countless cultural influences, but on the contrary as the actual source from which the particular manifestations of the people emanate.'[28] Weber was not here dismissing the notion of national character as meaningless, only insisting that it should be analysed as a complex of individually definable characteristics, each subject to historical explanation. Thus in an article he wrote on 'Church and Sect in North America', in which he contrasted the democratic ethos of the USA with the authoritarian mentality of the Germans, he attributed these traits not to some meta-physical 'Geist' but (in part at least) to the differences in the development of Protestantism each had experienced. In North America Protestantism developed as a religion of sects, whose emphasis on the 'qualified individual' deeply influenced the character of her democracy with its 'typically elastic structure and individualist quality'. In Germany, on the other hand, Protestantism remained a 'church', with an authoritarian structure that strengthened the power not of the individual but of officialdom. 'Thus every attempt to emancipate the individual from authority . . . had to take place in opposition to the religious communities.'[29] In Weber's view the character of a people depended upon a multitude of individual historical factors of this kind.

The central concept Weber uses most frequently to indicate the complex of characteristics which make up the individuality of a national community is 'Kultur'. Like 'rationality', 'Kultur' is one of the most familiar concepts in Weber's vocabulary, and at the same time one of the most difficult to define.[30] There is the very wide sense he gives the term in his methodological writings, in order to distinguish the subject matter of the 'cultural' from the natural sciences; their subject is men (*Kultur*, menschen'), who are capable of taking a value attitude towards the world, of finding significance within it.[31] In this sense 'Kultur' embraces the whole realm of human values, to include anything that men might attach significance to. The sense of 'Kultur' that we are concerned with here is a narrower one: it indicates those *particular* values which distinguish a group or society from others—which constitute its individuality ('Eigenart')—and which are given self-conscious formulation, typically in the art or literature of the society. Although art and literature are the most typical *vehicle* for the expression of this individuality, Weber does not confine the term 'Kultur' narrowly to artistic or literary *values*; it embraces values of whatever kind—manners, character, patterns of thought ('Geist')—which distinguish the society qualitatively from others, and which are recognised as such by its members. Thus Weber talks, for instance, of the Prussian spirit, expressed in the achievements of the great Prussian reform officials as well as in the literature of Scharnhorst, Gneisenau, etc, as a 'significant element in German culture'.[32]

Weber regarded 'Kultur' in this sense as particularly bound up with national communities. The individuality which characterised and defined a 'Kultur' was distinctively a national individuality. 'All culture is national culture,' he once wrote.[33] Within the national community it was the characteristic function of the intellectual or 'cultural' strata to preserve and give expression to this individuality, and hence they were particularly closely associated with the concept of the nation. In his chapter on the 'nation' in *Economy and Society* Weber writes about '. . . those privileged strata . . . who feel themselves to be the specific "sharers" in a particular "culture", which is diffused among the members of the political community'.[34] In a later passage the link between the concept of 'culture' and the individuality of a national community is made even more explicit:

> The significance of the 'nation' is usually anchored in the superiority, or at least the irreplaceability, of the culture values that can only be preserved and developed through the cultivation of the individuality ('Eigenart') of the community. It is self-evident, therefore, that the intellectuals'. . . will be among the foremost proponents of the 'national' idea.[35]

Weber defines the 'intellectuals' here as 'those who have special access to certain achievements which count as culture values because of their distinctive individuality'.

This concept of 'Kultur' which is so central in Weber's thought contains both a universal and a particularist element. The universal element is the assumption of certain common standards of literary or artistic achievement implicit in any 'Kultur'. Weber never defined what these standards were; it is clear, however, that he regarded the possession of a literature as a minimum prerequisite. Communities without this, however distinctive their customs, were 'kulturlos' (uncultured) or, more explicitly, 'Analphabeten' (illiterates). The masses were 'kulturlos', until they came to share in cultural values disseminated by elites. 'Language, and that means the literature based upon it, is the first and for the time being only culture value at all accessible to the masses attaining to participation in culture.'[36] The particularist element in 'Kultur' is the individuality, mentioned above, which distinguishes one community from another, and which is typically embodied in its literature and art. Both elements are necessary to Weber's concept of 'Kultur'. He seems to have seen them as interrelated. The capacity of a community to develop and self-consciously sustain values which were distinctive and qualitatively different from those of other communities was linked to the capacity for developing a literary culture. Thus, writing about the Poles in Upper Silesia before the war, Weber called them 'lacking in culture', both in terms of their low level of education and literacy, and also in terms of their inability to develop a sense of individuality over against the Prussian political community. 'They were loyal, if passive, Prussians . . . and had, at least the majority of them, no self-consciousness nor any strong need to distinguish or separate themselves from their German-speaking fellow citizens.'[37] All this changed as a result of the Prussian language policy and the development of an indigenous press. They achieved a level of 'Kultur', that is both literacy and a sense of their own distinctive identity together, that made them a political force to be reckoned with.[38]

This concept of 'Kultur' provides the bridge between Weber's empirical and normative conception of the nation. On the empirical level, 'Kultur' embraced both the objective differences of language and custom, and the subjective appreciation of their distinctiveness, that constituted the essence of a 'nation', and against which 'reasons of state' were often powerless. At the same time 'Kultur' was for Weber a value concept. This is most obvious in that it embodied a conception of minimal literacy or artistic standards, in relation to which certain groups or peoples could be judged as 'uncultured'. But more important, the self-conscious development of group distinctiveness and individuality that was equally a criterion of 'Kultur' was also a value for Weber; indeed it can be regarded as an extension of his central commitment to individualism at the personal level, since it was based upon the same belief that distinctiveness was more valuable than uniformity, and that the capacity to articulate distinctive values was among the highest human achievements. It was as a vehicle for, and embodiment of, 'Kultur' in this sense that the nation had supreme value for Weber.

It is important to emphasise here that Weber's commitment to the nation was thus based on a more universal premise than simply allegiance to the specific value of *German* culture. He held no simplistic belief that German culture was superior to any other; indeed he explicitly rejected such a view. He confessed that he knew of no criteria by which one could decide between, for example, the value of French or German culture.[39] More significantly, he frequently insisted on the equal importance of the culture values of small nations, such as the Swiss, Danes, Dutch or Norwegians. The following passage is typical:

It is naïve to imagine that a people which is small in terms of numbers or power is any the less 'valuable' or 'important' in the forum of world history [sc. than a 'great' power]. It simply

has other tasks and thus other cultural possibilities. . . . It is not
only a question of the simple civic virtues and the possibility of a
more real democracy than is attainable in a great power state;
it is also that the more intimate personal values, eternal ones at
that, can only flourish in the soil of a community which makes
no pretensions to political power.[40]

Weber could speak equally favourably of the 'ancient' cultures of
the East, of the Indians, Burmese and Chinese, who were held
under the colonial yoke, though it must be admitted that the
same did not apply to the Africans, who were 'kulturlos' and could
therefore be legitimately colonised.[41] There are also passages,
discussed later in the chapter, which appear much more chauvinis-
tic than anything so far examined. Yet this does not alter the fact
that Weber was committed to the value of national culture as
such—that is, to a principle—and therefore his specifically
German nationalism found its limits at the point where it threatened
the needs of other nations and their cultures. This can be most
readily demonstrated from his attitude towards the Poles during
the World War, when he argued that the demands of the German
state for military security in the East had to be reconciled with
the need for Polish cultural autonomy. This will be discussed
more fully below.

The final aspect of Weber's general theory of the nation to be
considered here is its explicitly political dimension: the relation
between nation and state. For Weber a community only counted
as a nation in so far as it was, or desired to be, incorporated in its
own autonomous state; it was the striving for political power that
made the Hungarians, Czechs and Greeks into nations.[42] This
was a striving which in modern circumstances arose naturally out
of the recognition of the distinctive value of one's 'Kultur' and the
desire to preserve and develop it. Thus nations usually came to
coincide geographically with states. However, this did not make
them identical. The nation belonged to those groups that Weber,
following Tönnies, called 'Gemeinschaften', that is, which were
based upon a feeling of the members that they belonged together,
a sentiment of solidarity. The state was an example of a 'Gesellschaft', an association developed consciously for specific purposes.
The nation was concerned with the realm of 'Kultur'; the state
with the realm of power. The essence of Weber's conception of
the nation state was that though nation and state belonged to
fundamentally different categories, they were also reciprocal.
The state could only survive in so far as it harnessed the solidary

feelings of the national community in support of its power. The nation could only preserve its distinctive identity, its 'Kultur', by the protection it received from the power of the state. Both aspects can be briefly illustrated.

Weber held that a sense of national identity was one of the essential supports for the modern state. What a state could achieve by means of military power alone without the voluntary support of the population was limited, especially in wartime. The following passage is a good example:

> What then is the 'realpolitisch' significance of 'Kultur'? . . . The war has powerfully increased the prestige of the state: 'The state, not the nation,' runs the cry. Is this right? Consider the fundamental difficulty confronting Austrian officers, which stems from the fact that the officer has only some fifty German words of command in common with his men. How will he get on with his company in the trenches? What will he do when something unforeseen happens, that is not covered by this vocabulary? What in the event of a defeat? Take a look further east at the Russian army, the largest in the world; two million men taken captive speak louder than any words that the state can certainly achieve a great deal, but that it does not have the power to compel the *free allegiance of the individual*. . . .[43]

This was the political significance of 'Kultur', of the nation. On the other side the nation needed the power of the state for the protection of its own individuality. Weber recognised that in the past it had been possible for Germany to be a leading 'Kulturvolk' in a period of political impotence.[44] But those had been 'unpolitical' times. The conditions of the modern state, and the imperialist tendencies of the larger powers, made the protection of political power a necessity. The state was the necessary context for the protection and promotion of national culture; hence a striving for power in the sense of political autonomy was a necessary prerequisite of national groupings.

If, however, the state and nation were usually co-extensive, Weber recognised that this was not universally so. 'There are three rational components of a political boundary,' he remarks in a wartime article: 'military security, economic interest, community of national culture; the three just do not coincide like that on the map.'[45] Some compromise between them was inevitable. This was particularly true where a great power required the incorporation of small national communities for the purpose of military security, or where such incorporation had happened historically, as in the Russian and Austrian empires. Such states generated problems both for the state and the nations within it. The problem for the state was how to harness the support of local nationalisms, a problem particularly acute in the war. The problem for the national communities was how to maintain their own distinctiveness without the protection of an autonomous state. Weber had been particularly concerned with this latter problem in his articles on Russia in 1905–6, and was impressed with Dragomanov's solution for maintaining together the unity of the Russian state and the ideal of cultural autonomy for the individual nations within the Reich. One of his suggestions had involved a federal arrangement with internal self-government for the larger minorities in clearly defined areas, such as the Poles and Lithuanians, together with cultural autonomy for the smaller minorities, that is, the right to their own language as the medium of instruction in schools, not simply as an object of education. What particularly impressed Weber was Dragomanov's combination of a commitment to cultural autonomy with a clear grasp of economic and political realities:

> Against the centralist-great Russian character of the revolutionary movement and against its exclusively economic programmes, he maintained the significance of the national cultures even for the 'plebeian' stock of the respective nationalities. Against the separatism of the extreme nationalists, he insisted on the 'political' necessity of the federal unity of the Reich. Against the protagonists of 'nationalist legitimacy' in the form of whatever boundaries the nation happened historically to have chanced upon, he contended his basic thesis: the idea of national *cultural* autonomy. . . .[46]

Dragomanov's writings strongly impressed Weber, and were clearly influential in framing his own views on how to reconcile the needs of national cultures with the realities of political power.

This discussion should make clear that, to Weber, state and nation, though reciprocal, belonged to different categories, which he was careful to distinguish conceptually, even where they coincided in practice. He drew a clear distinction between 'staatspolitisch' questions, which concerned the power and integrity of the state, and national or 'kulturpolitisch' questions, which concerned the maintenance and promotion of national individuality. The former were the particular concern of the 'staatspolitisch' groups, the army and civil service, who were 'the natural and primary exponents of the desire for the power-oriented prestige of their own political structure' and 'the chief bearers of the concept of the State'.[47] The latter questions were the concern of the 'kulturpolitische' groups, teachers, writers, artists, journalists, who were the 'specific bearers of culture and the idea of the nation'.[48] Weber identified himself with the latter rather than the former groups. The former were always prone to the pursuit of power prestige as an end in itself, which, in his mature work at least, he criticised and explicitly rejected. For Weber, 'Kultur', the promotion of what was individual to a community, was among the chief ends which alone could legitimate the exercise of state power.

The summary of Weber's theory given above has presented his idea of the nation and of nationalism as a principle only at its most general 'ideal-typical' level. The second part will look at his nationalism in practice, to see how far it can be understood in terms of the considerations outlined, and also to show the development in his thinking between his early and mature period.

GERMANY AS A 'MACHTSTAAT'

In the first part of the chapter Weber's conception of the nation state was treated only at a very general level. The second part will consider his specifically German nationalism. In the light of the preceding analysis one aspect of this can be regarded as relatively unproblematic, and that is his justification of the use of state power for the preservation of German cultural identity, whether in the 1890s in face of the 'influx' of Poles on the eastern frontier, or during the war against the more open threat of Russian 'imperialism'. One distinctive feature of Weber's early writings was that he regarded the process of economic development as itself posing as great a threat to national identity as external military power. The development of capitalism and the internationalisation of economic activity had not made nationalism redundant, but rather an insistence on national distinctiveness more necessary. This will be illustrated briefly, to show that, in Weber's view, though nationalism could not be reduced to a 'reflex' of economic activity, yet its intensity in modern society was in part the product of capitalist development.

The main points of Weber's discussion of the 'Polish threat' have already been treated in Chapter 2, and can be briefly summarised. His studies on East Prussia convinced him that the process of economic development, if left to itself, posed a threat to the preservation of German culture in the east. With the development of the large estates into capitalist enterprises, their owners' main interest was in cheap labour from whatever source, and the result was the progressive replacement of Germans by Poles. The course of economic development and the direct economic interest of the landowners alike threatened the national interest, which Weber defined as 'the preservation of German culture in the east, and the defence of our eastern border and of the German nationality, in peace as well as war'.[49] The view that economic competition could offer as much a challenge as war to national integrity was most clearly expressed in the Inaugural Address:

> The economic conflict of nationalities takes its course . . . even under the illusion of 'peace'. It was not in open struggle against a politically more powerful enemy that the German peasants and day-labourers of the east were forced off their native soil, but in the unobtrusive conflict of the daily economic round. . . . There is no peace in the economic struggle for existence.[50]

Weber went on to argue that it was mistaken to imagine that, because economic development had created an international community, therefore nationalism was an anachronism; on the contrary, the assertion of national interests was even more vital:

> The economic community is thus only another form of the conflict of nations with each other, a form which has not moderated but rather intensified the struggle for the assertion of one's own 'Kultur'.[51]

The conclusion Weber drew, as we have seen, was that the goals of economic policy could only be *national* ones.

However, if this aspect of Weber's nationalism is relatively unproblematic, other aspects are less so. His nationalism clearly went beyond the defence of German 'Kultur', to embrace considerations of Germany's special position as a 'Machtstaat' (great power state), and the possibilities which this opened up for the use of power externally. Weber held that the unification of Germany had put her in the league of great powers, and that she could not afford to ignore the possibilities this presented. In a much quoted passage from the Inaugural Address he remarked that the unification of Germany could only be considered a 'childhood prank' if it were to be the conclusion and not the starting point of a German 'Weltmachtpolitik'.[52] It is this aspect of Weber's nationalism that is more controversial. What is problematic about it can best be expressed in terms of the analysis given in the first part of the chapter. If Weber's commitment was to 'Kultur' rather than to the state as an end in itself, how could an *expansive* state power be justified in terms of cultural values?

A variety of different interpretations of Weber's nationalism has been given by commentators, though none satisfactorily answers this question. One view, taken by Wolfgang Mommsen and more recently by Christian von Ferber,[53] is that Weber's interest lay in the extension of state power for itself. Von Ferber writes that, for Weber, the readiness to use physical force contained a 'value of its own', a legitimating power'; even that the 'right of the stronger' provided him with an inner justification for political action.[54] Such an interpretation not only fails to account for the place of 'Kultur' in Weber's thought, but overlooks his repeated insistence that the power of the state as such had no intrinsic value, but only as a means to the realisation of values external to it.

A different view is suggested by Hans Bruun. He argues that Weber saw Germany as forced into power politics by the configuration of international relations. According to Weber, he writes, a power state 'represents an obstacle and a danger in the eyes of other power states, and may consequently, simply because of its *potential* ability to play a role in foreign affairs, be drawn into the manoeuvres of international politics'.[55] In other words, Weber regarded a vigorous external policy as the best form of national defence. While there are passages in his wartime writings which will bear this interpretation,[56] on its own it is hardly sufficient to account for the vigour of Weber's nationalism.

Raymond Aron takes the concept of 'Kultur' in Weber's thought more seriously, but argues that it was the prestige rather than the quality of German culture that Weber was concerned with, and that he regarded power as a means to its wider dissemination.[57] Prestige considerations were certainly a feature of Weber's nationalism, though perhaps 'honour' would be a better translation for the term 'Ehre' which occurs frequently in his political writings. He wanted Germany to have a say in world affairs, and to be treated by the other powers in a manner appropriate to her size. Thus he considered the responsibility for the war to lie not only in the inadequacies of Germany's political system, but also in the refusal of the other powers to allow her the right to exert an influence overseas.[58] It was a question of honour, he wrote, that was a stake in the war, of Germany's claim 'to have some share in deciding the future of world affairs'.[59] In the same vein he wrote after the war: 'as a private individual one can overlook damage to one's interests, but not to one's sense of honour; so it is with a nation.'[60]

This interpretation, however, still leaves unanswered the question of 'Kultur'. As will be argued below, it was not only national honour, but the quality and character of her culture that Weber believed to be bound up with Germany's external power. The development of a world political role had decisive implications for the character of her 'Kultur' and the quality of her internal life. For Weber it was the choice between an inward- and an outward-looking society, between a narrow preoccupation with the nation's internal affairs and the development of a wider consciousness through the pursuit of 'world-political tasks'. This aspect of Weber's nationalism will be considered in the next section, together with his justification for imperialism on economic grounds, which was more typical of his time.

The 1890s and imperialism

There are two main elements in Weber's imperialism in the early years. One was straightforwardly economic. Imperialism was a response to the 'intense seriousness' of the population situation and to the rising economic demands of the working class in a world of intensifying economic competition.[61] It was no accident that Weber's most forthright imperialist pronouncements were made in speeches to the Protestant Social Congress. A speech he made to the 1896 Congress on the subject of unemployment was typical. Unemployment, he argued, was not merely a technical economic problem, which required the reform of the social and economic structure, though Weber admitted the need for that. Behind it lay the serious problem of over-population. Every year half a million new hands came on the market. Where was the room for them? He then went on:

> We need more room externally, we need an extension of economic opportunities through the expansion of our markets . . . and that is nowadays in the long run absolutely dependent upon the expansion of our political power abroad. A dozen ships on the East Asian coast are at certain moments of more value than a dozen trade agreements which can be terminated. . . . It is a vital matter for us that the broad masses of our people should become aware that the expansion of Germany's power is the only thing which can ensure for them a permanent livelihood at home and the possibility of progressive improvement.[62]

As already mentioned, the context of such statements (and there are similar ones in his speeches to the Congress in 1895 and 1897) is significant. The Christian Social movement was dedicated to

improving the lot of the working class, and Weber regarded imperialism as an essential part of this task. The period of reform
in government social policy had come to an abrupt end in 1895, and
imperialism offered a way of satisfying the rising aspirations of the
working class without intensifying social conflict at home. It is
this that made Weber's imperialism so readily acceptable to
Friedrich Naumann and other members of the Congress. However, even when Weber advocated a policy of external expansion
outside the context of the Protestant Social Congress, the economic justification—in particular the economic improvement of the
working class—remained evident. In the autumn of 1897 the
Münchene Allgemeine Zeitung sent out a questionnaire to test
public opinion on the building of a German fleet. Weber's answer
again emphasised the sharpening of economic conflicts between
nations as the central consideration. Only a 'naïve optimism',
he wrote, could fail to recognise that an expansion of trade was
indispensable for industrial nations, and that after a period of
apparently peaceful competition they had now reached the point
'where *only power* can decide the share each enjoys in the economic conquest of the earth and the extent of economic opportunity
available to its population, especially to its working class'.[63]

If the expansion of economic opportunities thus provided one
reason for the exercise of external power, it was also at the same
time a means to it. An expansive economy was a necessary condition for attaining a great power role,[64] which was itself desirable
on other, more political grounds. In the Inaugural Address Weber
speaks of the 'great power-political tasks' of a 'Machtstaat' as
something desirable in themselves; he compares the apolitical
spirit of Germany's leading strata unfavourably with the 'resonance of a world power position' enjoyed in England and France;
he speaks of his own generation's 'responsibility to history' and
to its descendants to ensure a new world political role for Germany.[65] Such statements go beyond a purely economic justification for imperialism to a concern for Germany's political standing
in itself. It is here that the cultural implications mentioned above
are important. Just as Weber argued that small and large powers
had different 'cultural' possibilities, so he believed that playing a
role as a world power would have a marked effect on the character
of German life and values.

This dimension is particularly apparent in Weber's contribution
to a debate on 'Germany as an Industrial State' at the Protestant
Social Congress in 1897. Weber's position on the tariff issue was
that, while nothing could really prevent the progress of capitalism,

the question of free trade was crucially important to the character of Germany's development, cultural and political as well as economic. In response to the fear that Germany was taking a great risk if it chose to become an exporting nation, Weber replied:

> This is the same risk that all great trading and industrial peoples of the past, all peoples outstanding in the development of culture, all the great nations of world history in the period of their greatness have taken upon them. In my view it is not a policy of comfort and ease that we are after, but one of national greatness, and this is therefore the risk we must take, if we want to pursue a form of national life which is different, say, from the Swiss.

If Germany renounced this challenge, Weber went on, it would mean saying to her best children: 'seek another home; I want peace and quiet'. The most vigorous elements of the German people would emigrate; only 'indolent rentiers and an apathetic, traditionalist-oriented mass' would remain behind.[66]

The element of exaggeration in the speech reveals the characteristically Weberian values at work. They are the same values that led him to pronounce as the goal of 'Sozialpolitik' for the workers of East Prussia, not their happiness, but the creation of the conditions which would stimulate the development of vigorous physical and spiritual qualities; not their 'well being' but the 'characteristics which make for human greatness'.[67] It was in terms of the same values that Weber extolled the risk-taking entrepreneur in contrast to the indolent rentier, and the politician's struggle for personal responsibility in contrast to the bureaucrat's love of 'order'.[68] In each case it was not only the distinctive achievements of the capitalist and politician in their respective spheres that had value, but the human qualities developed in the course of that achievement. So too, the successful pursuit of a world political role on Germany's part would produce very different qualities of national life from those developed by a policy oriented solely to considerations of 'peace and quiet'.

There is one further element of Weber's nationalism that requires mention in this context. A noticeable feature of all his nationalist pronouncements is an emphasis on the tasks ('Aufgaben'), the duties ('Pflichten'), the responsibility ('Verantwortlichkeit'), facing Germany as a power. Thus Weber wrote that Germany had a 'duty' to be a power state, that she had a responsibility to future generations for their economic provision, a responsibility to history for the future of world culture, etc.[69] One of his short wartime articles, 'Zwischen zwei Gesetzen', can be taken as typical. Here he argued that it would not be the smaller nations, such as the Swiss or the Danes, who would have to bear responsibility for the world being carved up between the 'regulations of Russian officialdom' on the one side and the 'conventions of Anglo-Saxon society' on the other, but *Germany*:

> It is because we are a power state, and thus, in contrast to those 'smaller' peoples, can throw our weight into the scales of history—it is because of this that there lies heavy on us, and not on them, this duty and obligation towards the future, to oppose the complete domination of the world by those two powers. Were we to renounce this obligation, then the German Reich would become an expensive luxury whose vanity would be harmful to culture . . . a luxury which we ought to renounce in favour of a small federation of politically powerless cantons . . . and return to cultivate the comfortable cultural values of a small people, values which ought always to have remained the meaning of our existence.[70]

What Weber emphasises here is the responsibility of power. Certainly he attributes to power an ethical significance, yet this is not to power itself but the responsibility associated with it. To pursue power for its own sake, or to have power and not use it when one should, is irresponsible; better to have no power at all, than that it should have no 'meaning':

> There is no more pernicious distortion of political power . . . than the worship of power for itself. The pure 'Machtpolitiker', as glorified among us by a passionate cult, may produce a powerful effect, but his work has no meaning and leads nowhere. In this, the critics of 'power politics' are absolutely right.[71]

On the other hand, power as the possibility to affect the future, and the consciousness of a moral responsibility associated with it, had not only an ethical significance but a cultural one also, in that the consciousness of a nation which 'held in its hands a nerve fibre of historically important events'[72] could only be different from the 'quiet' values cultivated by the smaller states.

The question of the relationship between Germany's external power and her 'Kultur' can thus be answered as follows. To Weber it was not power in itself that was important, but rather the quality of national life that was associated with a 'world political' role, and the ethical and cultural significance he attached to exercising a responsibility towards the future in the use of that power. It may be argued that those who talk about the 'duties' of power are more dangerous than those who pursue power for itself. However, if Weber provided an ethical and cultural legitimation for a German world political role, an ideology of nationalism, the concepts of 'Kultur' and 'Verantwortlichkeit' themselves set limits to the legitimate exercise of that power. This will be illustrated by looking at the change in Weber's attitude to imperialism between the early and wartime periods.

Germany's Tasks in the First World War

Most writers on Weber who discuss the nationalist element in his political thought do so as if his wartime writings can be regarded as a straightforward continuation of the early period; as if, after an interval of dormancy, the nationalism of the Inaugural Address returned with renewed vigour on the outbreak of war. Such a view is misleading, in that it overlooks the different character of his nationalism in the later period. The war, which Weber regarded as a disaster as well as a challenge, made him highly critical of 'the politics of national vanity' that had helped bring it about.[73] There is now much less of the enthusiasm for imperialism that was such a marked feature of his outlook in the 1890s. The main reason for this lay in the damaging political consequences which, Weber believed, had followed from the way Germany's colonial policy had been carried out. Germany's colonial possessions were distinctly modest. Yet they had been achieved, as had the building of the German fleet, with an amount of noise 'as if Germany were intent upon swallowing up half the world'.[74] The chief consequence had been the intensification of national conflicts, and the consolidation of a world coalition against her. Germany still required security for her world trade and spheres of influence overseas; but these were better secured by political and economic agreements than by a policy of colonial expansion accompanied by military blustering. 'There are still strong German interests in the Orient,' Weber wrote in 1915; but these should be guaranteed by agreements on mutual aid rather than by 'a policy of brazen and obtrusive self-display'.[75]

However, despite this admission of the bankruptcy of German prewar policy (the policy which he had himself advocated in the 1890s), it is Weber's wartime writings as much as the earlier ones that are cited as evidence for his expansive nationalism. Thus when he writes about Germany's 'responsibility for deciding the future of world culture', to prevent the world being divided up between 'Russian bureaucracy' and the 'conventions of Anglo-

Saxon society',[76] this is taken as evidence that he wanted Germany to compete with these other countries in the extension of her power and in a form of cultural imperialism. Weber's statements, however, need to be judged and interpreted in the light of the very specific aims that he advocated for national policy during the war. Here one is struck immediately by a surprising feature. If it had been the extension of Germany's power, and prestige through power, that had been Weber's goal, one would expect this to have been most clearly demonstrated at the point of Germany's maximum territorial gains, when it seemed that she was winning the war. Yet this was precisely the point where Weber was at his most critical of the political and military policy of the government, and of the definition of war aims accepted by the majority of his compatriots. In his writings of 1916–17, in which he set out his critique of the government and his own assessment of war aims, he repeated two important distinctions which have not been adequately noted by his critics: first, a distinction between military power and political influence; secondly, a distinction between cultural imperialism and cultural prestige. These distinctions will be examined in turn.

In his writings of 1916–17 Weber insisted that the freedom to strike alliances with other great powers was much more important for Germany's future political influence than the annexation of territory or external displays of military power.[77] The latter were both a source of weakness rather than of strength. The central weakness of Germany's position before the war had been that whenever she sought to take some action in external affairs, she 'stumbled upon a coalition of world powers' directed against her. This 'unnatural' coalition was itself the result of Germany's military power. The occupation of Alsace Lorraine had made a permanent enemy of France.[78] The building of a fleet had offered a direct challenge to England.[79] A wartime policy of territorial annexation in Europe was simply repeating the same mistake, and could only perpetuate Germany's political weakness. Weber called demands for the annexation of Belgium 'unbelievable madness', and attacked every definition of war aims that assumed territorial gain as the only possible justification for the war.[80] The proper aim of the war, according to Weber, should be a political settlement which would enable Germany to break out of the prewar stranglehold of hostile alliances, and give herself some room for manoeuvre in foreign policy. This goal of 'Wahlfreiheit' in future foreign policy should dictate Germany's war policy in the West: military security; no annexations; above all a settlement that would open the possibility of detaching England and France from Russia and from each other. 'On our own we can defend ourselves *against* a world of enemies,' he wrote, 'but not have any influence *within* it' ('in der Welt mitreden nicht').[81]

If a striking feature of Weber's Inaugural Address in 1895 had been his insistence that the conflict between nations was as bitter in peace as in war, and required similar methods of national defence, his wartime writings were characterised by a contrary insistence on the distinction between force as an instrument of war and politics as the appropriate instrument for peace. 'The army makes the war . . . the statesman makes the peace,' he wrote in 1915. 'While this means proper consideration for military requirements, it also means the recognition that the interests of the country after the war . . . can and should be guaranteed only through the peaceful medium of politics.' A peace which simply ensured 'that Germany's boot trod on every foot in Europe' would lack the essential political element necessary to secure Germany's future interests and influence in the world.[82]

The break with Weber's early period is thus a marked one. Of course he still remained committed to the value of a world political role for Germany and to the expansion of German capitalism, but he now recognised that these ends could be more effectively secured by political alliance than by military blustering and 'a dozen ships on the East Asian coast'. What this indicates is that, contrary to the assumptions of some of his critics, he did not regard military power as an end in itself; indeed, that he came to recognise the limitations of power, even as an *instrument* of policy. This recognition is equally apparent in the other distinction in Weber's writings of this period, between cultural imperialism and cultural prestige.

Weber defined Germany's war tasks in the East in cultural terms. These involved the containment of Russian imperialism in its threats not only to the German state and nation but to the autonomy of the other cultures of Eastern Europe.[83] Weber saw Russia as a typical imperialist power, its pressure for expansion coming from a combination of elements within Russian society: from the landhunger of the peasants; from the power interests of the bureaucracy; from the cultural imperialism of the intelligentsia, who, 'too weak to secure even the most elementary demands for a constitutional order and guaranteed freedoms at home . . . find a support for their damaged self-esteem in the service of a policy of expansion, concealed under fine-sounding phrases'.[84] The same policy of cultural supremacy already pursued towards the minority nations within the Russian state, could be expected by any others who came within her orbit. It was Germany's task to challenge this cultural imperialism, not by establishing an alternative cultural dominance of her own, but rather by using her power to guarantee the autonomy of the smaller nations. Weber believed that Germany could present herself as a much more convincing patron of national self-determination than any of her enemies, who between them had been responsible for subjugating some 350 million foreigners, now 'being exploited for use as cannon fodder'.[85] The espousal of such a principle would itself enhance the prestige of German culture in contrast to the cultural imperialism of her enemies. This contrast is very clear in the following passage:

> A state does not have to be a 'national state' in the sense that it concerns itself exclusively with the interests of its one dominant nationality. It can serve the cultural interests of a number of nationalities, a policy from which its own dominant nationality can also benefit, if its interests are properly understood. In the light of changing needs it is now also in the cultural interest of the German nationality to demand that our state increasingly undertake such a task. The Russian state may then as a result, through the challenge of our example, be induced to guarantee its foreign peoples the measure of cultural autonomy that Dragomanov and other like-minded politicians made the centre-piece of their reform programmes some fifty years ago. If so, it will not find that this diminishes its power, but only perhaps that the pressures for expansion on the part of its bureaucracy and the one-sided myth of Greater Russia will recede.[86]

The decisive arena for this 'cultural task' lay in German policy towards the Poles. In 'Germany among the European World Powers' Weber argued that Germany was in a position to offer the Poles in Prussia and Congress-Poland far more than they had themselves demanded in 1905, namely an independent state with full self government, as an ally of Germany. In return Germany would need to guarantee for itself the security of the north-east frontier against Russian threats. Weber admitted that he had a reputation as an enemy of the Poles to live down. But the issue in the 1890s had been a quite different one of national competition over the import of cheap labour; this was a question of cultural autonomy for the Poles as a nation. Further, as he frequently insisted, even the Poles in Prussian territory had now developed a cultural awareness, a national solidarity, they had not had at that time. This made the language policy of Prussia towards its Poles inconsistent with the interests of the German Reich in securing autonomy for the Poles outside German territory, which in Weber's view should be a central aim of the war in the East.[87]

It is in the light of this definition of Germany's 'cultural tasks' that Weber's statements about Germany's 'responsibility for the future of the world' need to be read. Preventing the world from being dominated by Russian bureaucracy and Anglo-Saxon conventions (with a dash of Latin 'reason') did not mean vying with their various forms of cultural imperialism, but seeking to secure a sphere of autonomy for smaller cultures against their supremacy. In a world of power states, the independence of small nations could only be guaranteed by the tension of one great power against another. It was in this sense that Germany had a *duty* to be a 'Machtstaat'.

> The small nations live around us in the shadow of our power. What would become of the independence of the Scandinavians, the Dutch, the people of Tessin, if Russia, France, England, Italy, did not have to respect our armies? Only the balance of the great powers against one another guarantees the freedom of the small states.[88]

The critique of cultural imperialism contained in these writings demonstrates that Weber held no simplistic belief that the prestige of a nation's culture was dependent upon the mere extension of its power. Whatever prestige Germany might derive from the proposed cultural policy in the East, would not be a result of her power as such, but rather of the way it was used and the purposes to which it was put. While it might be argued that this was merely a plausible rationalisation of Germany's involvement in the war, this would be to ignore the distinction, central in Weber's thought, between power and the uses of power, and would fail to explain the restraint implicit in his condemnation of territorial annexation and in his policy towards the Poles at the time of Germany's maximum military success. The reason for this restraint, it is argued, was that the concept of 'Kultur' which underlay Weber's commitment to the nation as an end had a more general significance for him than simply *German* 'Kultur' and that the ethical notion of 'responsibility' which provided a justification for the power of the 'Machtstaat' itself set limits to the legitimate exercise of this power.

Those who regard Weber's wartime nationalism simply as an extension of the nationalism of this early period thus overlook two developments in his thinking. One of these was his critique of Germany's prewar foreign policy, the 'politics of national vanity', which made its contribution to the outbreak of war. The other was his confrontation with the situation of national minorities in his Russian studies of 1905–6, and with the problem of how to preserve the cultural identity of smaller nations in face of the aggrandisement of a larger power. The more universal reference he gave to the concept of national culture after this time is already apparent in his critique of Prussian attitudes to the Poles as early as 1908.[89]

This is not to deny that Weber was emotionally committed to the German nation, nor that he had his share of national prejudice, particularly in respect of the Russians. At the end of the war, after Germany's defeat, he wrote to Ferdinand Tönnies that he had 'never felt it so much a gift of destiny to have been born a German'; and in another letter he wrote that at least Germany had the glory of having prevented world domination by the Russians:

> It is all over with a *world* political role for Germany: the Anglo-Saxon dominance over the world . . . is a fact. It is highly disagreeable, but we have been responsible for preventing something much worse—the Russian knout! That glory remains to us. America's supremacy was as irresistible as that of ancient Rome after the Punic War. It is only to be hoped that they never share it out with the Russians.[90]

This is not denied. What is being denied is that Weber's profession of a world political role for Germany involved the pursuit of power and aggrandisement for its own sake, and that his national commitment can simply be reduced to the 'Gefuhlspolitik' (politics of emotion) of which he was himself so critical. Instead, we can apply to Weber himself in this context the conclusion he drew from his later studies on the world religions, that the ideas which are used to justify and give meaning to a particular way of life themselves set limits to the range of conduct possible within it.

The analysis given here of the relationship between power and 'Kultur' in Weber's thought helps to make clear in what sense his nationalism can be considered as an expression of bourgeois values. The weakness of the interpretation which sees Weber as striving for the extension of state power as an end in itself is not only that it is false, but that it leaves this aspect of his political thought unintelligible in relation to his other values. There is nothing distinctively 'bourgeois' about the pursuit of power in itself; it is a different matter, however, with the *ideas* Weber uses to justify its exercise. Both the limitation of cultural values to a national context (whether German or otherwise), and the particular qualities of national life Weber associated with pursuing a world political role, had their origin in the character of bourgeois society, as Professor Francis has recognised:

> It is difficult to avoid the conclusion that Weber remained bound by the typical categories of thought of the bourgeois age, to which belonged not only the concept of the 'Kulturnation', but also the idolatry with which the bourgeoisie pursued the national culture as the final value.[91]

This 'bourgeois' character of Weber's nationalism will be explored further in the concluding section of the chapter.

NATIONALISM AND THE PROLETARIAT

To complete the account of Weber's nationalism, its significance in relation to internal politics will be briefly considered. This will involve anticipating the discussion of his theory of society in subsequent chapters. As will be shown there, Weber recognised the phenomenon of class interests and class conflict as a central feature of modern politics. In this context, the significance of the national idea and a strongly national policy was that it encouraged the degree of social unity which was a necessary concomitant to a successful world political role.[92] The 'idea of the nation' provided a common consciousness which transcended that of class; in particular, it offered a means of drawing the working class away from an attitude of total opposition to the existing social order. Weber held that, though the immediate economic situation of the proletariat encouraged attitudes which were hostile to social unity, alongside this they enjoyed both a common interest in overseas economic expansion and a potential common consciousness as members of the German nation. 'Political education', as set out in the Inaugural Address, involved strengthening the latter features at the expense of the former.[93]

Implicit in the account given so far is Weber's recognition that a conscious commitment to the idea of the nation was not spread uniformly throughout society. Certain sections of the community had a particular interest in it: the army and civil service in extending their power and prestige; the cultural strata in preserving or developing the character of national culture; the propertied classes in the profits that accrued from overseas trade and colonisation.[94]

Such interests were not shared, at least immediately, by the proletariat. Their immediate class situation of opposition to these privileged groups determined an attitude of lukewarmness at best towards the national idea, particularly in its imperialist manifestation. This did not prevent the working class from becoming the most fervent supporters of nationalism; but, if so, it could only be because they were drawn away from the outlook which derived from their immediate social situation.

In relation to the economic aspect of nationalism, which was at its strongest in imperialism, Weber held that the immediate circumstances of class conflict tended to induce a pacifist outlook in the proletariat, who 'generally show no interest in forcibly participating in the exploitation of foreign colonial territories'.[95] In contrast to ancient Athens, where colonial tribute was distributed direct to the people, there was no such immediately comprehensible advantage for the modern masses. That such an advantage in fact existed, would be shown by the effect on employment if the overseas markets were ever lost; but it was an advantage which the situation of class conflict obscured. The proletariat therefore had to be brought to perceive an interest in nationalism beyond its immediate class situation. Weber laid frequent stress on this necessity in the writings and speeches of his early period.[96] The support shown for imperialism by the English working class, he argued, was a sign of their political maturity, of their ability to see beyond the ends of their noses; they supported it because they recognised that they could not maintain their standard of living for long if the external power of the nation ever declined. 'This needs to be brought home to our proletariat also.'[97] In contrast to the English working class, the German was gripped by a 'petty-bourgeois' mentality, which Weber defined as:

> The absence of great national power instincts, the restriction of political goals to material ends or at least to the interests of their own generation, the lack of any sense of responsibility towards the future.[98]

He could only express the hope that this mentality would be overcome, that in future it would be possible to 'stretch the hand over the heads of the petty-bourgeoisie to a proletarian movement, which in this respect thinks bigger than it does today'. Similar sentiments were expressed in the Inaugural Address also, where Weber described the German proletariat as having the character of a 'politically uneducated petty-bourgeoisie'. If one looked to England and France, he argued, one could see that the main factor which contributed to the political maturity of their working classes was, apart from the economically educative role of the trade unions, 'the resonance of their world power position, which continually confronts the state with great political tasks, and involves the individual in a constant political education, of a kind which occurs with us only when the frontiers are threatened'.[99]

If an appreciation of the national idea in its economic and political aspects could draw the working class from its narrow class outlook, so could its cultural aspect. When Weber spoke of the masses as 'attaining to participation in culture', it was as something that was brought to them, rather than something they created for themselves out of their own situation.[100] The cultural values they would attain, for example, through the extension of literacy, were specifically national ones. Weber's attitude towards the possibility of an autonomous working-class culture was an ambivalent one. In a debate on 'Technik und Kultur' at the first meeting of the German Sociological Association in 1910, he said that the outstanding feature of the modern proletarian movement had been the hopes it raised that it might create 'out of the bour-geois world entirely new values in all spheres'. He had to confess, however, that these hopes were disappointed, particularly in the realms of art and literature.[101] On a different level, he elsewhere spoke approvingly of the comradeship and solidarity of the trade union movement as a 'cultural value', particularly in contrast to the authoritarian relationships men had to endure at the work place.[102] This needs to be seen, however, within the general context of Weber's assessment of the trade unions as a vital agency in educating the working class to an acceptance of the existing social order. This view was particularly obvious in his wartime writings, where he singled out this 'comradeship' as an essential element in ensuring mass discipline, and emphasised the role of trade union leaders in securing working-class confidence in national policy.[103] The following passage, in which Weber is arguing for greater trade union autonomy, shows clearly that the perspective from which he judged their 'cultural value' was itself a national one:

> A state which seeks to base the spirit of its mass army on feelings of honour and comradeship should not forget that it is precisely these feelings which, in the everyday economic struggle of the workers, provide the one decisive moral force for the education of the masses, and that they should therefore be allowed to develop freely. From a purely political standpoint, it is this and nothing else that is meant by 'social democracy'

in an age which must inevitably remain capitalist for a long while to come.[104]

It was wholly characteristic of Weber's standpoint that he should seek to judge working-class institutions by their capacity to generate and sustain the elusive quality of 'Kultur'. This was for him always the decisive consideration, in contrast to the values of social justice or material well-being. But it was also characteristic that, when it came to making such judgements, his criterion for what counted as a 'cultural' value was itself dependent upon his own national and class cultural perspective. Thus when, for example, the same qualities of comradeship and discipline came to be exercised in opposition to the capitalist order, he could only describe them in much less flattering terms.[105]

Weber's nationalism was thus an expression of a bourgeois outlook not only in its linking of 'Kultur' with a national identity, but also in its self-conscious role in relation to class conflict. Certainly he made no crude identification of the national interest with the immediate interests of his own class, much less with how they perceived their interests at any one moment. Nevertheless, as shown in his speech on 'Deutschland als Industriestaat' and subsequently, he perceived a close connection between a world political role for the nation and the expansion of German capitalism, both in the sense that the two were mutually interdependent, and in that both found a similar cultural justification in terms of the vigour they brought to national life. Further, his conceptions of Germany's national honour' and her 'duty' as a great power formed part of a national ideal which was seen self-consciously as an instrument in the political education of the working class, to draw them away from their own class outlook. Finally, even the distinctive values of working-class institutions themselves—their solidarity and comradeship—came to be seen in his eyes as so many means of national discipline and national defence.

This class element in Weber's theory, not only in the sense of his own outlook, but as a central feature of his empirical analysis, will form the subject of the following chapters.

REFERENCES

1 'The structure of a state must be related exclusively to the actual world- and culture-political tasks, which confront the nation.' GPS, p 213; cf pp 296–7, 427.
2 GPS, p 282.
3 e.g. GAW, pp 151–5; MSS, pp 54–8

4 See page 22.
5 O Stammer, ed, op cit, p 93.
6 A Mitzman, op cit, p 147.
7 GARS, vol 1, p 258; GM, p 286.
8 ibid.
9 GPS, pp 18–19.
10 WG, pp 527–8; ES, pp 921–2.
11 ibid.
12 The following account is drawn from all these sources: WG, pp 242–4, 527–30; ES, pp 395–8, 921–6; GASS, pp 456–62, 484–91. The first of these latter was actually on the subject of race, but is relevant to the following discussion.
13 GASS, p 484.
14 WG, p 528; ES, p 922.
15 ibid.
16 WG, p 529; ES, p 924.
17 WG, p 239. Weber was actually speaking here about ethnic communities, but the point applies equally to nations.
18 Hence the distinction Weber drew between 'race' as an anthropological category and 'ethnicity' as a cultural or sociological one. WG, pp 234–6; ES, pp 385–7.
19 GPS, pp 2, 4, 9.
20 GASS, pp 489ff, 456–62; GAW, 167–8. Weber's last statement on the subject, in his introduction to the studies on the world religions, was more positive: 'The author admits that he is personally and subjectively inclined to attribute a great importance to biological heredity. But . . . as yet I see no way of even vaguely ascertaining, much less measuring, the extent and, more important, the character of its influence . . . .' GARS, vol 1, p 15; PE, p 30. The problem of isolating hereditary from environmental factors had been a major concern of his industrial studies, 'Zur Psychophysik der industriellen Arbeit'.
21 WG, p 242; ES, p 395.
22 GPS, p 164.
23 WG, p 526; ES, p 919.
24 GPS, p 172; cf p 234.
25 GASS, pp 485–6.
26 GPS, pp 169, 174–5.
27 For what follows, see WG, GASS, ibid.
28 GAW, pp 9–10; cf pp 141–2.
29 J Winckelmann, ed Max Weber, Soziologie, Weltgeschichtliche Analysen, Politik, 4th edn (Stuttgart, 1968), pp 393–6.
30 What follows is the best sense I can make of Weber's use of this elusive concept, though this still leaves certain complexities out of account. The only attempt in the literature on Weber to explicate this concept is Emerich Francis, 'Kultur und Gesellschaft in der Soziologie Max Webers', in Engisch, Pfister, Winckelmann, eds, op cit, pp 89–114. Francis is more concerned with the change in Weber's scientific work from the concept of 'Kulturwissenschaft' to 'Soziologie', though he mentions briefly the use of the concept in the political writings. He remarks that Weber 'worked with a traditional concept of culture, which was current among the idealist-oriented German bourgeoisie, but which remained scientifically unanalysed', op cit, pp 95–6.

31 GAW, p 180, and passim.
32 GPS, pp 269–70.
33 GPS, p 125.
34 WG, p 528; ES, pp 925–6.
35 WG, p 530; ES, p 926.
36 GASS, p 485.
37 WG, p 234, ES, p 396.
38 ibid; GPS, pp 174–5; GASS, p 486.
39 GAW, p 588.
40 GPS, p 139; cf p 170.
41 GPS, p 170.
42 WG, p 244; ES, p 398.
43 GPS, pp 164–5.
44 GPS, p 274.
45 GPS, pp 169–70.
46 *Archiv*, 23B, pp 267–8.
47 WG, p 520; ES, p 911.
48 GPS, p 248; WG, p 530; ES, p 926.
49 GASW, p 456.
50 GPS, p 12.
51 GPS, p 14.
52 GPS, p 23.
53 C von Ferber, *Die Gewalt in der Politik* (Stuttgart, 1970).
54 ibid, pp 53, 68, 72.
55 H H Bruun, *Science, Values and Politics in Max Weber's Methodology* (Copenhagen, 1972), p 255.
56 GPS, pp 140–1. See WG, p 520; ES, p 911, where Weber talks of the 'dynamic of power' inherent in international relations.
57 O Stammer, ed, op cit, pp 87–8.
58 GPS, pp 112–4.
59 GPS, p 171.
60 'Gegen Frankreichs Anspruch auf Pfalz und Saarbecken' (Archive Document no. 28, Max Weber Institute, Munich), p 36.
61 GPS, p 12.
62 *Verhandlungen des 7. Evangelisch-sozialen Kongresses* (1896), pp 122–3.
63 Weber's reply to the questionnaire is published in W J Mommsen, op cit, pp 420–1.
64 On more than one occasion Weber extols the 'profit motive' of British capitalism for building up her political power. GPS, p 239, GASS, p 416.
65 GPS, pp 23–5.
66 *Verhandlungen des 8. Evangelisch-sozialen Kongresses* (1897), pp 108–9.
67 See page 42.
68 See page 57.
69 GPS, pp 12, 24, 140, 171, etc.
70 GPS, p 140.
71 GPS, p 535; GM, p 116.
72 GPS, p 533; GM, p 115.
73 GPS, pp 125, 154–5, etc.
74 GPS, pp 111, 129, 154–5.
75 GPS, p 125.
76 GPS, pp 140, 171.

77 GPS, pp 127, 135, 156–7.
78 GPS, p 128.
79 GPS, p 112.
80 GPS, pp 117, 131, 156.
81 GPS, p 157.
82 GPS, p 124.
83 GPS, p 164.
84 GPS, pp 122–3.
85 GPS, pp 169–70.
86 GPS, pp 125–6.
87 GPS, pp 167–9, 121–2, 173–8.
88 GPS, pp 171–2.
89 *Lebensbild*, p 406.
90 GPS, 1st edn, pp 483–5.
91 Engisch, Pfister, Winckelmann, eds, op cit, pp 97–8.
92 GPS, pp 23–4.
93 ibid.
94 For what follows see the sections on 'Machtprestige und "Grossmächte" ', 'Die wirtschaftlichen Grundlagen des "imperialismus"', WG, pp 520–7; ES, pp 910–20.
95 WG, pp 526–7; ES, pp 919–20. He calls this a 'natural product of the immediate class situation'.
96 It is repeated in his later writings also, e.g. GPS, p 239: 'Despite all their social opposition there is one decisive respect—that of economic rational-isation—in which the interests of the workers are identical with those of the great entrepreneurs; both are in turn identical with the political interest in maintaining the world position of the nation; in both respects they stand opposed to the interests of all those who enjoy "security of tenure for life" and their associates in economic stagnation.'
97 *Verhandlungen des 5. Evangelisch-sozialen Kongresses* (1894), pp 81–2. 'No one has a greater interest in the power of the nation state than the proletariat, if it looks beyond tomorrow.'
98 ibid.
99 GPS, p 23.
100 GASS, p 485.
101 GASS, pp 452–3.
102 'Rundschreiben', p 2.
103 GPS, p 293.
104 GPS, p 306.
105 See page 190.

Chapter 6

Society, Class and State: Germany

Previous chapters have concentrated on the more exclusively political aspects of Weber's theory. His theories of bureaucracy, of Parliamentary government, of the nation and nationalism, have been considered largely in abstraction from his theory of society. Although this has the advantage that each can be isolated for purposes of analysis and discussion, it is not intended to imply that Weber regarded the political as independent from society. The political values that Weber sought to realise, whether liberal or national, and the system of Parliamentary government itself, were not simply a matter of designing appropriate institutions and policies, but also of identifying the constellation of social forces, in particular class forces, which supported the existing structure, and of assessing the chances for change in this social basis of support. Most of Weber's writing on contemporary politics was concerned with the interaction between the social and the political, and with the political significance of class structure and attitudes, rather than with constitutional questions pure and simple. The next two chapters will look at Weber's accounts of the relationship between society and state in Germany and Russia respectively, and clarify what kind of theory is implicit in them.

It should be said that Weber's immediate purpose in much of the writing discussed here, at least on Germany, was not to conduct an exercise in political sociology, but to comment on some specific issue of policy—tariff reform, industrial relations, the system of land ownership. Invariably, however, such issues could only be made intelligible in terms of a wider analysis of the social and political forces involved. It is possible to build up a remarkably consistent picture of these from the different periods of Weber's writing. Historians of Germany and Russia may find nothing particularly novel in his account, yet for all that it shows a charac-

teristic perceptiveness of insight. At the same time it has a significance beyond the particular situation Weber was confronting.
His analysis of the authoritarian state in Russia and Germany, and
of the failure of both societies to achieve a liberal Parliamentary
system, contains an implicit theory of the historical preconditions
of liberal institutions. It also embodies a general theory of the
relationship between society and state in the modern world. As
pointed out in Chapter 1, nowhere in his academic writing does
Weber attempt to set out an account of the interrelationship of
those forces in modern society which are particularly significant
for the political structure. What follows is therefore of some importance to our understanding of Weber as a political theorist, while
also showing once again his characteristic values at work.

THE SOCIAL BASIS OF THE AUTHORITARIAN STATE

Weber's account of the German political system has been outlined in previous chapters. It was a type of 'Obrigkeitsstaat' or
authoritarian state, its political direction in theory in the hands of
the monarchy but in practice determined by the bureaucracy, with
a façade of Parliamentary institutions, or 'token Parliamentarism'.
Such a system could only persist because it enjoyed the support of
the dominant groups, and because the class most hostile to the
system, the proletariat, had come to adopt political attitudes
which in practice helped to sustain it. It was not simply a question
of class, but of the political physiognomy of class. In what follows
Weber's account of the different classes and their relation to the
state will be taken in turn, beginning with the Junkers.

The Junkers

The most direct support for the existing political structure came
from the Junkers, the landowning aristocracy of East Prussia.
The changing economic situation of this class, and the political
consequences of this change, formed a central theme of Weber's
early studies. The traditional country estates of the east had been
not merely economic concerns, but 'Herrschaftszentren', centres
of political authority:

> They were destined, according to Prussian traditions, to provide
> the material foundation for the existence of a social stratum into
> whose hands the state was accustomed to entrust the exercise
> of its military and political power . . .'[1]

Two features of this 'material foundation' were of particular political significance. First, the large estates of the east had provided an appropriate standard of living for their occupants, without absorbing all their energies; as a result the sense of acquisitiveness in the typical Junker was 'relatively underdeveloped', and, although he was no absentee landlord, he had plenty of time to devote himself to political and administrative activities.[2] The estates provided a source of political consciousness dispersed throughout the countryside.[3] A second feature of the rural economy was that it had been organised on a patriarchal basis. The labourer owed total allegiance to his master, but in return he received the use of some land and a share in the harvest. Despite the authoritarian relationship, therefore, there was a substantial community of interest between the owner and his tenants, which had an important political significance. The Junker could not merely claim to be, but in fact was, the 'born representative of his people's interests'.[4] This not only ensured him their automatic support, but also gave him a political outlook which transcended that of his own immediate self-interest. This community of interest formed the 'basis of the landowner's historical power position in the state.'[5]

The economic changes of the nineteenth century had now eroded this material basis of Junker power. This was partly the unwitting consequence of their own achievements in unifying the nation, which had given a further impetus to the development of capitalism. 'It is the tragic fate of the German east,' wrote Weber, 'that in the course of its powerful achievements for the nation, it has dug the grave for its own social organisation.'[6] The features of its economic position which had been so politically decisive were now vanishing. The country estates could no longer provide the secure and trouble-free existence they had in the past. International competition forced their owners into a ceaseless struggle to maintain their standard of living. The centre of economic importance had moved decisively to the towns. Weber was convinced that *in the long term* these changes could only undermine the political power of the Junkers. 'In the long term, political power cannot be maintained intact on this basis.'[7] In the short term, however, the Junkers were still able to cling on to power through their hold over the institutions of government. They still exercised political power, but the economic changes gave it a completely different significance from formerly. Where, before, the economic security the Junkers enjoyed had nurtured a political outlook which transcended that of class, and provided the basis for a policy of national greatness, now their economic insecurity compelled them to use their political power to prop up their declining economic position. 'Political power, instead of being based upon a secure material foundation, has now, on the contrary, to be put to the service of economic interests.'[8] Their demand for protection, Weber went on, was already assuming the tone of a 'dissatisfied receiver of charity'.

It was not only that the economic position of the Junkers was now weaker; it had also completely changed its character. They had been compelled to change from patriarchal lords into capitalist businessmen.[9] As with the typical capitalist, economic interest had to become the dominant consideration, or they faced seeing their estates decline into smallholdings. The striving for profit, which had always been a secondary factor with them, now became all-important. The chief goal of their policy was cheap labour and a good price for their products. At the same time capitalism destroyed the ties of common interest which had bound the serf to his master. He became a free labourer, with no share in the product, his interests opposed to those of the landowner. Class conflict emerged. The Junker could thus no longer support the claim to represent the common interest of society as a whole; he represented only himself. His politics became class, not national politics. The situation on the eastern frontier was a paradigm of this change. The landowner's economic interest in cheap labour from any source put him on the side of the Polish immigrant against the indigenous German; it set him in opposition to the national interest, which required a secure defence for the eastern frontier and the maintenance of German culture in the east.[10] The Junkers were no longer capable of pursuing national goals, only class ones. Though they continued to claim a national significance for their policies, this was no more than a hollow pretence.

If the significance of the Junkers' political power had changed, however, their power itself had not. Despite their economic decline, they maintained their traditional dominance through their hold over the institutions of state. 'The power of the eastern aristocracy in the army and administration remains as great as ever,' Weber complained, 'and it has many sources of access to the ear of the monarch which are not available to other citizens.'[11] A major source of this power, within both the Prussian state and the Reich as a whole, lay in its monopoly over recruitment to the army and civil service. This monopoly was reinforced by the system of *fideicommissum* or entailed land, which guaranteed an aristocratic title to the owners of particular estates, and a place in the administration to their sons.[12] Even where other classes were admitted to the civil service, they were quickly socialised into the values of the agrarian aristocracy, which prescribed the norms of official social behaviour. 'Countless characteristics of the social behaviour of officialdom,' Weber wrote, 'continue to be determined by their conventions.'[13] This capacity of the Junkers to influence the attitudes of other classes through their monopoly of social conventions was a major feature of their power in Weber's account.

In practice, then, the bureaucracy was not independent, as the 'conservative' view maintained. It did not stand above class but was subordinate to it, and the trend of government policy reflected the interests and values of those groups from which it was recruited. This was a frequent refrain of Weber's writing, in the later, as well as the earlier, period. In an article on the system of *fideicommissum* in 1905 he complained that Germany had 'an administration, which has no knowledge or understanding of the broad strata of the modern bourgeoisie and working classes, and confronts them with a vague feeling of antipathy, coloured by agrarian prejudice.'[14] In a lecture on rural society, given the previous year in the USA, he spoke of 'the imprint of the Junker character' on Prussian officials and on German diplomacy, and how this determined 'many of most important presuppositions of German foreign policy'.[15] In his articles on 'Parliament and Government' in 1917 he explicitly rejected the view that the system of bureaucratic rule could be independent of party or class:

> Our state of affairs can teach everyone, that because a bureaucracy is all-powerful does not mean that there is no *party* rule. Anything except conservative governments in Prussia are impossible, and German token Parliamentarism rests in all its consequences on the axiom: every government and its representatives must of necessity be 'conservative', apart from a few patronage concessions to the Prussian bourgeoisie and the centre party. This and nothing else is what is meant by the 'above party' character of bureaucratic rule. . . . The party interests of the conservative officialdom in power, and of the interest groups associated with them, control the direction of affairs alone.[16]

Any social or political reforms could only be achieved at the expense of substantial concessions to this agrarian interest. The reform frequently cited as an argument against the 'plutocratic' character of the Prussian state—the income tax introduced by Von Miquel in the 1890s—proved just the opposite in Weber's view. It showed rather the power of the landowner within this plutocracy, since the price of its introduction had been the abolition of a separate tax on landed property. There could in any case be little harm to agrarian interests from a tax system in which the calculation of their income lay in the hands of officials who were 'politically and socially entirely dependent upon them'. It was only a further indication that all reforms would come to nothing which did not make major concessions to these interests.[17]

Other sources of continued Junker power, besides their monopoly of administrative (and also military) recruitment, lay in the constitutional arrangements of the Prussian state. The three-class voting law ensured a permanent conservative majority in the Prussian Landtag.[18] The special position of Prussia within the Reich, as 'Hegemoniestaat', gave them power over the Reich as a whole. Although the influence of the Reich and Prussian governments on affairs of common concern was in theory reciprocal, in practice 'the inner structure of the Reich and its individual states ensures that it is generally the latter influence, that is, the great Prussian character of the Reich government, that prevails'.[19] This dominance of the landowners within Prussia and the Reich (and the capitalist interests allied with them) was naturally cloaked with fine sentiments—monarchist, nationalist, and so on; in reality, however, it was a system of class rule. The main purpose for which political power was exercised was to bolster up the declining economic and political privileges of a class, who no longer had any genuine concern for the nation as a whole:

> For fifty years now the Prussian conservatives have never shown a spark of political character in the service of great political or ideal goals. Anyone can see for themselves that it was when either their financial interests, or their monopoly of office or patronage, or their voting privileges . . . were at stake, that their state electoral machine got ruthlessly to work, if necessary against the king himself. The whole sorry apparatus of 'Christian', 'monarchist' and 'national' slogans then sprang into action, and continues to do so.[20]

The Junker class, then, provided the most direct support for the authoritarian state. It was their system, and its authoritarian character reflected the patriarchal relationships of the traditional estates of East Prussia. Yet, as Weber insisted, the class was in a process of economic decline. On this basis alone the system of bureaucratic rule could not persist for long, if it did not also enjoy the support, or at least the acquiescence, of the economically powerful class of the bourgeoisie. It was the political character of the bourgeoisie that was central to understanding the persistence of the authoritarian state.

The bourgeoisie

'The broad strata of the bourgeoisie,' Weber wrote, 'are still excluded by feudalism from a share in the exercise of political authority.'[21] Their exclusion from formal power, however, was distinguished by a marked acquiescence in the system which excluded them. Weber gave a variety of reasons for this. The most obvious one lay in their political character: their cowardice ('Feigheit'), their 'will to powerlessness', their desire for peace and quiet.[22] Bismarck had achieved German unity—without them. What was there left to accomplish?

> So once the unity of the nation was achieved, and its sense of accomplishment satiated, the German bourgeoisie, growing up drunk with success and thirsty for peace, was seized by a peculiarly 'unhistorical' and apolitical spirit. German history seemed to be at an end. The present was the final culmination of the previous thousand years—who bothered to ask if the future might judge differently?[23]

Bismarck's success had led them to expect that others would achieve their political goals for them; it had deprived them of all political independence. Part of the bourgeoisie looked for the appearance of a new Caesar; part had long since sunk into the political apathy typical of a petty-bourgeois mentality.[24]

This lack of political spirit on the part of the German bourgeoisie was nothing new. Yet it was not on its own a sufficient explanation of why a class which was increasingly powerful economically acquiesced in a system which excluded it from a share in government. Weber's analysis was in fact more complex than this, and included other factors which accounted for their support. One of these was the ability of industrialists, particularly the large syndicates, to exert an influence on government policy through the activity of employers' associations, and to pursue their economic interests by means of direct liaison with the bureaucracy. Weber complained of 'the liaison behind closed doors', and 'the disastrous political influence of the leaders of heavy industry' on the regime.[25] As in his Russian articles, he observed that the interests of capitalist industry and the system of bureaucratic rule had become closely intertwined,[26] and that 'the great capitalist powers . . . stand as a man on the side of the bureaucratic "Obrigkeitsstaat" and against democracy and Parliamentary government'.[27] Since they could successfully satisfy their interests by direct influence on the bureaucracy, Parliament became an unnecessary complication.

Thus, though the conservatives enjoyed a monopoly of formal office, from which the bourgeoisie were largely excluded, this was only maintained by an uneasy compromise with the interests of large-scale capitalism. While industry had to make concessions to the agrarian interests,[28] it in turn received the support of the state for its economic goals. A reactionary social policy, and a highly authoritarian system of industrial relations, were among the most pernicious consequences of this coalition, in Weber's view.[29] The laws which gave workers the right of association were empty, because at the same time they allowed employers to dismiss them with impunity, while also giving full protection to the strikebreaker. In addition, the courts invariably sided with the employer. In the Saarland 'anyone who is a state official dances to the tune of these people'.[30] The whole character of industrial relations took its tone from the authoritarian nature of the state, of which the factory was a microcosm. Indeed, an insistence on showing who was boss within the factory became the employer's substitute for his lack of formal authority within the state:

> The less political say the German citizen has officially in the German Reich, the more the government is carried on over his head, the more he is treated as merely an object of statecraft, so much the more is he determined that where he is actually paterfamilias—and that includes the large firms particularly— he will show those under him that he now has something to say, and the others must fall into line.[31]

Weber's account of industrial relations illustrates a central feature of his analysis of the German bourgeoisie; they acquiesced in the 'Obrigkeitsstaat', not only because they were able to pursue their economic interests successfully within it, but because they had themselves imbibed the patriarchal attitudes of its dominant landowning class. The clearest example of this was the increasingly widespread practice among the bourgeoisie of buying up country estates in order to purchase the accompanying aristocratic titles, which ensured a social position for themselves and political privileges for their offspring. The amount of agricultural land subject to *fideicommissum* was extending rapidly under their pressure. If there was one thing more than any other which characterised· for Weber the condition of the German bourgeoisie, it was this striving of the *nouveaux riches* for social status. Economically and politically debilitating, it ensured that they remained captive to the existing system. Economically, it meant that industrial capital became tied up in land, and that the attention of the bourgeoisie was diverted from entrepreneurial activity, from 'the path of economic conquest in the world', to a concern with securing the placid existence of a rentier.[32] Ownership of land was the method chosen by satiated capitalists to 'rescue their earnings from the stormy sea of the economic struggle into the safe harbour of "peace with honour".'[33] This 'feudalisation' of bourgeois capital distorted the rural economy, since ever more land was needed in order to secure an adequate rent. But Weber's main fear was that Germany would become, like France, a 'Rentnerstaat', a stagnant society, choosing to live off rent rather than engage in vigorous entrepreneurial activity. Thus, when in the middle of the war proposals were made by the Prussian government to extend still further the system of land entailment, to provide a safe home for the profits made in the war, Weber could not contain his disgust:

> This proposal breeds not entrepreneurs, but rentiers, and those of the most despicable kind. . . . The ideal of secure rents hovers in front of an increasing portion of the nation, and the stupid clamour set up against capitalism only intensifies it. The decisive problem for our whole future is how to free ourselves from the resulting rentier character. If we do not succeed, then Germany will become an economically stagnant country, far more even than France. . . .[34]

It is, however, the political significance that Weber attached to the system of *fideicommissum* that most concerns us here. In offering the bourgeoisie, or at least some of their number, the chance to achieve an aristocratic social position and political privileges for their children, it reconciled them to the 'Obrigkeitsstaat' and to the exclusion of their class from formal power. Weber pointed out that the aristocratic ideal they pursued was in fact a thing of the past; the spirit of the traditional Junker could not be re-created in an age when the rural estate was beset by economic worries. All they attained was the 'physiognomy of the *parvenu*'. The dance round the golden calf' was as eagerly pursued in the country estates as it was anywhere, only here it was mixed with seigneurial pretensions.[35] It was these pretensions, though, that the ruling circles in Prussia knew how to play on, in order to reconcile the bourgeoisie to their own lack of power:

The current political wisdom which is dominant in Prussia is to reconcile bourgeois money-bags to the negligible political influence of the bourgeoisie, by conceding a type of 'second-class aristocracy'; and nothing would be more unpopular in the circles which are receptive to this policy than to put difficulties in the way of the 'ennoblement' of capital won in the course of trade, industry or the stock exchange, and its transformation into country estates.[36]

This inculcation of the bourgeoisie with the social attitudes of the Prussian ruling class extended to all areas of life. Even the newly founded trade and business schools, which were springing up everywhere, instilled their entrants not only with commercial skills but also with the social qualifications for reserve officer status. Anyone who aspired to be a full member of the commercial class had to acquire this characteristic qualification of the feudal social order.[37] What this striving after the prestige symbols of a previous age could contribute to commercial success Weber found hard to imagine; indeed it was quite inappropriate to the hard task of economic competition.[38]

Although Weber's account of the German bourgeoisie contains an element of caricature, it is clear that, in his view, they did not fully measure up, either economically or politically, to the type image of a true bourgeois class. Economically, they did not show that degree of devotion to the work ethic which was the central feature of the capitalist spirit, but were easily diverted to a rentier existence. Politically, the achievement of quasi-feudal aspirations reconciled them to their exclusion from formal political power. Marx or Engels would have called this 'false consciousness'. Weber eschewed such loaded concepts, but the exact terms matter little. The attitudes of the German bourgeoisie, or a section of it, were in Weber's view inappropriate to their economic situation, and belonged to a different age. That they held such attitudes was due, in part at least, to the conscious efforts of a ruling class to hold on to its political power after the point of its economic decline. He could only express the hope that the bourgeoisie would 'free itself from its *unnatural* association' with the Junkers, and 'return to the self-conscious cultivation of its own ideals'.[39]

The acquiescence of the bourgeoisie in a system of government from which they were excluded was sealed, finally, by the threat of an organised and self-conscious working class. The industrialists had no confidence in their ability to withstand the working class on their own in a fully democratic system.[40] Universal suffrage had come before they had had a chance to find their feet in the practice of Parliamentary government. In this article, 'Wahlrecht und Demokratie,' Weber questioned whether it would not have been better from a political point of view if in the early stages of the Reich there had been a more restricted suffrage, like the British, so that the more prominent classes could have accustomed themselves to responsible Parliamentary co-operation with the government. As it was, fears of further democratisation among the bourgeoisie could always be played on to ensure their support for the existing system:

> The division of the characteristic strata of modern society into two interlocking and hostile classes, bourgeoisie and prole-tariat, made it possible... to exploit the cowardice of the bourgeoisie in the face of democracy for the preservation of bureaucratic rule. The effects of this cowardice are felt to this day.[41]

The political situation and character, then, of the bourgeoisie was crucial to the persistence of the 'Obrigkeitsstaat'. Although formally excluded from political power, the large industrialists were able to pursue their interests through the influence of em-ployers' associations, and formed an uneasy 'coalition' with agrarian capitalism. This coalition was strengthened by the assimi-lation of a section of the bourgeoisie into a pseudo-aristocratic stratum. Their support for the system was confirmed by the fear of their inability to resist working-class strength under more demo-cratic political arrangements. The next section will consider briefly the political character of the working class which reinforced such fears.

The proletariat and social democracy

While it could not be said that the working class supported the existing system of government, yet the character of their political activity and organisation contributed, in Weber's view, to its persistence, in that it pushed the bourgeoisie into the arms of the conservatives. This view was expressed somewhat crudely in a speech in 1896. 'Because Social Democracy has set itself against the bourgeoisie,' Weber said, 'it has smoothed the path for reac-tion.'[42] Later this was developed with rather more subtlety into a critique of the character of the Social Democratic Party itself. Its combination of a revolutionary ideology on the one hand, with a network of full-time activists who had a direct material interest in the persistence of the party structure on the other, was a combination which could only serve to reinforce the existing political system. The revolutionary ideology frightened the bourgeoisie. The material interests of the party officials and others directed that the party should prosper within the system rather than that the system itself should be changed.

Weber recognized at least as early as Robert Michels that behind the façade of revolutionary zeal in the SPD was a party of a very different character. One of the earliest attempts at a social analysis of the party's electorate was published in the *Archiv für Sozialwissenschaft und Sozialpolitik* in 1905, and Weber added some comments of his own at the end.[43] He argued that the character of the party was affected not only by the social composition of its electorate, but also by the interests of those immediate supporters who made a living from it. For them the party was an end in itself ('Selbstzweck'), and their interest lay in maintaining the party as it stood, because their livelihood depended on it. The influence of these 'conservative' interests had made itself felt in the crisis over revisionism. The demand for a formal surrender of the ancient faith, which everyone had been able to interpret as he found convenient, and the attempt to substitute a new one, had presented a serious threat to the party and had had to be resisted. In all major questions of strategy their concern was that under no circumstances should there be any risk to the existing state of the party. In respect of this constellation of material interests ultimately involved in its fortunes, the SPD was increasingly coming to resemble the American political parties, albeit under very different political circumstances.[44] In a speech to the Verein two years later Weber spelt out more fully what these interests were.[45] The party, he said, was in the process of becoming a powerful bureaucratic machine, creating a huge army of officials, a 'state within the state'. Just like the state itself, it had its own hierarchy of offices, its own universities with professors, its own 'enemies of state', its regular assemblies. Above all it had an increasing army of people who had an interest in 'advancement', including not only party employees, but the innkeepers whose premises were patronised, the editors of socialist journals, and so on. If ever the socialists achieved power, and it came to a conflict between the revolutionary ideologists and the material interests of those whose livelihood depended on the party, the power of the latter would become apparent.[46]

In the meantime, however, it was in the interests of these groups to maintain a revolutionary ideology and a total opposition to the existing order so as to preserve their electoral support. Weber discerned a kind of unholy alliance at work between the ruling classes and these interests within the SPD. It was in the interests of the Junkers and the large capitalists that the electoral strength of revolutionary socialism should be kept up, since this would lessen the chance of social reform and would keep the bourgeoisie as a whole in line. At the same time it was in the interest of those who made a living from the SPD that as reactionary a social policy as possible should be pursued by those in power, so as to maintain their electoral support and their own positions secure. This symbiosis of opposites was well expressed in another of Weber's speeches to the Verein:

> Have the representatives of large industry and their allies in the field of social policy, the agrarian parties, any real interest in the restriction of Social Democracy? Anyone at all intelligent politically must answer, no! Every additional socialist non-entity in the Reichstag, elected at the expense of parties of social reform, is pure gain for them. Every upsurge of radicalism within Social Democracy, every increase of Social Democracy at the expense of liberalism, especially of the Left, means pure gain for them, just as on the other side it means pure gain for the dependants of Social Democracy, when we pursue a reactionary policy. And on the other side, have any of the numerous people who are economically dependent on the increase in numbers of the SPD, on the increase in the readership of social democratic newspapers, and so on, any interest in the state's pursuing a reforming social policy? The closer the state allies itself with property and maintains a common interest with the syndicates, and the more reactionary its policies, so much the better for the material interests of these people—since even Social Democracy itself will have to allow its representatives to be put under the microscope of their own so-called materialist principle of explanation. Reactionary policies mean pure gain for these party dependants. Despite all their mutual opposition in economic affairs, therefore, there exists no closer community of interest politically than between the representatives of agrarian capitalism and the industrial syndicates on the one hand, and the representatives of Social Democracy on the other.[47]

Although opposed to the existing social and political order, those who made their living from Social Democracy thus had an interest in its perpetuation, so that they could continue to benefit from opposing it. While their revolutionary ideology no longer corresponded to the actual condition of the party, it nevertheless played a part in sustaining the existing system of government.

This completes our account of Weber's analysis of the social basis supporting the authoritarian state. The latter persisted because the Junkers managed to hold on to their traditional monopoly of office; because the bourgeoisie acquiesced in it and had, to an extent, assimilated its values; because, finally, the political organisation of the working class reinforced the alliance between Junkers and bourgeoisie. This analysis determined the character of Weber's strategy for reform, which will be discussed in the next section.

A STRATEGY FOR BOURGEOIS DEMOCRACY

Weber's strategy for change was intimately linked with the socio-political analysis outlined in the first part of the chapter. At least until late on in the World War, this strategy was less concerned with constitutional reform itself, than with bringing about a new alignment of social and political forces which would undermine support for the existing system of government. One part of this strategy lay in detaching the bourgeoisie from their subservience to the authoritarian state—by seeking to drive a wedge between the interests of industrial and agrarian capitalism, by attacking the social status system which reconciled the bourgeoisie to the existing order, and by exposing their fears of Social Democracy as empty. The other part of the strategy involved seeking to draw the working class away from a negative, oppositional attitude to capitalist society by means of a social policy which encouraged co-operation rather than outright opposition. In this way a social coalition could emerge capable of supporting bourgeois democracy.

To speak of Weber having a 'strategy' can perhaps be misleading. It is not meant to imply that he was himself engaged in any sustained campaign to construct the kind of coalition he saw as necessary. He was not a professional politician of this kind. Yet it is possible to talk of him having a strategy in the sense that his various interventions as a propagandist in policy issues formed a coherent and consistent whole, which made sense in terms of the social analysis just considered. What is important here is not so much the actual political effectiveness of Weber's interventions, but rather the coherence of his perception of his own society. The different aspects of this 'strategy' will be considered in turn.

A recurrent theme of Weber's political speeches and writings was the necessity for a complete break between the forces of industrial capitalism and the rural landowning class. A typical example of this theme is a speech he made at the founding meeting of Naumann's National Social Party in December 1896, in which he insisted that there was only one meaningful choice in German politics: either to support the feudal reaction or to promote bourgeois independence.[48] Although Weber had himself been partly responsible for the change of direction in Naumann's political development, which led to the foundation of the new party, he was critical of the venture because Naumann failed to recognise the necessity of this fundamental choice. Naumann's concern to make the party a supporter of the economically disadvantaged, wherever they might be, threatened to turn it into a kind of 'jumping jack', turning against the agrarian interests one moment, and against large-scale industry the next. A viable party could not be constructed out of this kind of purely ethical motivation, but only on the basis of a clear political recognition that there was only one choice available: 'either to promote bourgeois development or unconsciously to support the feudal reaction'.[49] A party of the 'fourth estate' could only serve to strengthen one or other of the dominant forces, whether it wanted to or not. The question was: which one? Weber insisted that the new party must become a 'national party of bourgeois freedom', since this was what Germany needed above all.

Two areas of policy that Weber regarded as particularly crucial to driving a wedge between the bourgeoisie and the rural landowners were the tariff issue and the system of entailed land. He was outspoken on both. In the speech he made to the Protestant Social Congress in 1897 on 'Germany as an Industrial State' he treated the tariff issue both as a touchstone for the kind of society Germany was to become, and as crucial to the independent development of the bourgeoisie. The consequence of tariff protection and of the 'internal market' it created was to make the bourgeoisie inward looking, and to confirm the coalition of interests between industrial and agrarian capitalism. While nothing, in Weber's view, could hinder the development of German industry—it was an irreversible process—the ending of tariff protection was a necessary step to the political independence of the bourgeoisie. He said at the end of his speech:

Everyone here is looking for a bourgeois politics; they want the bourgeoisie to free itself from its unnatural coalition and show an independent outlook; they want it to return to the self-

conscious cultivation of its own ideals, in the interests of a pros-
perous social development and the development of the country's
political freedom.[50]

Weber was equally explicit about the need to check the extension
of the system of entailed land and close the avenue to the 'feudalisation of bourgeois capital'. In both 1904 and 1916 proposals
were made by the Prussian government to extend the amount of
land subject to *fideicommissum*, so as both to secure more rent for
existing holders and to satisfy the demand for new estates. On
each occasion[51] Weber wrote articles attacking this further
capitulation to the interests of agrarian capitalism, 'which sacri-
fices hundreds of thousands of acres of German soil to the con-
temptible striving for aristocratic titles or a pseudo-aristocratic
position'.[52] In both articles he put up counter-proposals, which
would have the effect of restricting the extension to families of at
least two generations' standing on the land and to areas of wood-
land only, and of giving protection to the small independent
farmer.[53] A central argument was the consideration of social
policy: the desirability of maintaining a strong rural population of
independent farmers. But Weber linked this, typically, with the
wider political consideration, of the necessity to close off this
avenue to satisfying the quasi-feudal aspirations of his own class.

The question of tariffs and the system of entailed land were only
two of the critical issues on which Weber sought to detach the
bourgeoisie from the Junker ruling class. He also set out to expose
their fears of the 'red spectre' as illusory. A particularly notable
example of this was a speech he made at the Mannheim meeting
of the Verein in 1907.[54] The subject for debate was the constitution and administration of local government, and it developed
into an argument on the extension of the suffrage, with many
fears being expressed of the consequences of the Social democrats
attaining power as a result in the large towns and cities. Weber
sought to ridicule such fears. In the event of the socialists attaining office, he argued, one of the first consequences would be the
emergence of a conflict between the bearers of its revolutionary
ideology and the host of its supporters with a material interest
in their own advancement. The former would be the ones in real
danger. In the long run it would not be Social Democracy which
conquered city and state, but rather the latter which conquered
Social Democracy.[55] The faint-hearted should take a lesson from
the Mannheim party congress, Weber went on. The Russian
socialists, who attended as spectators, must have been shaking

their heads at the spectacle of a self-confessed revolutionary assembly behaving like a collection of petty-bourgeois innkeepers. There was no word of revolutionary enthusiasm, only 'a feeble, niggling, pettifogging style of argument and debate, instead of the Catalinarian energy of faith', which the Russians were accustomed to in their own assemblies.[56] But what would be the actual effect of socialist economic policy carried out in practice? Weber asked. They should take a look at towns where socialists were already in power, such as Catania, the main industrial centre of Sicily. The policy of the socialist council there had been precisely the same as the bourgeois one it replaced, of attracting the maximum amount of industry to the town. Only the motive was different. Bourgeois councils wanted industry so as to ease the tax burden on the citizens, socialists so as to bring favourable employment opportunities for the workers. As to the attempt to municipalise the bakeries in Catania, that had collapsed and led to the discredit of the socialist administration, not, however, without the citizens enjoying some good cheap bread for a while. Any similar attempt, Weber concluded, to carry out futuristic socialist policies in Germany on the basis of its existing social and economic order would pay the same penalty. 'The first to leave the party in the lurch would be its own supporters, the working class.'[57]

Robert Michels wrote to Weber after the meeting, expressing some consternation at the savagery of his attack on Social Democracy. Weber replied that his purpose had not been to criticise Social Democracy itself, so much as to make fun of those who were afraid of it.[58] In a further letter he urged Michels to regard the speech which he found so puzzling as the exhortation 'of a class-conscious bourgeois to the faint-hearts of his own class'.[59] While fairly representing Weber's views on the SPD, the speech was thus also a typical example of his concern to free his class from the fears which kept them in thrall to the existing order.

The animosity Weber showed towards the SPD did not extend to the working class itself. If one part of his strategy involved seeking to detach the bourgeoisie from its support for the system, the other part sought to encourage in the working class a readiness to co-operate with bourgeois democracy, by means of a progressive social policy. This did not mean the kind of paternalist welfare policy traditional in Germany, which was only another expression of the Junker social outlook. It meant rather one which gave the working class increased opportunity to exercise responsibility for themselves. Central in this policy was the position of the trades unions, which Weber regarded with as much favour as he showed

disfavour towards the SPD. They offered the means for developing a spirit of independence and political maturity within the
working class. But they could only do so if they were freed from
the legal obstructions with which they were encumbered.

The issue of trade union rights formed one of the central areas of
controversy within the Verein für Sozialpolitik, and is one of the
chief criteria used by Lindenlaub for distinguishing between a
'liberal' and a 'conservative' wing.[60] The main figure in the controversy was Lujo Brentano, who from the 1860s onwards had
been a student and admirer of British industrial practice, and who
advocated the development in Germany of trades unions with the
effective right to collective bargaining on the British pattern.[61]
In theory German workers were accorded the rights to free
association and withdrawal of labour under the constitution. But in
practice these were rendered ineffectual by clauses which gave full
legal protection to blacklegs and forbad the use of any pressure on
workers to take part in industrial action.[62] The 'liberals' in the
Verein demanded the removal of these offending clauses, so that
the unions would be strong enough to bargain with employers on
an equal footing. This was partly an indication of their faith in the
power of the market to produce a balance between the two sides
of industry. More important, however, was the value they placed
on the development of an independent labour movement, capable
of standing up for itself, and taking its own decisions on the social
and welfare interests of its members. The 'conservative' fear of
too much trade union power, and their preference for bureaucratic regulation as the solution to social conflict, was characterised
by the liberals in the slogan: 'Everything for the people, nothing
by the people'.[63]

Weber was firmly on the 'liberal' side in this controversy. In
the Verein debate on industrial relations in 1905[64] he made a
scathing attack on the patriarchal relationships within German
industry, on the 'authoritarian mentality, the need to have everyone regimented, ordered about, constructed, which grips the state
and the system of industrial relations in present-day Germany'.[65]
Characteristically, he linked it with the political system as a whole.
The attitudes of the typical industrialist reflected the qualities
which 'a history of past suppression had stamped on him and
which the pressure of the authoritarian system may make permanent'.[66] These attitudes were in turn responsible for dictating the
character of the working class, and were reflected in the laws
which governed industrial relations. The law which punished a
striker for putting pressure on those who stayed at work was 'a law

for old women, a protection for cowardice'. It was also completely one-sided, since it gave full protection to those who took no part in a strike, while enjoying its advantages, yet at the same time permitted a striker to be dismissed with impunity. What was needed was a system of free and independent trades unions, enjoying the effective protection of the law. Weber went on to contrast the trades unions favourably as agents for the education of the working class with Social Democracy as a whole. They provided the 'only defence of idealism' within the SPD, the only 'guarantee of a political, manly, free independence of outlook'.[67] It was therefore essential that they be defended.

A rather more systematic exposition of Weber's position on social policy is contained in a memorandum he wrote in 1912.[68] The context of this was the attempt by a group from the Verein to create a new initiative for social policy by propagating an agreed set of minimum aims, if necessary through creating a special organisation for the purpose. In the end the initiative came to nothing because of disagreement over whether members of the SPD should be invited to join in, but Weber's memorandum provides a useful indication of what he thought these minimum aims were. In the sphere of workers' rights, they rejected all approaches to the problem from the standpoint of the rights of owners, or of patriarchalism, or treating the workers as objects of bureaucratic regulation. Workers should have an equal right to participate in collective agreements on working conditions and their organisations should be strengthened to this end. They regarded the increasingly one-sided power of employers' associations, backed by the support of the police and the courts, as an evil, as also the total supremacy of capital in the areas of heavy industry in liaison with the power of the state, since 'we wish to live in a land of citizens, not of slaves'.[69]

There is no doubt that Weber regarded the increased autonomy of working-class organisations as valuable in itself. At the same time he was alive to its wider political significance. A strong trade union movement, capable of pursuing its interests successfully through collective agreements with employers, would have a powerful educative influence on the working class towards co-operation with a bourgeois democracy.[70] A hope he had expressed in the Inaugural Address had been for the development of an aristocracy of the working class, which, partly through the economically educative influence of an organised labour movement would move towards political maturity and become a fitting ally for the bourgeoisie.[71] The British model of industrial relations, as

advocated by Brentano, thus had for Weber a political significance also. Where the SPD was caught in the sterility of the
German political structure, the trades unions, in his view, offered
the working class a more positive way out.[72]

It has often been pointed out that Weber's political position,
as represented in these and similar proposals, was one which cut
across the existing political parties. Since he broke with the
National Liberals at the end of the 1880s for their failure to take
issues of social policy seriously and their commitment to an
'outdated economic dogmatism', and at the same time criticised
the more left-oriented 'Freisinnige' for their apolitical and anti-
national character, there was no natural home for him in the
German political system.[73] He was always at odds with the policies
of the existing parties. The failure of the kind of programme he
advocated to achieve anything has been taken as evidence either
of his basic unsuitability for politics[74] or else of the incompetence
of the Verein in propagating a progressive social policy. Certainly
the Verein was largely ineffectual as a propagandist body, as
Weber recognised. Yet the failure of the progressive national
liberalism he represented was itself a product of the system and its
incapacity for change. His analysis of the 'Obrigkeitsstaat' was
acute, and his strategy for bourgeois democracy made good sense
in terms of his own assumptions. That such a strategy never came
to anything was mainly because the interests in perpetuating the
existing system were too powerful and too deeply entrenched.
Weber himself realised this. As he wrote in one of his wartime
articles, 'There is no doubt at all that only the pressure of some
absolutely compelling political circumstance could bring about
any change here. Certainly a Parliamentary system does not arrive
of its own accord.'[75] In the event it was only the threat of military
collapse that could bring any change at all. Weber's reaction to
this will be discussed briefly before proceeding to some conclusions.

WAR AND REVOLUTION

In the first instance the effect of the war, in Weber's view, was to
strengthen the hold of the existing dominant groups over German
politics. The influence of heavy industry on government policy
increased, as did also the hold of the Prussian conservatives over
the formal institutions of state. The characteristic product of this
alliance was the proposal of the Prussian government in the middle
of the war to extend the system of *fideicommissum* still further,

which Weber described as the 'most intolerable thing that could be ventured against the nation by a minority clinging to power by means of a plutocratic suffrage'.[76] As the war progressed, however, it also increasingly exposed the weakness of the German political system. The same defects which, Weber believed, had been responsible for the débâcles of prewar diplomacy, in particular the lack of any clear line of responsibility for policy, now revealed themselves in the conduct of the war itself. This was demonstrated not only in the chronic uncertainty over war aims, but in specific decisions as well, among which the decision to engage in unlimited U-boat warfare was to Weber the most damaging of all. The appeal of the admirals to public opinion against the Chancellor took the decision away from the sphere of careful strategic calculation and into the arena of demagogy and 'Gefuhlspolitik', and showed a degree of irresponsibility that would have been impossible in a Parliamentary system.[77] Previously the problem had been the political control of bureaucracy but now the military was added as well. As he wrote in an article towards the end of the war, there had existed in Germany from the start of the war, and openly from the beginning of 1916, not one but a number of governments, all contending with each other for the control policy. All the official steps taken towards peace had been discredited by the publication of contradictory speeches and telegrams from dynastic or military circles, which were never placed before the appropriate political authorities for approval. This was the 'fatal weakness' which prevented the creation of a common political will in the German people.[78]

The regime was further weakened by its persistent failure as the war progressed to make any political concessions to the troops at the front. Weber argued that giving them the opportunity to participate in the postwar reconstruction through the ballot box was not merely a matter of justice, but increasingly urgent if a bitter social conflict was to be avoided, which would make a German victory impossible and undermine her postwar development. 'If there is any further "no" to reform,' he wrote at the beginning of 1918, 'no one will be able to hold them back.'[79] It was in these circumstances, when the inability of the system of government either to maintain political direction over the war, or to meet the political aspirations of the men at the front, had become clear, that Weber published his two major series of wartime articles on the suffrage and Parliament respectively, which marked the culmination of his thinking about political institutions up to this point. The content of these articles has already been dis-

cussed, and will not be repeated here. Two considerations, however, are worth emphasising. The first is that Weber's series on
'Parliament and Government' contained an important final section, omitted from the analysis in Chapter 4, since it was not so
relevant to his general theory of Parliament, in which he delivered
a sustained attack on the Prussian three-class voting law and on the
privileged position of Prussia within the Reich.[80] Both of these
provided important supports for the perpetuation of Junker
power. In the context of Weber's social analysis, democratisation was not merely a formal political device for encouraging
leadership, but also a substantive measure to reduce the power of a
particular class. Secondly, it is significant that Weber only turned
to constitutional discussion at a point when a widespread mood
for change had already developed, and when its introduction was
now a more realistic possibility. Thus it was not simply a question
of Weber himself becoming more alive to institutional factors at
this point. It was equally a question of a change in public attitudes,
which made institutional reform a more serious possibility.

The circumstances in which Parliamentary democracy was
finally instituted, however, were very different from those Weber
had expected or hoped. It came 'burdened with the debts' of the
old regime,[81] its first task being to incur the odium of suing for
peace at the insistence of the generals. It was further weakened by
the refusal of the Kaiser to resign, which fanned the flames of
revolution, and led directly to the proclamation of a republic.[82]
Finally, it was threatened by the 'antics' of the revolutionary
socialists, which Weber believed could only pave the way for reaction.[83] In his letters and speeches at the end of 1918 he directed
most of his animus at the activities of the revolutionary groups
associated with the Munich and Berlin soviets. Their 'ecstasy of
revolution', he argued, was a kind of narcotic, protecting them
from the real hardship facing the country.[84] Their schemes for
industrial reorganisation and for a revolutionary leap to a socialist
society were pure fantasies, which bore no relation to the shattered
state of industry, and would only breed disillusion if ever tried.
'I fear,' he wrote to Else Jaffe, 'that when it becomes clear that
faith can certainly move mountains, but not save ruined finances
and lack of capital, their disappointment will be intolerable, and
leave them inwardly bankrupt.'[85] The only consequence of an
uprising would be the invasion of the enemy and the consolidation
of reactionary forces. It would follow the typical course of revolutions, and end up with the same powers in control as when it
started.[86] The 'mad Liebknecht bands' would have to make their

putsch; this was unavoidable. The important thing was that they should be suppressed as quickly as possible, so as not to give an opportunity for wild reaction.[87] When the end finally came for Liebknecht and Rosa Luxemburg, Weber could express no sympathy. 'Liebknecht called up the street to fight,' was his comment; 'the street has dispatched him.'[88]

Weber was much more favourably disposed towards the majority socialists of the SPD. He welcomed the sense of responsibility they had shown in seeking to control the revolutionary upsurge, and get the better of the 'Bolsheviks'.[89] This favourable attitude should not, however, be interpreted, as some have done, to mean that Weber was moving towards the left. This, like a number of other misconceptions about Weber's politics, can be traced to J P Mayer's book, in this particular instance to a mistranslation of one of Weber's speeches at the end of 1918, in which Mayer has Weber saying that he was 'so near to Social Democracy as to be indistinguishable from it'.[90] In fact what Weber said was that his position was indistinguishable from 'many of its economically sophisticated members'—that is, those who recognised the necessity of capitalism!—and in fact he went on in his speech to explain why he could not be a Social Democrat.[91] Marianne Weber says explicitly that in his speeches for the Democratic Party at the end of the year he sought to move the party against the Left, which he criticised particularly for its 'stupid hatred of the entrepreneur'.[92] A central theme of all these speeches was that the reconstruction of German industry could only be achieved by the entrepreneurial class, not by means of socialist experiments.[93] One reason for this was the desperate need for foreign credit, which would only be made available to a regime which had the confidence of the bourgeoisie. Any capable bourgeois entrepreneur, he argued, however penniless himself, would receive this credit much more readily than a socialist *apparat*. Upon this 'iron fact' all schemes for industrial reorganisation on socialist lines by a dictatorship of the proletariat would fall down.[94] The bourgeoisie would only co-operate in getting the necessary credit if they were guaranteed an equal share in political power and a free hand in industry.[95] Besides the problem of international confidence, which Weber was concerned to spell out to any who were thinking of trying socialist experiments, he also stressed the indispensability of the business skills of the bourgeoisie to any reconstruction. A civil servant was no substitute for these, much less some half-baked theoretician from the Munich or Berlin soviet.[96] It was equally illusory to imagine that the skills of the bourgeoisie could somehow be used without giving them a profit-making context to work in. Without their *free* co-operation, he insisted, a viable industrial order was impossible.[97]

The issues involved here, and the contrast between the 'extreme' socialists in the soviets, and those who 'responsibly' accepted the need for a capitalist order, are treated in a more theoretical form in Weber's student address on 'Politics as a Vocation', in his distinction between the ethic of pure conviction and the ethic of responsibility.[98] The distinction he makes is between two different ways of holding to principles, the absolute and the contingent. On the one hand is the demand that a person should act rightly, regardless of the consequences. What matters is remaining true to principle, 'keeping the flame of pure intention undampened,' even where this might lead to harmful results.[99] On the other hand is the ethic of responsibility. As its name implies, this involves the demand that the individual take responsibility for the total consequences of his action. If by acting on principle, consequences ensue which are damaging to his cause, this cannot simply be shuffled off on to the evil world or the stupidity of others. The individual must accept the ethical ambiguity of the world—the fact that good does not follow from good, nor evil from evil—and be ready to compromise on principle, if this is the only way to ensure that the cause he seeks to promote is not set back or rendered ineffectual.[100] Of the two types of ethic, Weber regarded only the second as appropriate to the condition of politics. The first was an apolitical, other-worldly attitude, since it failed to recognise that the consequences of an action often stood in paradoxical relation to its intention, and that the means the politician used (the achievement and maintenance of *power*) were frequently at variance with the ends he sought to achieve.

Although in this distinction between the two types of ethic, Weber was highlighting a universal problem of political morality, its polemical purpose and context should be obvious.[101] The distinction was a useful device for banishing his political opponents to a category of the apolitical, where they could be shown to be caught in self-contradiction: they were trying to achieve aims in the world with attitudes which were essentially other-worldly. Thus, in the case of pacifists, the consequences of their position would not be to bring peace, but only make war more likely; their only consistent position was complete retirement from the world.[102] Weber used a similar argument against syndicalists, who believed that any industrial action as an expression of class solidarity must be right, even if in practice it produced reaction and class oppression. This made sense as an ethic of conviction, but those who held it should give up the pretension that their aim was this worldly achievement. In reply to Michels, who argued that every strike must work in the direction of socialism and therefore be right, Weber wrote:

> Now we have the perfect syndicalist, Michels. Michels the syndicalist might (and should) say: the conviction which a strike expresses is always the 'right' conviction.... But what weakness to pay any attention to its results! And then to do violence to the clear facts![103]

In Weber's view the clear facts were that lost strikes not only damaged the trade unions, but could delay the progress of the class movement for decades.[104] Weber extended this argument to the socialist position in general. It was argued, for example, that the war should be prolonged in order to achieve revolution. But what could such a revolution produce? Only a bourgeois economy, stripped of its feudal elements.[105] As Weber frequently insisted, any attempt to impose a socialist economy would discredit socialism for centuries.[106] Such a position made sense in terms of an ethic of conviction, but it was inconsistent with this-worldly achievement.

Weber's argument sought to put socialists into a category which would rule them out as serious politicians—men with passion, perhaps, but no perspective. The weakness of his argument was that it presented as a difference of moral categories what could equally be presented as a disagreement about the consequences of political action, or about whether the longer-term rather than the short-term effects should be considered. A syndicalist who insisted on the unity of class action, or a socialist who demanded prolongation of the war to achieve revolution, would presumably disagree with Weber about the consequences of such policies. Not everyone would agree that a lost strike produced reaction, or, if so, that there might not be longer-term consequences to justify it. Nor would everyone agree that the only outcome of a revolution would be a bourgeois economic system, even if this was what 'every scientifically trained socialist' accepted.[107] Weber was right to insist that, if his opponents were serious about this-worldly achievement, rather than the salvation of their souls, they should stand on the ground of empirical argument about consequences. But he was wrong to speak as if there could be only one possible correct view about these consequences. Lenin provided an effective, if crude, answer to this. Weber had written in one of his

articles on Russia that the December uprising of 1905 was a
'senseless *putsch*', since it no longer enjoyed the support of the
bourgeoisie, and could only strengthen the forces of reaction.[108]
In reply Lenin pilloried the 'cowardly bourgeois professor' for
his 'scientific' view. Weber's assessment of the possibilities was
not only mistaken; it was 'a subterfuge on the part of the representatives of the cowardly bourgeoisie, which sees in the proletariat its most dangerous class enemy'.[109] Lenin was naturally
quick to appreciate the polemic context of Weber's assessment.

Any appearance of a move leftwards by Weber at the end of the
war is thus something of an optical illusion, and is evidence of a
change in the Social Democrats as much as in Weber himself.
In so far as he approved of them, it was because they had now
demonstrated the political maturity that he had found lacking in
the prewar SPD, and which he had looked forward to one day in
his early writings as the necessary condition for a working-class
movement to which the bourgeoisie could 'extend the hand of
co-operation'.[110] In the economic sphere, he believed, most of
them now accepted the necessity of a social order led by the bourgeoisie, not the proletariat, at least for the time being. Politically,
they had shown a realistic grasp of possibilities, and a sense of
responsibility in keeping a curb on their wild elements. They had
thus proved themselves fitting partners in a bourgeois democracy.

The crucial question for the future of Parliamentary democracy,
therefore, remained for Weber what it had always been: whether the
bourgeoisie as a class could develop the political character capable
of supporting free Parliamentary institutions. As he wrote in his
article on Germany's future constitution, this was more important
than constitutional details:

For decades now they have been dominated by the spirit of
'security': of feeling safe in the protection of authoritarianism,
of frightened concern at the riskiness of any change—in short,
a cowardly will to impotence. It was precisely the technical
excellence of the administration, and the fact that as a result
things by and large went well for them materially, that reconciled whole strata of the population (not only the bourgeoisie) to
this cage, and stifled that sense of civic pride, without which
even the freest institutions are a mere shadow. The republic
has put an end to this 'security. . . .' The bourgeoisie is now
cast as exclusively on its own resources as the working class has
been for a long while. Under the social conditions prevailing
for the foreseeable future it must not be afraid to face the test of

its indispensability and its unique qualities. It is just this test that, we hope, will do good for its self-confidence.[111]

Weber's hope was, however, tinged with pessimism. It could only be bad for this self-confidence, he went on, that democracy had not come to Germany, as it had to other nations, as the result of a victorious struggle or an honourable peace, but as the consequence of defeat. The shadow of the 'Obrigkeitsstaat' hung heavy over it. 'The shameful bankruptcy proceedings of the old regime, with which the democracy is burdened, intervene to darken its political future.'[112] And it was not many months before Weber was himself to question the advantages of the new Parliamentary system.[113]

POLITICS AND CLASS

A fuller discussion of the theoretical assumptions involved in Weber's account of German politics will be given in later chapters, but a number of points can be emphasised here briefly. The first of these concerns Germany's failure to develop Parliamentary institutions. Of the different reasons Weber gave for this, the chief one was the way the bourgeoisie came to be assimilated into the traditional system of the Junkers. In an academic lecture on rural society which he gave on his visit to the United States in 1904, he singled out the tension between the traditional rural society of the east and the industrial west as the chief problem in Germany's political development. 'For Germany,' he said, 'all fateful questions of economic and social policy and of national interests are closely connected with the contrast between rural society of the east and the society of the west, and with its further development.'[114] He went on to congratulate the United States for not possessing an ancient aristocracy and for thus avoiding the 'tensions caused by the contrast between an authoritarian tradition and the purely commercial character of modern conditions'. The nub of his analysis of Germany's socio-political structure, as portrayed in this chapter, was that these tensions were kept in a state of balance by the developing needs of industry being met within the Junker political system, and by the assimilation of the bourgeoisie into that system. Weber recognised the irreversible character of industrial development in Germany,[115] and saw that the entrepreneurial class would inevitably wield a political influence consistent with their economic power. The question was, what form this political influence would take: whether a 'liaison behind closed doors' with the bureaucracy, support for the

'Obrigkeitsstaat' and the assimilation of industrial life to its authoritarian outlook; or alternatively that of a challenge to the system, and support for Parliamentary democracy. Either was possible. Which development took place was not determined by economic conditions alone; indeed, as we shall see particularly from his analysis of Russia, Weber saw no particular connection between modern large-scale industry and free political institutions. It was a question rather of the political character of a class, and the variety of historical and contemporary factors which conspired to mould it.

Professor L M Lachmann, in an essay in which he attempts to deduce a theoretical structure from Weber's articles on 'Parliament and Government', detects in Weber's analysis a functionalist model 'of a crude kind'.[116] According to Lachmann, Weber assumed as a principle 'the need for homogeneity among all the institutions of modern industrial society' and thereby made the kernel of his critique of Germany's political structure its inappropriateness to its developing industrial base.[117] This interpretation entirely misses the point of Weber's analysis, and what he conceived the central problem of German politics to be. The problem was that it was perfectly possible for capitalist industry to find 'security' and satisfaction of its material goals within an authoritarian political system. All it needed for this was an efficient administration of a modern bureaucratic type,[118] and this of course the German system provided in ample measure. In so far as there is an argument from appropriateness and 'homogeneity' in Weber's account, it is of a different kind. Weber argued that there must be a compatibility between the tasks set by a government, and the political system necessary to carry these out. In the case of Germany he detected a basic inconsistency between its attempt to play a world political role and its traditional structure of government. The deficiencies in the definition of policy and in the consistency of political determination shown by the 'Obrigkeitsstaat' demonstrated its inadequacy for world politics, as evidenced by its prewar foreign policy and the conduct of the war itself. If Germany wanted a world political role it could only achieve this through a Parliamentary democracy. This argument of Weber's was not a 'functional' one, but a question of choice, of the means appropriate to a given end. Germany could choose whether to be a world power or not; it if did, then its political arrangements must measure up to the task.

Central to Weber's analysis, in fact, was not so much an assumption about the functional interrelationship of institutions, but rather an assumption about class and classs power. Regimes persisted or changed according to the configuration of classes which supported them. The German 'Obrigkeitsstaat' persisted, despite the declining economic position of the Junkers, because the particular interrelationship between the country's economic and political development had put the bourgeoisie on its side, and because the Junkers knew how to use their monopoly of political position and social status to reinforce this support. In like manner, Parliamentary democracy was only possible if the configuration of class support changed, and the political character of the bourgeoisie was altered. The necessary complement to Weber's account of Parliamentary institutions, as set out in Chapter 4, was thus a theory of class. A similar assumption about the relationship between class and political structure will be seen to underlie Weber's analysis of Russian politics, considered in the next chapter.

REFERENCES

1 GASW, p 471.
2 ibid.
3 GPS, p 20.
4 SVS, vol 55 (1892), p 796; GASW, p 474.
5 ibid; cf *Mitteilungen des Evangelisch-sozialen Kongresses*, 6 (1892), p 5.
6 SVS, vol 55 (1892), pp 802–3.
7 GASW, p 473.
8 ibid; cf GASS, p 388.
9 SVS, vol 55 (1892), p 773; GASW, pp 449, 475–6.
10 'It is impossible for him in the long run to promote the national interest, when his workers are Poles.' GASW, p 454. SVS, vol 55, pp 795–6.
11 ibid; GPS, p 19.
12 See Weber's article 'Agrarstatistische und sozialpolitische Betrachtungen zur Fideicommissfrage in Preussen', GASS, pp 323–93.
13 SVS, vol 55, pp 795–6.
14 GASS, p 389; cf pp 380–1.
15 GM, p 373.
16 GPS, p 351; cf pp 401–2.
17 GPS, p 401, n 1.
18 GPS, pp 178, 282–3, 351, 400–1.
19 GPS, pp 405ff.
20 GPS, pp 300–1. cf p 402: 'Whenever the material or the social power interests of the strata which stood behind the ruling party were at stake, the throne always remained powerless . . . .' There is a splendid example of Weber's exposure of the conservative ideology in GASS, pp 380–90. The conservatives sought to hide the material interests involved in the *fideicommissum* proposals under a screen of 'romantic idealism'.
21 Quoted in W J Mommsen, op cit, p 109.

22 GPS, pp 20–2, 393, 441–2.
23 GPS, p 21.
24 ibid.
25 GASS, p 403; GPS, p 448.
26 GPS, pp 276–7.
27 GPS, p 337.
28 e.g. in the 'internal market' policy. *Verhundlungen des 8. Evangelisch-sozialen Kongresses* (1897), p 109.
29 GASS, pp 395–9.
30 GASS, p 395.
31 GASS, pp 396–7.
32 GASS, p 391.
33 GASS, p 331.
34 GPS, pp 184ff.
35 GASS, p 386.
36 GASS, p 379.
37 'Verhandlungen des IV. deutschen Hochschullehrertages', Dresden, 12–13 Oct 1911 (Archive Document no 35, Max Weber Institute, München), pp 67, 86; also Weber's reply to criticism of his speech in *Berliner Tageblatt*, 27.10.11. (Arch Doc. no. 38).
38 'Neither membership of a reserve regiment nor the possession of letters patent are in themselves any indication that their possession is suited to that hard, sober work, without which our bourgeoisie will be unable to maintain Germany's dominant world position in the sphere of trade and industry.' ibid, cf GASS, p 390, n 1.
39 *Verhandlungen des 8. Evangelisch-sozialen Kongresses* (1897), p 113.
40 GM, p 373.
41 GPS, p 233; cf p 402: 'The fear of the bourgeois plutocracy in the face of "democracy", which it saw embodied in the Reich suffrage and the Reichstag itself, gave support to the dominant party interests in Prussia.'
42 GPS, p 28.
43 *Archiv*, vol 20 (1905), pp 550–3.
44 ibid.
45 GASS, pp 407–12, especially 408–9.
46 ibid.
47 GASS, pp 404–5.
48 'Zur Gründung einer national-sozialen Partei', GPS, pp 26–9.
49 ibid.
50 *Verhandlungen des 8. Evangelisch-sozialen Kongresses* (1897), p 113.
51 GASS, pp 323–93; GPS, pp 178–86.
52 GASS, p 393.
53 GASS, pp 377–9; GPS, pp 185–6.
54 GASS, pp 407–12.
55 GASS, p 409. 'And I do not see what danger bourgeois society should see in that.'
56 GASS, p 410.
57 GASS, p 411.
58 Letter to R Michels, 15.10.07, quoted in W J Mommsen, op cit, p 123.
59 Letter to Michels, 6.11.07: ibid.
60 D Lindenlaub, op cit, pp 198ff. Boese talks instead of a Left and a Right wing, and shows how the conflict broke out into the open at the Mannheim meeting of 1905 over the issue of trade union rights. The two Webers and

Sombart were leaders of the Left, he writes, with Brentano their 'authoritative protector'. Schmoller's attempt to maintain a middle line from the chair with a savage criticism of Naumann for demagogy led to a demand for his resignation from Weber. F. Boese, op cit, pp 108–20.

61 See J J Sheehan, op cit, passim.
62 D Lindenlaub, op cit, pp 198–203.
63 ibid, p 204.
64 GASS, pp 394–9.
65 GASS, p 396.
66 ibid.
67 GASS, pp 398–9.
68 'Rundschreiben' (copy in Max Weber Institute, München). For a discussion of the context see B Schäfer's article in *Soziale Welt*, 18 (1967), pp 261–71; also W J Mommsen, op cit, pp 133–7.
69 'Rundschreiben,' pp 2–3.
70 Thus he contrasts such a movement with the sterility of the SPD and the subservient attitudes towards the party authorities it generated. GASS, pp 405–6.
71 GPS, p 23.
72 In a wartime discussion Weber compared the German trade union leadership favourably with the unruly 'politics of the streets' in other countries. In contrast with those irresponsible elements, he wrote, the industrial proletariat was 'a power, which is at least *capable* of ordered and disciplined direction under its leaders, i.e. when they are rational thinking politicians. Everything now depends on these leaders, and that means in Germany the trade union leaders, achieving supremacy over the instincts of the moment.' GPS, p 275. In Weber's view, a liberal social policy would strengthen the position of such leaders.
73 *Jugendbriefe*, pp 234, 249, 297–9.
74 W J Mommsen, op cit, p 137.
75 GPS, p 356.
76 GPS, pp 185–6.
77 GPS, pp 218–19, 284.
78 GPS, p 433.
79 GPS, p 282.
80 'Parlamentarisierung und Föderalismus', GPS, pp 394–431.
81 GPS, p 442.
82 GPS, 1st edn, pp 477–9.
83 He was hostile to the revolution, writes Marianne, and called it a 'bloody carnival which does not deserve the honourable name of revolution'. *Lebensbild*, p 642.
84 GPS, 1st edn, pp 481–2.
85 ibid.
86 GPS, p 473.
87 GPS, 1st edn, pp 481–2.
88 Quoted in *Lebensbild*, p 653.
89 ibid, p 644.
90 J P Mayer, op cit, p 97.
91 GPS, p 472.
92 *Lebensbild*, p 653.
93 GPS, pp 446–8, 470–1, 473–5.
94 GPS, p 474.

95 ibid.
96 GPS, p 448.
97 GPS, pp 441, 471.
98 GPS, pp 539ff; GM, pp 120ff; cf GAW, pp 491–2; MSS, p 16.
99 GPS, p 540.
100 ibid.
101 Weber's lecture 'Politics as a Vocation' is often discussed as if it had no context. Yet it was given in the winter of 1918–19 in the middle of the revolutionary events. Weber was apparently only persuaded by the student association to give the address at all because of the threat that they would invite Kurt Eisner, the Bavarian revolutionary, instead. (H H Bruun, op cit, p 271.)
102 GPS, pp 141–2.
103 Letter to R Michels, 9.2.08, quoted in W J Mommsen, op cit, p 122.
104 ibid.
105 GPS, pp 540–1.
106 e.g. his letter to Dr Neurath, GPS, 1st edn, p 488: 'I consider all proposals for a planned economy to be a totally irresponsible and dilettantist frivolity, of a kind which can discredit socialism for a century.'
107 GPS, p 541.
108 Archiv, 23B, p 166.
109 Lenin, Selected Works (3 vols, Moscow, 1960), vol 1, p 840.
110 Verhandlungen des 5. Evangelisch-sozialen Kongresses (1894), p 82.
111 GPS, p 442.
112 ibid.
113 See Chapter 8.
114 GM, p 384.
115 Verhandlungen des 8. Evangelisch-sozialen Kongresses (1897), p 109.
116 L M Lachmann, The Legacy of Max Weber (London, 1970), p 124.
117 ibid, pp 125–6.
118 WG, pp 562–3; ES, p 975.

Chapter 7

Society, Class and State: Russia

Weber's articles on the Russian revolution of 1905–6 form the most substantial of his political writings, at least in extent. The material for them was drawn entirely from Russian sources, though he admitted that they were written too close to the event to count as history.[1] They were no mere chronicle, however, but an attempt to grasp what was 'essential and characteristic'[2] about Russian developments, a portrayal of the 'general social and political situation'[3] in which the events of the revolutionary period took place. It is this attempt to distil the essential interrelationship of society and government that gives the articles their value as examples of political analysis.

Like Weber's writings on Germany, indeed more explicitly so, his Russian articles were concerned with the question of how a movement for Parliamentary government was possible within an authoritarian state, and what social forces were capable of sustaining it. At the same time Weber recognised obvious differences between the political structure of Russia and that of Germany. Russia lacked the basic civil freedoms which were taken for granted in Western Europe. Richard Pipes is wrong when he says that Weber was looking to Russia for entirely new possibilities of freedom which existed nowhere else.[4] On the contrary Weber was explicit that the demands of the Russian liberals 'for us in the West have long since lost the charm of novelty'.[5] What was new was the problem of establishing these freedoms for the first time under the conditions of advanced capitalism and a modern bureaucracy. Besides the absence of basic freedoms, Russia was also distinguished by a sharp divorce between society and state. The absolute power of the Tsar, as Weber described it, 'after the breakdown of the organic structures which gave Russia of the seventeenth and eighteenth centuries its character, now hangs in the air in a completely "unhistorical" freedom'.[6] Although

Weber's own account showed this 'suspension' to be by no means total—the system of Tsarist autocracy enjoyed a measure of support from the Church and sections of the landowning aristocracy, as well as from emerging capitalism—yet its degree of alienation from society was remarkable and could only be a source of political weakness. This fragility of the system was further emphasised by the conflicts within society itself. If a feature of German development was the tension between the rural aristocracy of the east and the urban society of the west, Russia was distinguished by an even more violent contrast: the 'importation of great capitalist powers in their most modern form on to a basis of archaic peasant communism'.[7]

For all these differences, however, Weber raised a similar question in his Russian studies to the one that concerned him in relation to Germany: what social forces were there capable of generating and sustaining Parliamentary government? This was the explicit theme of his first article, entitled 'The Situation of Bourgeois Democracy in Russia'.[8] The first part of the present chapter will follow the account given in this article, of the main forces at work in Russian society, albeit in a more systematic manner, and omitting some of its detailed discussions of the various liberal programmes. Weber's second article was devoted to a political analysis of the Tsarist system, and contains an account of a more dynamic kind of the way it responded to the various revolutionary crises. This will form the subject of the second part of the chapter. The third section will consider the article Weber wrote on the April revolution of 1917 and his subsequent reactions to Bolshevism. The chapter will conclude by drawing out some of the theoretical implications common to his writings on Germany and Russia together, among others his theory of the historical conditions for liberal democracy.

THE OUTLOOK FOR BOURGEOIS DEMOCRACY

The immediate subject of Weber's first article, written at the end of 1905, was the reform proposals published by the Constitutional Democrats under Peter Struve earlier in the year.[9] Part of the article was taken up with a discussion of this document and a comparison of its proposals with those of other groups. Weber's analysis, however, went deeper, to involve a consideration of the political forces which generated these proposals, and the question of whether there existed a sufficient social basis in Russia to support a liberal democratic regime.

His starting point was an analysis of the liberal movement itself. Though supported mainly by the urban intelligentsia and the liberal landowners it was not tied to any particular economic class, but was largely an idealist movement. From an economic point of view, Weber noted, its supporters were 'Nicht-Interessenten', bearers of a political and social idealism of a kind that was impossible to organise into an effective political force in Germany.[10] In the years preceding the revolution, this movement had found its focus in the 'Zemstvos', the organs of local government, which Weber described as the 'most lively institutions of Russian public life'.[11] The Zemstvos offered a basis for the liberal movement in a number of ways. They provided a sphere for the exercise of self-government, which, in the range of tasks they performed, gave the lie to the belief that the Russians were 'unready for a free administration'.[12] At the same time the national Zemstvo congress provided a forum in which the liberal landowners and the intelligentsia could organise legally for constitutional reform.

However, Weber questioned the real strength of this Zemstvo movement. The Zemstvos themselves were being increasingly undermined by the central bureaucracy, which sought to restrict their activities and take over their functions. They were increasingly restricted to the role of a 'passive organisation for raising taxes decreed and spent by the state'.[13] In the light of this trend Weber expressed his amazement that the various liberal reform programmes contained so little mention of the autonomy of local government, which was one of the central constitutional questions of the time.[14] Another weakness of the liberal movement was that it was so largely a movement of the intelligentsia. These were 'bourgeois' in terms of their life-style and education but not strictly in terms of economic class.[15] Although Weber was ready to acknowledge the strength of this tradition in Russian life, he clearly saw it as having only a limited political effectiveness, apart from the support of major classes or institutions of society.[16] The rest of this section will consider Weber's assessment of the main forces of Russian society, from the standpoint of their possible support for the liberal movement, beginning with the Church.

In Weber's view the character of a society's religion and religious institutions was historically one of the most important factors in determining its political outlook, in particular whether it developed a liberal tradition or not. Those forms of Protestantism which rejected all worldly powers as usurpations of divine authority had a special influence on the development of political individualism.[17] The historical character of Russian orthodoxy, in contrast, was authoritarian. 'The history and form of organisation of the orthodox Church,' Weber wrote, 'makes it quite improbable that, however transformed, it could ever set itself up as a representative of civil liberties against the power of the police state.'[18] This was not only a question of its own authoritarian internal structure, but also of its historical implication in the state. The doctrine of the Church provided Tsarism with a powerful ideological justification, and its priests acted as instruments of police rule in rural areas. The orthodox Church was the 'religious foundation of absolutism'.[19]

Weber recognised the existence of a radical movement among the clergy, reflecting the wider movement in society. Basing itself on a theology which emphasised the this-worldly element in the Christian message and the desire to realise God's kingdom here and now, it demanded the end of absolutism and a programme of social reform.[20] This was linked with the demand for various internal reforms within the Church, such as increasing the importance of the laity and subjecting the episcopacy to election from below. The movement was only of limited consequence, however. It was essentially urban-based, and made little impact on the countryside.[21] Further, as Weber pointed out in his second article, these attacks from below on the authority of the episcopacy, only served to strengthen the alliance of the hierarchy with the state administration.[22] An episcopacy whose internal authority was threatened, far from joining in the challenge to the power of the state, would have every incentive to make common cause with it, in order to win external support against its own rebels. In this respect, Weber argued, Russian Orthodoxy was in a crucially different position from Roman Catholicism:

> The Church has no Archimedian point outside the sphere of the state, in the form of a pope, and will never get one. Given the choice between dependence on those under them through election, and dependence on those above, the hierarchy will have no doubt which is preferable for its own interests; indeed, the choice has already been made.[23]

If it was in vain to expect support for the liberal movement from the chief historical institution of Russian society, what of its social classes?

Of all the classes in Russian society, Weber regarded the peasants as most crucial to its future political development. The decisive question, he wrote, for the success of the movement for constitutional democracy and for the chances of a liberal development of the Western European kind 'is and must remain the position of the peasants'.[24] The space he devoted to the agrarian situation in his articles reflected not only his long-standing interest in the economics and sociology of agriculture, but also the centrality of the issue in Russian society at the time. Proposals for agrarian reform held a central place in all the liberal programmes.[25] The need to satisfy the demand of the peasantry for more land was generally accepted, and the failure of the Tsarist regime to tackle the issue contributed to its weakness. The important question to Weber, however, was how far the peasants could be won for a liberal *political* programme, and whether their economic demands could be satisfied in a way which would strengthen the cause of bourgeois democracy. The liberals in general assumed that agrarian reform and political reform were two sides of the same coin, and that they would reinforce each other.[26] Weber questioned this assumption on the basis of his analysis of the economic demands the peasants were making.

The demand for more land, Weber argued, by and large did not take an individualistic form, but was shaped by the traditional communist ideals of the Russian 'Mir'.[27] In opposition to the capitalist principle of the 'selection of the fittest' on the basis of private ownership and technological development, the peasant movement demanded the principle of the equal right of all to a livelihood from the land, on the basis of traditional methods of agriculture.[28] Paradoxically, this principle was itself only strengthened by the development of industrial capitalism in the urban centres; it was the 'reflex image' of capitalism.[29] The peculiarity of the Russian situation, Weber argued, was that 'an increase in capitalist development . . . can also bring with it an increase of archaic agrarian communism'.[30] The broad mass of the peasantry were not to be won for an individualist agrarian programme in the Western European sense.

If the peasant movement were successful in its demands, Weber believed, it would set Russia's economic development back a generation.[31] But it was the political consequences that concerned him more. The result of satisfying the peasants' demands could only be to strengthen the anti-individualist forces in Russian society and make the cause of liberal democracy more difficult. The liberal reformers were thus caught in a dilemma.[32] They accepted the need for agrarian reform and made it the centrepiece of their social and economic proposals. But its achievement could only weaken the chances for success of a genuinely liberal political programme:

They have no choice but to support an agrarian reform, which, in all probability, will not strengthen the cause of an economically and technically 'progressive' socialism of a voluntary kind, but will rather confirm an essentially archaic peasant communism . . . as the main feature in the economic practice and outlook of the masses, and thus postpone the development of a Western European individualist culture that most of them consider inevitable.[33]

A further feature of the peasants' demands, which made their support for liberal democracy questionable, was that they were almost exclusively economic. In so far as they had any political aims, these were entirely negative ones: the abolition of bureaucratic supervision at the local level, and the election of representatives to negotiate directly with the Tsar—a conception which, as Weber pointed out, had absolutely nothing in common with modern Parliamentary government.[34] The main emphasis of their demands, though, was economic, and Weber could only express a general scepticism about where 'the masses would find the impulse from to participate in a movement which went beyond purely material demands'.[35] While this also applied to the urban masses, it was particularly true of the peasantry, who possessed no consistent political character of their own. Foreign observers, Weber noted, tended to regard the Russian peasants as extreme reactionaries, whereas the Russians themselves considered their temper to be that of extreme revolutionaries.[36] Both could be equally true. The historical experience of modern European revolutions was for the peasants to switch 'from the most thoroughgoing radicalism to a state of apathy or political reaction, once their immediate economic demands had been satisfied'.[37] The basic assumption of the liberals was that it was impossible for these demands to be satisfied under Tsarism, since it would involve the dispossession of the landed aristocracy, and that therefore the peasants must be the allies of Parliamentary reform. But Weber himself would not rule out the possibility that by some act of force the autocracy might 'stop up their mouths with land'. If this happened, or if the peasants simply seized the land for themselves in an outburst of anarchy, 'any further interest on their part in constitutional reform would evaporate'.[38]

To regard the peasants as committed supporters of liberal democracy was thus a mistake in Weber's view. While they might join in a coalition of forces for the overthrow of Tsarism, they could not offer any long-term basis of support for Parliamentary institutions. But nor could the more 'modern' social classes, the urban proletariat or the bourgeoisie, either. The non-liberal character of the former was reinforced by Social Democracy. The latter were able to attain their ends by interest-group pressure on the administration.

Weber's account of Russian Social Democracy is characteristically hostile, though the article contains an acute analysis of the divisions between Lenin and Plekhanov.[39] The reasons for the split, he observed, were not so much a matter of principle, as of a personal and tactical nature. It also had its origin in the ambiguities of Marxism—as demonstrated by Marx himself in his attitude to the Paris Commune and similar events—as well as in the particular character of the Russian tradition of socialism. The emphasis on revolutionary uprising and the opposition to fixed laws of social development lay 'deep in the blood' of Russian socialism, as the consequence of specifically Hegelian ideas. What Weber called the 'pragmatic rationalism' of this tradition—its emphasis on the creative character of human thought—was never completely submerged under the 'naturalistic rationalism' of a theory of inevitable social development.[40] Not surprisingly, though, Weber could find nothing in either faction which bore any relation to liberalism. Both declared it the party's duty to support the liberal movement against Tsarism, but at the same time did their best to discredit all the liberal groups in the eyes of the workers. What particularly destroyed the hope of any unity in the opposition to Tsarism was the dogmatic and sect-like character of Social Democracy. The chief aim of the rival groups was to maintain the purity of their doctrines, to win a few extra souls for their sect, to secure the exposure of the 'enemies of the people' in the neighbouring factions rather than to work for any long-term political success. 'Any agreement among the oppositional elements is thereby made impossible,' Weber concluded.[41]

As in his writings on Germany, Weber was also concerned at the educational effect of Social Democracy on the character of the working class, and its inculcation of attitudes far removed from the spirit necessary to the operation of free institutions. Although a year or two later he was favourably to compare the Russians' 'Catalinarian energy of faith' with the qualities shown by the German party,[42] here he criticised them for the same ineffectual posturing which was his standard reaction to revolutionaries. Nothing that he wrote elsewhere was quite as scathing as this:

'Correct' Social Democracy drills the masses into a spiritual parade march, and dismisses them, not to an other-worldly paradise (which, in Puritanism, at least had respectable achievements in the service of this-worldly freedom to its credit), but to a this-worldly one, and makes from it a kind of vaccination for all those with an interest in the existing order. Social Democracy accustoms its pupils to submissiveness in the face of dogmas and party authorities, to the futile spectacle of mass strikes and the passive enjoyment of the spine-chilling ragings of their press hacks, considered as ridiculous as they are harmless by their opponents—accustoms them, in other words, to a hysterical excess of emotion, which acts as a substitute for economic and political thought and action, and renders it quite impossible. On this sterile soil, when the 'eschatological' epoch of the movement is past, and generation upon generation has clenched its fists and gnashed its teeth in vain, can only spiritual dullness grow.[43]

Whatever the adequacy of Weber's assessment of the revolutionary potential of Russian Social Democracy—and he was not alone in underestimating it—he was at least correct in his judgement that it did not have much in common with liberalism, and that whatever alliance it might make with bourgeois democracy would be a matter of temporary convenience only.[44] Under its tutelage, the working class was unlikely to provide reliable support for the liberal movement.

The last of the social classes to be considered in Weber's account—the petty-bourgeoisie merited only a few lines in its capacity as Jew haters and police agents[45]—was the 'thin stratum' of the bourgeoisie itself. In effect, Weber's conclusion was the same as Lenin's, that this was a bourgeois revolution without the bourgeoisie.[46] The liberal intelligentsia were 'bourgeois' in lifestyle and outlook alone,[47] whereas the bourgeoisie proper, the capitalist entrepreneurs, kept aloof both from the party of Constitutional Democracy and from the Zemstvo movement.[48] None of its leading figures were to be found within the ranks of liberal reform. A few industrialists might support a progressive social policy and resent their exclusion from formal political power, and the class as a whole could not be assumed without further question to be on the side of Tsarism. But they were not decisively in favour of the liberal movement either.[49]

This assessment was emphasised by the events Weber analysed in his second article. Even though the industrialists were largely unrepresented in the Duma elected in the spring of 1906, they were perfectly happy with the system of 'token constitutionalism', because they could get the economic changes they wanted by means of direct pressure on the bureaucracy.[50] They had been interested in political reform only so as to secure social order and a relief from revolutionary turmoil, but they had no desire to turn the token constitutionalism into an effective Parliamentary system. 'The class of the large capitalist entrepreneurs and the bankers,' Weber wrote, 'is the only stratum apart from officialdom itself, that would pronounce itself in complete agreement with the rule of the bureaucracy in token constitutional form, always under the assumption that a free hand were given to profit. . . .'[51]

Weber recognised at work in Russia the same feature of modern large-scale capitalism that he had found in Germany: that its material demands could be met without a system of effective Parliamentary government, provided it was able to maintain its influence with the bureaucracy. Under modern circumstances economic liberalism, in the sense of 'a free hand for profit', was perfectly compatible with a political system which embodied a widespread denial of civil liberties and constitutional rights. Indeed the Russian civil service, on Weber's analysis, itself demonstrated this combination; economically liberal in outlook, it administered a repressive police state.[52] There thus existed no 'inner affinity' at all between modern high capitalism and liberal democracy.[53] This made the outlook for bourgeois democracy particularly bleak, when the bourgeoisie themselves were no longer necessarily in favour of 'bourgeois' political reforms. The Russian dilemma, as Weber concluded at the end of his second article, was that capitalism was being imported into the country in its most advanced form.[54] Thus 'all the forms of development are excluded which in the West put the strong *economic* interests of the possessing classes in the service of the movement for bourgeois liberty.'[55]

There is much more in Weber's first article than can be included in this brief summary, in particular an exhaustive account of the programmes of the various political parties and groups, but what has been mentioned here constitutes the essence of his social analysis. The problem for bourgeois democracy, according to this, was that, whatever the extent of opposition to the Tsar, there was no major social interest decisively behind a specifically liberal programme. The latter was a movement of ideas only, and such a movement, without the support of significant material interests, could only have a limited political effect. Although the elections to the Duma were to bring a temporary triumph for

Constitutional Democracy, this did not lead Weber to modify his assessment.

THE PATHOLOGY OF ABSOLUTISM

Where in his first article Weber was more concerned with the social forces at work in Russian society, his second article, entitled 'Russia's Transition to Token Constitutionalism',[56] was devoted to a political analysis of Tsarism itself, and its response to the revolution. It was written in August 1906, after the election and subsequent dissolution of the Duma, at a point when it was possible to attempt some overall assessment of the events of the previous year. In his first article Weber had described the Tsarist system as 'suspended above society' like the monarchy of Diocletian.[57] The gulf between society and government was a recurrent theme of his second article, a gulf which he largely explained in terms of the 'vanity' and 'prestige interests' of the Tsar and the bureaucracy, and the steadfast refusal of the regime to share any of its power, even with those social groups which were otherwise its natural supporters. In the absence of this support it was forced to rely on the police and the army, and to have recourse to 'the typical instrument of the Roman emperors in their period of decline: massive donations to the troops'.[58] As a result, its success in stemming the tide of revolution could only be temporary, Weber believed, especially as in the process it had been compelled to make concessions to the liberal position— theoretical if not practical—which could only further undermine its rule.[59]

For the time being, however, Tsarism had survived, and Weber sought to show how it had done so. Its response to revolution had been to offer a façade of token constitutionalism, which created the illusion of reform without surrendering any essential powers, and provided a breathing space to regroup the forces of reaction.[60] The success of this strategy was already evident in the Moscow strike in December 1905, which achieved nothing in comparison with the October ones, because it no longer enjoyed the support of the bourgeoisie.[61] Its failure marked the beginning of reaction. Weber did not, however, assign all the credit for this strategy to the regime itself; it was largely forced upon it by the insistence of foreign banks. The actions of the government were only intelligible, he argued, when one grasped its essential dependence on external creditors.[62] These demanded 'order'. The Manifesto of October 1905 was an attempt to secure order, but it failed. The bankers thereupon insisted that the proposals for a constitution should actually be put into effect. The Tsar was forced to bow to the necessity of empty coffers and 'show the requisite obedience towards the impersonal but all the more implacable power of the exchange market'.[63] In the light of its financial position, the regime was compelled to operate a kind of 'double account':

> On the one side it is obvious that the Tsar himself never seriously believed in the transition of Russia to a constitutional state, with 'effective' guarantees of individual rights, as they were naïvely termed in the October Manifesto, and this was made evident on every occasion that offered itself. The interests of the police were all he thought of. This fitted in very nicely with the power interests of the old type of police bureaucracy, and at the same time a policy of ruthless oppression could certainly impress the foreign exchanges with the appearance of 'strong' government. On the other side, however, the repeatedly fruitless missions abroad of finance officials showed that, in spite of all, the bankers believed they must insist upon the Duma's actually being summoned before any substantial loan could be entertained. So the promises of 17 October had formally to be observed, and the 'constitution' put into effect at least far enough to show the public abroad, on whose good impression the bankers were calculating, the outward semblance of constitutional guarantees.[64]

The task, then, assigned to the ministry under Count Vitte, was the establishment of token institutions which would give the appearance of carrying out the October Manifesto and create the necessary confidence abroad, without in fact yielding any of the arbitrary power enjoyed by Tsar and bureaucracy.[65] Weber proceeded to examine at some length the various freedoms which had been proclaimed, and showed each in turn to be a sham.[66] Thus freedom of expression had been declared in principle; in practice oppositional newspapers were harassed at will by local officials. All that was meant by freedom of conscience was that certain sects were tolerated; unbelief itself was not admitted. Freedom of association was never effective, least of all at the work place. The declaration of the freedom of the person was accompanied, from the beginning of 1906 onwards, by the extension of martial law and emergency jurisdiction, till the prisons were insufficient to cope with the numbers. In general the government 'by means of every judicial manipulation subordinated the new freedoms to administrative arbitrariness. . . . The machinery grinds on, as if nothing had ever happened.'[67]

However, as Weber was quick to point out, this kind of double game, of formally conceding rights on the one hand, while taking them away with the other, was more dangerous than naked repression, and only increased resentment.[68] In practice the only effective reform dating from October was an administrative one, which eroded liberties still further.[69] The traditional method of government was by means of autonomous departments, each answerable to the Tsar, without any co-ordinating first minister. These separate 'satrapies' were usually in a state of war with one another or, at best, enjoyed a relationship of uneasy peace. On the outbreak of 'war' they would bombard each other with massive papers of state, running into hundreds of pages and full of learned erudition. It was only this obstructionism that made life at all tolerable for the subjects of autocracy.[70] From the standpoint of individual freedom, Weber remarked, 'every obstruction which the "system" of absolutism set in its own way . . . provided a protection for the human dignity of its subjects'.[71] The reform of October put an end to this chaos, and created a modern centralised bureaucracy under a single ministerial council. Such a 'rationalisation of autocracy' strengthened the position of the bureaucracy at the expense of the Tsar himself, who now received all questions pre-digested from the council. At the same time it made the position worse for the subjects. The whole of Russian society, Weber wrote, apart from the industrialists and the bankers, opposed this development of ancient absolutism into a modern rational bureaucracy. With it, the war of society against the bureaucracy became chronic.[72]

The centrepiece of token constitutionalism was the Duma, which itself reflected the absence of effective rights in society and the opposition between the society and its government.[73] Its constitutional position was very weak and restricted, in terms both of its powers to propose change in the laws and to supervise the administration. It was denied the usual rights associated with a Parliament, such as the right of petition and the right to approve the budget; the latter it had in token form only, since in the absence of its approval, the previous year's budget was automatically renewed. The only right it possessed was to veto legislation, which epitomised the whole relationship between Russian society and government in its assumption that 'the representative assembly is the natural enemy of the government . . . and the government the natural enemy of "the people" '.[74]

While the earlier parts of Weber's article were concerned to examine the framework of token constitutionalism and the emptiness of the rights it embodied, the later parts were devoted to an account of the circumstances leading up to the election of the Duma, its summoning and subsequent dissolution. Despite the universal hostility of society towards the government, Weber remarked, everything in the early months of 1906 seemed to conspire to make the circumstances unfavourable for a liberal democratic outcome to the elections. The electoral system was carefully rigged by the regime to exclude whole groups of the population and diminish the voting strength of others.[75] The campaign in the countryside was hampered by continuous police harassment.[76] The most radical leaders were in jail. In addition, the parties themselves were in some disarray. The decision of the Social Democrats to boycott the Duma proved a considerable obstacle to the cause of democracy throughout the elections. It was no thanks to them that the elections did not produce a reactionary outcome: 'they had done all they could to play into the hands of the government'.[77]

Worst of all, in Weber's view, was the situation in the party of Constitutional Democracy itself, the Kadets.[78] They were increasingly divided over the question of land reform. Not only was there a chaos of conflicting interest among the peasants themselves, which it would require a government of dictatorial stamp to resolve,[79] but a crucial change could be observed in the attitude of the large landowners, who were the class most favoured by the electoral system. Under the pressure of continual peasant agitation and the threat to their land, they were becoming increasingly reactionary.[80] They had provided the spearhead of Zemstvo liberalism, but now that their material interests were threatened they could afford to entertain liberal ideas no longer:

After the suppression of the Moscow uprising and under the pressure of peasant unrest, the reaction began to infiltrate from the sphere of the bureaucracy into 'society', that is, in the first instance into the Zemstvos. In this respect it was the severe threat of peasant unrest to the economic basis of the private landowners, whose representatives formed the best minds of the liberal Zemstvo movement, that played the decisive role. The course events took is a good example of the conditions for ideological activity on the part of a propertied class, and of the limited effect of humanitarian ideals in the face of economic interests. So long as the economic basis of the landowners, who were dominant in the Zemstvos, remained undisturbed, they assumed the leadership of the numerous political and social ideologues who stemmed from their midst. But once the threat of immediate physical and economic ruin appeared, they were assailed by the force of conflicting interests which had remained latent before, and it was inevitable that, shaken out of their everyday existence and forcefully reminded of the material basis of their own position, their attitudes should undergo a marked transformation.[81]

In view of all these handicaps to the cause of democracy, and in particular of the increasing class conflict within the Zemstvos,[82] it required some special explanation why the elections turned out favourably for the Kadets. One point Weber had made earlier was that, once the fetters of absolutism were loosened, however momentarily, it unleashed such a flood of political activity as simply could not be controlled by the government.[83] But the main reason, he argued, was the government's own obstinacy. One would have thought that it would have been only too ready to make use of the class interests of the propertied strata, always prompt enough in the support of state order, and would have sought to forge an alliance with the moderate elements in the Zemstvo movement, which were increasingly fearful of revolution. Instead the bureaucracy steadfastly refused to make any sacrifice of its arbitrary powers, and went out of its way to affront the self-respect of the Zemstvos. No compromise of its supreme power was to be entertained.[84]

Even so, the results of the elections were quite unexpected.[85] The government was confronted with an almost totally hostile Duma, composed mainly of Constitutional Democrats. Their victory, though, needed careful interpretation, Weber argued. It was the product of an alliance between the urban voters, the peasants and some landowners, united in their opposition to administrative arbitrariness, but not necessarily in support of a full liberal programme. The success of the Kadets depended upon Social Democrat voters, who in the absence of their own candidates voted for the next best thing; in the few instances where Social Democrats put up at the last minute, they easily beat their Kadet opponents. The democratic victory thus rested on an uncertain foundation. Once the extreme left took part in elections, it would give the Kadets such a trouncing in the large cities that 'the balance would lie entirely between the socialist and the bourgeois class parties, and ideological democracy would be, eliminated'.[86] The vote had been primarily a negative vote, in which everyone who had an ounce of conviction 'joined under the flag of democracy to protest'.

The party of trade and industry, in contrast, proved completely ineffective in the elections. Its response was to dissolve itself into a powerful economic interest group, and concentrate on exerting influence on the government direct. In this it proved more successful.[87] The 'general agreement between the government and the industrialists' was shown when, immediately after the elections, they were invited to discuss a social programme of a far-reaching kind. They were offered all they wanted in the way of freedom from administration control and supervision, in return for some minimal recognition of workers' rights. From the point of view of the bureaucracy, Weber wrote, this was tactically just right: the Russian bourgeoisie, freed from state control in the pursuit of its economic interests, would become 'an even more reliable supporter of "strong government", though certainly not *inside* Parliament'.[88]

Apart from the bourgeoisie, the regime found itself faced with the united opposition of society in the Duma.[89] But it was the foreign banks which now 'had the game in their hand'.[90] It was they who had insisted upon the calling of the Duma in the first place; it now became a matter of urgency for them that the government loan should be effected before the Duma actually met, since they realised that it would never accept the terms they knew they could exact from the government. The government was in a hopeless financial position. It had the choice of submitting either to the Duma or to the banks. It preferred the latter, under almost any conditions, and they were the severest that any great power had ever had to agree to. At all events, the loan was brought safe into harbour before the Duma met. Count Vitte's ministry was now dispensable, its main purpose having been achieved, and it was promptly replaced by an assortment of correct thinking conservative officials, who were less 'compromised with society'.[91]

Under these circumstances of confrontation, Weber found it hardly surprising that the activities of the Duma should prove ineffectual.[92] All its proposals were simply ignored by the government. And at the first opportunity the Tsar dissolved it. Thus the opposition between society and government remained total; the 'two Russias' stood over against each other without any meeting point.[93] The immediate reason for this, as Weber had insisted, was a political one: the obstinacy of Tsarism. Its concern with its own prestige, with saving its face, always led it to make the necessary concessions too late, and then, 'as one concession after the next was forced from it, it sought to retrieve its lost "prestige" through the relentless use of arbitrary police powers'.[94] It was impossible for such a regime to bring any lasting peace to the country; the tireless energy of Russian radicalism would bring about the economic ruin of the country first.[95]

However—and here Weber returned to the theme of his first article—it was unlikely that a liberal government could survive for long under Russian circumstances. Underneath the political conflict lay a social crisis: the tension between peasant and landowner, the tension created by the superimposition of advanced capitalism on an archaic social structure, and the radical socialism this generated. Tsarism sought to keep these tensions in check. But 'the easing of the great pressure of police arbitrariness under a liberal ministry would have brought about a powerful increase, not only in aimless outbreaks by the radicals, but also in the intensity of class and national conflicts.'[96] The course of the revolution itself had also pushed the supporters of liberalism among the landowners to the right. Any government based upon property would therefore, in Weber's view, be reactionary rather than liberal.[97] The prospects for the liberal movement thus looked bleak. This had nothing to do with the Russian people's 'immaturity for constitutional government', as German readers might like to believe; it was the product of the circumstances themselves.[98] 'Never,' he concluded, 'when all is said and done, has a struggle for freedom been carried out under such difficult conditions as the Russian.'[99]

REVOLUTION AND BOLSHEVISM

Weber did not return to the study of Russian affairs till 1917. The article he wrote soon after the February revolution[100] largely confirmed the analysis of his earlier studies, particularly the impossibility of bourgeois liberalism under Russian conditions, and will be summarised here mainly as a postscript to the previous analysis. Weber admitted that he had thought the prospect of a revolution during the war unlikely.[101] The land reforms of Stolypin had divided the peasantry, one of 'the chief fighting forces of revolution', and created a new body of property owners allied with the regime.[102] Although the industrial proletariat had increased dramatically in numbers, it still remained comparatively small, and, as the previous revolution had indicated, could only bring Tsarism down by means of an improbable alliance with the bourgeoisie.[103] The large industrialists remained as reactionary as ever. As for the bourgeois intelligentsia, they had seen their self-respect broken by the failure of 1905–6, and sought compensation in external adventures:

> There appeared to be no doubt about the attitude of the majority of the Zemstvo circles and of the bourgeois intelligentsia, previously the main supporters of reform. Their self-respect, which had been broken by the disappointment of their internal power hopes, now transferred itself all the more fervently to the romanticism of external power. It is perfectly understandable: the members of the higher Russian civil service as of the officer corps are mainly recruited, as they are everywhere else, from these propertied strata. Constantinople and the so-called 'liberation' of the Slavs—which meant in effect their domination by the national great Russian bureaucracy—now replaced the earlier enthusiasm for 'human rights' and 'constituent assemblies'.[104]

A revolution had thus appeared improbable. The reason why it in fact occurred, however, was a familiar one: the persistent vanity of the Tsar, especially after Russia's defeats in war, and his determination to rule alone without sharing power, even with the socially conservative forces of bourgeois property.[105] Given Russia's situation after three years of war, it was no longer possible to rule the country by means of the police alone.

The revolution that in fact occurred, however, was not a real revolution, according to Weber. All that had happened, he wrote, was 'merely the removal of an incompetent monarch, not a "revolution" '.[106] The Kerensky regime was a transitional one, and the question was, which way it would go. The owners of property, who determined its character, would much have preferred a bourgeois constitutional monarchy or military dictatorship, but had had to make common cause with the proletariat in order to get rid of the Tsar.[107] This was a temporary alliance only. The Social Democrats and Social Revolutionaries in the government fulfilled the role of 'taggers-on', useful to the bourgeoisie 'because they created the illusion among the masses that the regime was really revolutionary'.[108] As soon as order was established, and an opportunity presented itself, the army would be used to remove them.[109]

The essential character of the Kerensky regime, as the title of Weber's article indicated, was that of 'token democracy'. Its bourgeois members could not allow real democracy, since this would mean a majority for a peasant movement committed to the expropriation of land and the renunciation of state debts. The constituent assembly had therefore to be delayed.[110] Above all, the peasantry had to be kept at the front so that there was no chance of their participating in any election. This was the crux of the situation, as Weber saw it. Continuation of the war was necessary for internal reasons, however hopeless its outlook:

> They [the propertied classes] are unconditionally for the continuation of the war for its own sake, however hopeless the prospect, in order to keep the peasants away from home. Only through continuation of the war can, first, the peasant masses be kept under the control of the generals far away in the trenches; secondly, the new-found power of the propertied classes be consolidated before the conclusion of peace; thirdly, the financial support of the banks at home and abroad be secured, in order to organise the new regime and suppress the peasant movement.[111]

Once more the banks and financiers played a central role. The regime needed credit for the purpose of war and internal suppression, and this reinforced the token character of its democracy.[112] As under Tsarism, democratic-sounding promises had to be made, but no genuine democracy could be allowed. Professions of peace were given, but peace had to be denied in practice.

The fate of social revolution, on the other side, was also intimately linked with the question of war and peace. So long as the war continued, the peasants would remain at the front, the power of finance would be supreme, and the 'revolutionaries' would be limited to the role of 'taggers-on'.[113] Weber confessed that he did not see the task of the revolutionary movement to be an easy one, such were the conflicts among the peasants, between those who owned land privately and those who did not. But he was clear about the necessary conditions for its success:

> These difficulties could only be overcome in the course of a social-revolutionary dictatorship lasting for years. . . . Whether the personalities for this are available, I cannot say. But they could only achieve lasting power if peace were concluded immediately. Only then would the peasants be available at home to support them.[114]

The possibility Weber was considering here was a peasant-based revolution, and its possible relationship to the urban proletariat was unclear. As he argued, there might be a degree of subjective solidarity between the proletariat and peasantry, for instance, on the issue of peace, but their interests were largely opposed.[115] Any settlement of the peasant demands would set back Russia's capitalist industrial development for years. Whatever the future prospects here, however, Weber was clear that the Kerensky government was a transitional one only, and could only develop in one of two directions, reactionary or revolutionary. In either case, the possibility of a liberal development was ruled out.

While subsequent events proved the correctness of Weber's analysis of the Provisional Government,[116] the Bolshevik uprising itself did not conform to the social revolution he had expected. 'It is a pure military dictatorship,' he wrote in February 1918, 'only one of corporals rather than generals.'[117] The longest he expected it to last was a few months. Too much stress should perhaps not be placed on instant analyses made in a rapidly changing situation, and Weber wrote no systematic account of Bolshevism as he had of the previous revolutions. Two points, however, are worth noting about the various brief references he made to Bolshevism, since they form characteristic assumptions of Weber's political writing.

The first of these was that the character of Bolshevism was determined, not by its ideas, but by the material interests of its followers. Whatever goals the Petersburg intellectuals might pursue, Weber wrote in February 1918, the instrument of Bolshevik power, the soldiers, demanded above all pay and booty.[118] The Red Guards could therefore have no real interest in peace, since it would leave them without any source of income. The fate of the Kerensky regime had been similarly decided by the instrument of power on which it relied, foreign finance. In order to get the necessary credit to establish its authority, it had been forced to deny its idealism, and sacrifice its citizens in a war for the interests of foreign bourgeois powers.[119] The Bolsheviks might aim for peace in their turn, but their military following would prevent it. This had been Weber's initial analysis, and though the situation changed, he believed that it would be the material interests of the Bolshevik following that would determine everything. Thus he spoke of the influence of those who lived 'not *for* but *off* the revolution', the parasites who made a living out of revolutionary activity as such, and were more interested in its perpetuation than in the achievement of ideological goals. This was the 'essence of Bolshevism'.[120] In his address on 'Politics as a Vocation' Weber used this as an example of the general problem confronting any crusader who sought to achieve this-worldly transformation:

He who wants to establish absolute justice on earth by force requires a following, a human 'machine'. He must hold out the necessary internal and external premiums—heavenly or worldly reward—to this 'machine' or else the machine will not function. Under the conditions of the modern class struggle, the internal premiums consist of the satisfying of hatred and the craving for revenge. . . . The external rewards are adventure, victory, booty, power and spoils. The leader and his success are completely dependent upon the functioning of his machine and hence not on his own motives. Therefore he also depends upon whether or not the premiums can be *permanently* granted to the following, that is, to the Red Guards, the informers, the agitators, whom he needs. What he actually attains under the conditions of his work is therefore not in his hands, but is prescribed to him by the motives of his following, which if viewed ethically, are predominantly base.[121]

In the case of Bolshevism, Weber argued, the need to satisfy the material interests of its proletarian supporters struck at the root of its socialist ideals, since it was forced to introduce practices into industrial life which denied all its principles:

> . . . The Soviets have preserved, or rather re-introduced, the highly paid entrepreneur, piece-work, the Taylor System, military and industrial discipline, and have instituted a search for foreign capital. Hence, in a word, they have had to take on again absolutely all the things they had fought as bourgeois class institutions, in order to keep the state and the economy going at all.'[122]

This passage illustrates a second assumption of Weber's, familiar from the previous chapter, that industrial development could only take place under capitalism, through the 'economically revolutionary' class of the bourgeoisie, and that any attempt to introduce socialist experiments prematurely was bound to fail.[123] In this respect, if not in accepting the values or desirability of socialism, Weber stood near the position of the 'evolutionary socialist' Mensheviks, who argued that 'this Bolshevik experiment, of superimposing a socialist order from above on the present state of bourgeois society, is not only a nonsense, but an outrage against Marxist dogma.'[124] This was the position of all 'scientifically trained' socialists, according to Weber.[125] If he did not agree with them on the advantages a socialist future would bring, he at least could agree that capitalism must come first. Thus in his analysis of Bolshevism we find Weber, in effect, appealing to orthodox Marxism against what he had called the 'Hegelian' tradition of Russian Social Democracy, with its emphasis on the 'creative character of human thought'.[126] The material interests of the proletariat, and their demand for jobs, would, he believed, make a capitalist organisation of industry in Russia a necessity.

THE CONDITIONS FOR LIBERAL DEMOCRACY

The account of Weber's writings on Russia given in this chapter may appear to have been unduly drawn out, but it is difficult to compress further without losing altogether the sense of his argument. Along with his writings on Germany, the aim has been to convey some idea of how Weber analysed the politics of a particular society in his own time, and what he conceived the most significant features in such an analysis to be. We are interested in these writings not merely as descriptive accounts, but also for the theoretical assumptions they contain. These assumptions can be treated at a number of different levels. At the most general level is a theory of the relationship between society and government. At this level, it should be clear that Weber's accounts of Germany and Russia differ in a number of respects from what is frequently regarded as the typically Weberian approach to political analysis, and that such supposedly Weberian emphases as the independence of the 'political' from the 'economic' (in particular from economic class), the importance of ideas, the role of legitimacy in explaining political stability and change, etc, are largely absent from these accounts and even at points explicitly denied. Thus class and class conflict are seen to be central features in explaining the exercise of power and the phenomenon of political change. If Tsarism managed to achieve a certain independence from society by reliance on the police and bureaucracy, this was only at the expense of internal instability and submission to the demands of foreign finance. So too Weber explicitly denies the power of ideological factors in the face of material interests. In Russia the liberal movement failed once the material position of the intelligentsia was threatened, and socialist ideals gave way before the need to satisfy the material demands of the proletariat.

These and other aspects of Weber's account will be discussed in a more systematic manner in the final chapter, when a comparison will be made between the standpoints of his political and sociological writings. For the moment, however, a different level of theory will be examined, concerning the historical conditions for liberal democracy. Weber found in Germany and Russia a common inability to develop a liberal constitutional state, or 'bourgeois democracy' as he called it. This was partly the result of conditions which were unique to each country. At the same time there were factors common to both his accounts, which together provide the basis for a theory of liberal democracy.[127] The most significant features of this can be summarised briefly.

First was the character of industrial development in the two countries, and the difference between mature and early capitalism. Political freedom, Weber argued, had grown historically out of the practice and idea of individualism, which was rooted in the economic and social structure of the early capitalist epoch.[128] The age of this individualism was now past. The development of capitalism itself had destroyed for ever 'the optimistic belief in the natural harmony of interests of free individuals'.[129] The impact of technology had created a uniformity in the external conditions of life through the standardisation of production. The organisation of industry required the aggregation of large numbers of men into hierarchical structures, while their welfare needs were met in ways directly opposed to individualistic self-help: 'American "benevolent feudalism", Germany's so-called "welfare organisations", Russian factory administration—everywhere the cage of a new bondage is ready'.[130] Nothing in all this development had anything to do with the individualism characteristic of the earlier epoch. Thus countries, of which Russia was the extreme example, which began their industrialisation late, with capitalism in its mature form, missed out that epoch of social and economic development which had provided the basis for free political institutions and a strong liberal tradition. If it depended only on material conditions, Weber wrote, and the constellation of interests created by them, one would have to conclude that 'all the *economic* weather signs point in the direction of increasing "unfreedom" '.[131]

A second reason Weber gave was also linked to the development of capitalism, but was of a more political kind, and concerned the political character of the bourgeoisie. In Germany and Russia the bourgeoisie was never given a chance to share in political power before the appearance of the proletariat and the development of modern class conflict.[132] Their fear of working-class power pushed them into an alliance with the existing authorities, and the interests of property became directed in support of a traditional system rather than against it.[133] This was exacerbated by the fact that the suffrage was extended to the working class, or parts of it, before the establishment of Parliamentary government, and made the bourgeoisie afraid of a Parliamentary system.[134] As Weber argued in his writings on both countries, the nature of modern capitalism made any sort of electoral system short of universal suffrage in the long run untenable. The continually changing character of industry made it impossible to limit the suffrage on the basis of economic or social function,[135] and the representation of one class by another could no longer be justified once their interests were in conflict.[136] It was therefore no longer possible to give the bourgeoisie a chance to find its feet politically by means of a suffrage weighted in its favour. As he said of Russia, 'the opposition of economic interests and the class character of the proletariat strikes all specifically bourgeois reforms in the back: this is its fateful work here as elsewhere.'[137] Germany provided the clearest example of this 'fateful work'. Although working-class representation in the Reichstag could not hinder the economic progress of capitalism, Weber wrote, yet 'it weakens the political power of the bourgeoisie and strengthens the power of the bourgeoisie's aristocratic adversaries. The downfall of German bourgeois liberalism is based upon the joint effectiveness of these factors.'[138]

Both the factors mentioned above were the product of a late development of industrial capitalism. A further factor—and according to the typically Weberian account it was related to the others—was the historical character of religion in both countries.[139] In each case this worked in support of the traditional state, rather than against it, and reinforced attitudes in the individual of submission to authority rather than of personal independence. This was true to an extreme degree of Russian orthodoxy; itself authoritarian in structure, it was bound intimately to the state, providing 'the religious foundation of absolutism'.[140] Although Germany, in contrast, had experienced the Protestant revolution, it had taken a form in Lutheranism which legitimated the authoritarian state, and established itself as a 'church' rather than a 'sect'. In his article on 'Church and State in North America',[141] Weber ascribed important features of American liberal democracy, in particular its strong tradition of individualism and of voluntary associations, to the influence of the Puritan sects. Two passages from this article are worth quoting. The first emphasises that Weber's account of liberal democracy involved a conception of society and not merely political institutions:

Whoever understands by 'democracy' ... a human mass pulverised into atoms, is fundamentally mistaken, at least so far as

American democracy is concerned. It is not democracy, but bureaucratic rationalism that tends to have this consequence of 'atomization', a consequence which is not avoided by its preference for imposing compulsory structures from above. Genuine American society . . . was never a sandheap of this kind, nor yet a building where anyone without distinction could just walk in. It was and is permeated with 'exclusiveness' of every kind. The individual never finds sure ground under his feet, either at university or in business, until he has succeeded in being voted into an association of some kind—in the past invariably Christian, now secular as well—and has asserted himself within it. The inner character of these associations is governed by the ancient 'sect spirit' with far-reaching consequences.[142]

The religious development in Germany had taken a very different form, with markedly different consequences for its political life, as Weber explained in a further passage:

It is even now still our fate, that, for numerous historical reasons, the religious revolution of that time meant for us Germans a development which did not promote the power of the individual, but rather the importance of officialdom. And so, because the religious community after the revolution as before took the form only of a 'church', a compulsory association, there arose that situation in which every struggle for the emancipation of the individual from 'authority', every manifestation of 'liberalism' in the widest sense, was compelled to set itself in opposition to the religious communities. At the same time we were denied the development of that tradition of voluntary associations which the 'sectarian life' had helped to encourage in the Anglo-Saxon world, so different in all these respects.[143]

It is of some interest that Weber should criticise the 'sects' of Russian Social Democracy for fostering precisely the opposite traits—subservience to dogmas and party authorities. This apparent inconsistency would seem to justify the doubts of those who confess to see no particular connection between religious sectarianism and political liberty. In Weber's view, however, it was a question of the interaction between a particular set of beliefs and the pressures of sect life. Not only did the sects reject all earthly authorities, but the continuous pressure they exerted on the individual to prove himself in the possession of distinctive personal qualities, led to the 'inner isolation of the individual' and the 'maximum development of his powers towards the external world' together.[144] This was the result of a very different kind of discipline from that of an authoritarian church. The continuous and unobtrusive ethical discipline of the sects, Weber wrote, was 'related to the discipline of the authoritarian church as the rational training and selection of qualities is to command and punishment'.[145] The contrast between sect and church was thus reflected in the contrast between the 'social elasticity and individualist quality' of Anglo-Saxon democracy, and the rigid authoritarianism of social institutions in Germany.[146]

Thus, in the course of their development, Germany and Russia had missed out on the particular combination of factors which defined the epoch of individualism. These were now unrepeatable. The particular quality of religious sect life could not be recovered, even if one wanted to. The bureaucratisation of industrial concerns was far advanced. The arrival of the working class on the heels of the bourgeoisie was irreversible. As was pointed out in Chapter 2, however, Weber did not regard individualism and political freedom as necessarily identical; it was possible for the latter to survive without the former. But the end of the age of individualism made it infinitely more difficult to *establish* civil liberties and Parliamentary institutions for the first time. This was the dilemma for bourgeois political development in both Russia and Germany.

The character of Weber's argument was largely a historical one. It concerned the particular societies of Russia and Germany, and the historical conditions for liberalism in the West. At the same time his accounts contain material of a wider significance, which raises questions about the concept of 'bourgeois liberalism' as such, irrespective of the particular circumstances of the two countries mentioned. Weber's critique of socialism, discussed in Chapter 3, was based upon an argument of a general kind—that some special connection existed between the bourgeoisie and political freedom, which would be denied under a socialist order. Capitalism provided a necessary tension between the bureaucracies of industry and the state: the bourgeoisie as a class provided the necessary social support for free Parliamentary institutions. The accounts given show that in practice Weber had reservations on both aspects of the argument.

First, Weber recognised that an increasingly common feature of large-scale capitalism was its forging of close links with the state, This was not only because of the needs of capitalism to secure a political climate favourable to its interests, but also for the state in the pursuit of its own ends. The result, however, of such links was not so much the state direction of industry as capitalist direction of the state, because of its superior knowledge in the field of business. Weber repeated this theme in a number of contexts. In a Verein debate in 1905 on the relations between cartels and the state, Weber opposed Schmoller's suggestion that there should be state-appointed directors in the major cartels.[147] Among other objections to this kind of liaison, he argued that, far from it producing a greater influence for state policy in their operations, it would only give *them* greater influence with the state;[148] in the act of embrace, the cartels would play the role of Brunnhilde, and the state would suffer the fate of King Gunther.[149] The reason for this, as he pointed out in *Economy and Society*, was that the expertise of businessmen in their own sphere was far superior to that of the state bureaucracy, and that as a consequence the measures taken by the state to influence economic life under capitalism were frequently 'made illusory by the superior knowledge of interest groups'.[150] It was not simply the question of who would influence whom, however, that concerned Weber, but the possible threat to freedom posed by the increasing tendency of large-scale capitalism to involve the state in its activities. The following passage from Weber's memorandum on social policy raises very explicitly the question of whether capitalism was necessarily preferable to socialism in this respect:

> The trends towards state ownership, municipalisation, syndicalisation, advance irresistibly together. Increasingly, administrative positions in the syndicates are adjusted to the career opportunities of state officials, and influential state positions to those of industrialists. For these and other reasons, it will in future be all the same from the standpoint of social policy, whether it is state ownership or state 'controlled' syndicalisation that takes place, or whatever else the formal relationship is between the state and municipal apparat on the one side and that of the large syndicates on the other. In the face of these overpowering corporations the traditional trade union policy breaks down, as does that of all social structures which can be considered as agencies of a decisively liberal social policy.[151]

It needs to be remembered here that Weber's view was coloured by the experience of an authoritarian state, and that Prussian conditions were no more satisfactory a guide to the future of capitalism than of socialism. Indeed Weber's commitment to capitalism as a system presupposed that a more liberal social policy was possible within it than existed in his own society, and that the formally free association of economic interests on the part of both capital and labour, which he saw as a distinctive feature of capitalism, could be structured so as to achieve a more even balance of power between the two sides of industry. In fact, it was in this context that he produced his only really democratic argument for the extension of the suffrage, when he wrote that, without it, the bankers and large capitalists would become 'the uncontrolled masters of the state'.[152] Possession of the vote by the working class would counteract some of the worst features of 'power exercised in the interests of profit'.[153] Against the reality of capitalism in his own society he thus set a counter-image of capitalism as it might be, which provided the basis for his critique both of German capitalism and of the socialist alternative in his speeches to the Verein für Sozialpolitik. Nevertheless, if Weber gave characteristic expression to the theory that a tension between the bureaucracies of industry and state was a necessary condition for social and political freedom in modern society, his writing also provided evidence that, unless there were strong counteracting factors, the interests of business would come to dominate the state, and that there was nothing in the nature of modern large-scale capitalism as such that was necessarily conducive to political liberty.

The same could equally be said of the bourgeoisie themselves, that there was nothing in their social or economic conditions of life, nothing in the ownership of property itself, to make them the natural supporters of free Parliamentary institutions. What was 'bourgeois' about the Russian liberal movement, on Weber's analysis, was the character of its ideas, not the social composition of its supporters; the capitalists were noticeably absent from its ranks. There was no particular connection between the freedom to make profit and political liberty. The desire of the Russian propertied strata for order was stronger than their zeal for constitutional rights,[154] and they were prepared to put up with a widespread denial of civil liberties provided a free hand was given to profit.[155] Equally, Weber wrote of the German bourgeoisie that, as a result of material prosperity and an efficient administration, it had found itself perfectly at home in the 'cage' of the authoritarian state.[156]

Taking Weber's account as a whole, therefore, it is clear that in practice he regarded the concept of 'bourgeois liberalism' as a historical rather than a living concept, as a set of ideas rather than a living relationship between a particular economic way of life and corresponding political institutions. The only ultimate guarantee of political freedom thus lay in the liveliness of a country's *political* tradition and in its determination to be free:

> Democracy and freedom are only possible where there exists a settled and determined *will* on the part of a nation, not to be ruled like a herd of sheep. It is 'against the stream' of material interests that we are 'individualists' and advocates of 'democratic' institutions.[157]

How it was possible to attain such a will when it did not already exist, to this Weber had no clear answer. But at least he recognized that it had nothing to do with modern capitalism as such, nor with the economic circumstances of the bourgeois class.

This discussion brings us to a final substantive issue to be considered in Weber's political theory. Weber's account of the dilemma of bourgeois liberalism exemplifies a more general problem which he discerned in the character of bourgeois society, arising from the phenomenon of class and class conflict. If the nature of class action was to pursue material interests to the exclusion of other considerations, and to see politics largely as an instrument of this, how was it possible for wider political goals of any kind to be achieved? When Weber wrote of the Russian masses that he doubted where they could find 'the impulse to participate in a movement which went beyond purely material demands',[158] he could well have said the same about any of the classes that he analysed in contemporary Russia and Germany. It is in the context of this problem that the next chapter will return to a reconsideration of his conception of political leadership, and in particular of the factors which led him to abandon some of the liberal constraints on the political leader in his postwar constitutional theory. It will be argued there that this is only fully intelligible in the context of his theory of society, discussed in the preceding two chapters.

REFERENCES

1 *Archiv für Sozialwissenschaft und Sozialpolitik*, vol 22 (1906), Beilage, p 234; vol 23B, p 165.
2 ibid.
3 *Archiv*, 23B, p 393; GPS, p 103.
4 R Pipes, 'Max Weber und Russland', *Aussenpolitik*, vol 6 (1955), pp 627–39, especially pp 629–30.

5 *Archiv*, 23B, pp 396; GPS, p 105.
6 *Archiv*, 22B, p 246; GPS, p 30.
7 *Archiv*, 23B, p 398; GPS, p 107.
8 'Zur Lage der Bürgerlichen Demokratie in Russland', *Archiv*, 22B, pp 234–353.
9 P Struve, ed, *Loi fondamentale de l'Empire Russe* (Paris, 1905).
10 *Archiv*, 22B, p 244.
11 ibid, p 246; GPS, p 31.
12 *Archiv*, 22B, p 247.
13 ibid, p 248.
14 ibid, pp 249–50.
15 ibid, p 244.
16 ibid.
17 ibid, p 280.
18 ibid, p 274.
19 ibid, p 279.
20 ibid, p 276.
21 ibid.
22 *Archiv*, 23B, p 199.
23 ibid, p 200.
24 *Archiv*, 22B, p 293; GPS, p 42.
25 *Archiv*, 22B, pp 293–335; GPS, pp 42–51.
26 *Archiv*, 22B, p 293.
27 ibid, p 320.
28 ibid, p 299.
29 ibid, p 321; GPS, p 47.
30 ibid.
31 *Archiv*, 22B, pp 317, 321; cf 23B, p 314.
32 *Archiv*, 22B, p 335; GPS, p 51.
33 ibid.
34 *Archiv*, 22B, pp 322, 332.
35 ibid, p 280.
36 ibid, pp 333–4; GPS, pp 49–50.
37 ibid.
38 ibid.
39 *Archiv*, 22B, pp 281–4.
40 ibid, p 283.
41 ibid, p 284.
42 GASS, p 410.
43 *Archiv*, 22B, pp 348–9; GPS, p 62.
44 *Archiv*, 22B, p 284.
45 ibid, p 293; GPS, p 41.
46 What made it 'bourgeois' was the character of its demands: guaranteed freedoms for the individual, a constitutional 'Rechtsstaat', etc. *Archiv*, 22B, pp 280–1.
47 ibid, p 244.
48 ibid, pp 292–3; GPS, p 41.
49 ibid.
50 *Archiv*, 23B, pp 371–3.
51 op cit, pp 231–2; GPS, p 79. 'The large capitalists will naturally *always* take the side of the bureaucracy against the Duma. . . .' ibid.
52 e.g. *Archiv*, 22B, p 352. Their policy was 'on the one hand to encourage the

development of capitalism, on the other to cut off every development towards bourgeois independence'. GPS, pp 64–5.

53 *Archiv*, 22B, p 347; GPS, pp 60–1.
54 *Archiv*, 23B, pp 398–9; cf p 324: 'One sees how in this respect also the country immediately jumps right into the middle of the most modern form of economic struggle, without repeating any of the intermediate stages of Western development.'
55 ibid.
56 'Russlands Übergang zum Scheinkonstitutionalismus', *Archiv*, 23B, pp 165–401.
57 *Archiv*, 22B, p 246; GPS, p 30.
58 *Archiv*, 23B, pp 175–6.
59 ibid, pp 249–50.
60 ibid, pp 171–4; GPS, pp 67–9.
61 *Archiv*, 23B, pp 167–70.
62 ibid, p 170; GPS, p 66.
63 *Archiv*, 23 B, p 171; GPS, p 67.
64 ibid.
65 For an analysis of Vitte's position in Weber's first article, see *Archiv*, 22B, pp 337–45; GPS, pp 52–8.
66 *Archiv*, 23B, pp 181–224.
67 ibid, p 224.
68 'One cannot treat a nation and its political freedoms like a "Hasch-Hasch" game with children, offering them the ball one moment, then hiding it behind one's back as soon as they make a grasp for it.' ibid, pp 224–5; GPS, p 71.
69 *Archiv*, 23B, pp 226–33; GPS, pp 72–80.
70 ibid.
71 *Archiv*, 23B, pp 228–9; GPS, pp 74–5.
72 *Archiv*, 23B, p 232; GPS, p 79.
73 *Archiv*, 23B, pp 233–50.
74 ibid, p 237.
75 A detailed account of the electoral arrangements is given, ibid, pp 251–74.
76 ibid, pp 275–6.
77 ibid, p 284.
78 ibid, pp 284ff.
79 ibid, p 312; GPS, p 90.
80 *Archiv*, 23B, pp 327–8; GPS, pp 93–4.
81 ibid. Weber gives a similar analysis in his first article: 'It was naturally also the hope of the government, and of Vitte especially, that anarchy would produce this result, and that, in Vitte's own words, "society itself" would finally come to demand order and recognition for their watch-cry "*Enrichissez-vous*". And so it happened. . . . The hour of the ideological gentry was over; the power of material interests resumed once more its normal function. The consequence of this process was to rule out, on the Left, any thoughtful political idealism, and on the Right, any commitment to the extension of the old kind of Zemstvo self-government. . . . Vitte was unlikely to lose any sleep over either.' *Archiv*, 22B, p 342; GPS, p 55.
82 *Archiv*, 23B, pp 333–55.
83 ibid, pp 270–2.
84 ibid, pp 359–60.
85 ibid, pp 360–71.

86 ibid, pp 363, 371.
87 ibid, pp 371–3.
88 ibid.
89 ibid, pp 377–8.
90 ibid, p 378.
91 ibid, p 379.
92 ibid, pp 380–90.
93 ibid, p 385.
94 ibid, p 394; GPS, p 103.
95 *Archiv*, 23B, p 396; GPS, p 105.
96 *Archiv*, 23B, pp 386–7.
97 ibid, p 395; GPS, p 104.
98 ibid.
99 *Archiv*, 23B, p 398; GPS, p 107.
100 'Russlands Übergang zur Scheindemokratie,' published in April 1917 and reprinted complete in GPS, pp 192–210. Lionel Kochan calls Weber's analysis 'remarkable'. L Kochan, *Russia in Revolution* (London, 1966), p 212.
101 GPS, p 192.
102 GPS, p 193.
103 GPS, pp 193–4.
104 GPS, p 194.
105 GPS, pp 196–9.
106 GPS, p 205; cf p 200.
107 ibid.
108 GPS, p 205.
109 GPS, p 206.
110 GPS, p 205.
111 GPS, pp 202–3.
112 GPS, p 203.
113 GPS, p 205.
114 GPS, p 202.
115 GPS, pp 204–5.
116 Thus he wrote later in the year: 'I believe that, in this as in other predictions that I made elsewhere about the Russian situation, I was unfortunately right.' GPS, p 325, n 1.
117 GPS, p 280.
118 GPS, p 281.
119 ibid; cf GPS, p 325, n 1.
120 GPS, p 440.
121 GM, p 125; GPS, p 544.
122 GM, p 100; GPS, p 517.
123 In his lecture on socialism (July 1918), having described how the Bolsheviks had compelled existing entrepreneurs, civil servants and army officers to serve their regime, Weber remarked that 'a state machine and an economy cannot be conducted for long in this manner'. GASS, p 514.
124 GASS, p 516.
125 ibid.
126 *Archiv*, 22B, p 283.
127 For a contemporary discussion of these issues, see Barrington Moore, *Social Origins of Dictatorship and Democracy* (London, 1967), though the

main focus of the book is on the role of the landed upper classes and the peasantry.

128 *Archiv*, 22B, pp 280–1, 347–50; GPS, pp 39–40, 60–2.

129 *Archiv*, 22B, p 280.

130 ibid, p 347.

131 ibid.

132 This is a familiar theme in the writing of Marx and Engels on Germany; e.g. Engels: 'It is the misfortune of the German bourgeoisie to have come too late—quite in accordance with the beloved German tradition.' F Engels, *The German Revolutions* (Chicago, 1967), p 7.

133 GASS, pp 404–5.

134 GPS, pp 233–4.

135 GPS, pp 243–4; GASS, pp 407–8.

136 *Archiv*, 22B, pp 250–1.

137 ibid.

138 GM, p 372.

139 This was a question of its influence in the past rather than in the present, which Weber regarded as much slighter.

140 *Archiv*, 22B, p 278.

141 In J Winckelmann, ed, *Max Weber, Soziologie, Weltgeschichtliche Analysen, Politik*, 4th edn (Stuttgart, 1968), pp 382–97.

142 ibid, pp 393–4.

143 ibid, p 395.

144 ibid.

145 GARS, vol 1, p 234. (This is a later reworking of the same article.)

146 J Winckelmann, ed, op cit, p 393.

147 GASS, pp 399–406.

148 GASS, pp 403–4.

149 GASS, p 415; cf GPS, p 79, n 1.

150 WG, p 574; ES, p 994. This is the main objection Weber makes in his lecture on 'Socialism' to state capitalism, which he speaks of as one of the possible forms of 'socialism'. As Germany's wartime experience showed, this would not mean control of industry by the state, but rather the opposite. GASS, p 503.

151 'Rundschreiben', p 8.

152 GPS, p 255.

153 GPS, p 256.

154 *Archiv*, 22B, p 342; GPS, p 55.

155 *Archiv*, 23B, p 233; GPS, p 79.

156 GPS, p 442.

157 *Archiv*, 22B, p 348; GPS, p 61.

158 *Archiv*, 22B, p 280.

Chapter 8

Class Society and Plebiscitary Leadership

While the earlier chapters of the book were concerned to present various aspects of Weber's political thought in isolation from their social context, the importance of this context to his theory should now be apparent. In practice Weber recognised that forms of government could not be considered in abstraction from their social basis of support, nor politics explained apart from the activities of class. His theory of politics rested on a theory of society. At the same time, however, while attention to this social dimension may bring some completeness to the consideration of his political theory, it also throws one major problem into relief: what relationship is there between Weber's advocacy of individual political leadership and his insistence on a class analysis of politics? What is the connection between his plebiscitary leader with a political base in a mass electorate, and the role of class in political action?

On the face of it, these belong to different categories of thought. Thus Christian von Ferber poses the question to Weber's political theory as follows:

> Who are the historical subjects, who can intervene by setting goals to the mechanism of historical development? Are these subjects collectivities, like social classes, who in the material reproduction of their life determine both their own social fate and the future of society as well? Or are these subjects 'political leaders', who make history on the basis of their appropriation of the means of power . . . ?'[1]

Having posed this alternative, von Ferber decides in favour of the latter. On his interpretation, Weber's political leader stood suspended above society, with a free sphere of operation on the basis of his monopoly of the means of physical force, a conception of politics which von Ferber rightly considers inadequate.[2] Such an interpretation, however, not only ignores Weber's theory of society altogether, but it grossly exaggerates the role of force in his political thought. While it is true that he defined the state in terms of the sanction which was specific to it, he was equally insistent that the use of force was not its normal mode of operation, nor by any means a sufficient one.[3]

Other answers to the problem, however, are equally unsatisfactory. Thus it is often said that Weber's work consists of an amalgam of Marxist and Nietzschean elements, a 'massive, but brittle, intellectual synthesis' as one commentator puts it.[4] Such a judgement simply restates the problem, rather than providing an answer to it. In a similar way Raymond Aron detects in Weber's 'Weltanschauung' a variety of components: Darwinian, Nietzschean, economic, Marxist, nationalist.[5] What we wish to know, however, is not merely what its components are, but what relationship they hold to each other. From this point of view it may seem more attractive to argue for a development in Weber's thought: to say that his emphasis on class was a phenomenon of his early period, and that it increasingly came to be replaced by an emphasis on the individual leader; that he began as a Marxist and ended as a Nietzschean.[6] However, as should be evident from the previous chapters, the concept of class remained a central feature of Weber's political analysis throughout his life, and therefore such a view, at least in this form, must also be regarded as inadequate.

This latter view can, however, provide a useful starting point for inquiry. It is true that there is a greater preoccupation with the figure and role of the individual leader in Weber's later writings. What he says about the individual leader, Bismarck, in the Inaugural Address, is mainly negative; Bismarck is criticised for his effect in stifling political initiative in society at large.[7] Leadership is here presented in terms of leadership by a class—hopefully the bourgeoisie—and is dependent upon their achieving a wider political and national outlook as a class. In contrast, political leadership in Weber's later writings is presented as leadership by an individual, within a context of political institutions and on the basis of a political relationship with a mass electorate.

To this extent there is a change of emphasis. But underlying the difference is an important element common to both early and later writings, and that is Weber's desire to secure a political dimension which would transcend that of narrow class interests. Central to an understanding of this is his analysis of the Junkers in his early writings. Not only did this stratum have the time to devote to politics, but they were also capable of transcending a merely class outlook, because their economic situation was one of shared interests with their workers. This, as Weber frequently insisted, was the secret of their political power and their value to the nation.[8] In the Inaugural Address Weber was still looking for a replacement to the Junkers in the bourgeoisie. His analysis of capitalist society, however, increasingly convinced him that it was no longer possible for any class to fulfil the same role under modern conditions. While the major classes provided the necessary social basis of support for parties and political systems, they were also too closely bound to a particular economic function and outlook to be capable of wider political achievement which went beyond that of class interest. As Weber wrote of the entrepreneurs in a wartime discussion of this problem, they were 'far too directly involved in the class conflict as an interested party to be of much value politically'.[9] Their existence was too much taken up with economic affairs for them to see any political issues beyond these. Hence the need for a distinctively political elite or leadership to counteract the dominance of class and economic factors. The plebiscitary figure of Weber's later writings is thus the necessary replacement, under modern conditions, of the Junkers as the bearer of a distinctively 'political' outlook and consciousness.

The significance of Weber's plebiscitary leader can therefore only properly be grasped in terms of his concept of society. Chapters 3 and 4 showed how his emphasis on political leadership was a means to ensure the supremacy of the political over the bureaucratic. It was also a means to secure the supremacy of the political over the *economic*, in face of the increasing influence on politics of economic interests, and to secure a focus for social unity in face of the divisiveness of class. We have already seen how a national consciousness fulfilled a similar function in Weber's theory; indeed, it was all the more emphasised because of the intensity of class conflict.[10] So too the political leader. This can be seen most clearly in Weber's final constitutional proposals, in which he divorces the political leader from Parliament altogether, and gives him an independent power base in the mass vote in order to transcend the conflicts and compromises of economic interests within Parliament itself.

There is thus no haphazard amalgam of elements in Weber's political theory, but rather a reciprocal relationship between class and politics. If social class and economic interests provided a necessary basis of support for political parties and constitutional structures, they in turn required to be transcended in the political sphere. The present chapter will consider Weber's conception of plebiscitary leadership from this standpoint, and will begin by drawing together some strands in his account of politics in capitalist society.

POLITICS IN CAPITALIST SOCIETY

Dieter Lindenlaub's study of the Verein für Sozialpolitik has emphasised the extent of the controversy in Weber's early years between those of its members who took Marx's work seriously, and those who regarded it at best with suspicion.[11] The younger generation accepted the concept of capitalism as central to their understanding of society, as 'the framework not only for scientific inquiry but for their political perspectives as well'.[12] This was as true of Weber as the others, and in his early writings on East Prussia, in particular when describing the changing position of the Junkers, he was concerned to define the distinctive character of capitalism and the extent of its consequences for modern society. Although his later *academic* work shows a different emphasis, particularly in subsuming capitalism under the wider concept of rationalisation, the features of capitalist society he underscored in this early work remained central to his writing on contemporary politics. At the expense of some repetition, these features can be briefly summarised.

One aspect of the change Weber observed in the Junker estates from patriarchal to capitalist organisations was the replacement of personal by impersonal relationships. The serf had been bound to his master by ties of personal dependence, and these were now replaced by the impersonal relationship of one class with another, mediated through the market. 'The characteristic feature of modern development,' Weber wrote, 'is the abolition of personal authority relationships . . . and their replacement by the impersonal dominance of the class of property owners.'[13] A second feature was the development of class conflict. Under the patriarchal system the landowner and his workers had shared a common interest in the harvest. But now that the worker had become a wage earner, 'he loses the manifest ties of common interest with the individual landowner, and becomes a member of the huge unified mass of the propertyless'.[14] These now became the natural opponents of the propertied and 'between natural economic opponents there can only be struggle, and it is a vain delusion to believe that the strengthening of the economic power of one side can benefit the social position of the other'.[15]

The inevitability of class conflict in capitalist society was a central theme in Weber's speeches on social policy in this period, particularly to the Protestant Social Congress, whom he sought to convince that any social policy would be ineffectual which did not make this recognition its starting point. He went further, and argued that the impersonal nature of class conflict made it impossible any longer to conceive social relationships in terms of the ethical categories of religion since the individual entrepreneur was only a 'class type' and acted as his class position compelled him to.[16] A speech he made to the Congress in 1894 contained a particularly sharp attack on the religious point of view. The context was his account of the development of capitalism on the rural estates:

> Above all there takes place a phenomenon of imcomparable significance: the replacement of personal relationships of dominance by the impersonal dominance of class. We know the phenomenon and its psychological consequences from industry. The individual entrepreneur banishes the worker, who approaches him for more pay, to the sphere of competition. Only class can bargain with class. The relationship of responsibility between individual master and worker disappears; the individual entrepreneur becomes so to speak replaceable, since he is now only the type of his class. The personal relationship of responsibility goes; the impersonal 'dominance of capital' takes its place. And above all this has natural psychological consequences. . . . The resignation of the subordinate masses disappears, and as personal relationships are replaced by the dominance of class, so personal hatred is replaced with natural inevitability by the phenomenon of 'objective hatred'—the hatred of one class for another.[17]

This development, Weber went on, presented religion with a fundamental challenge. It had been possible to comprehend the personal relationships of patriarchal society in ethical categories, in terms of the duties of one individual to another. But under capitalism the concept of personal responsibility had no place. It was in vain for the Church to condemn class hatred as 'godless', or even to ignore it. 'The class struggle is an integral element of contemporary society . . . the Church must recognise this fact.'[18]

Capitalism, then, replaced the personal relationships of patriarchal society with impersonal class conflict. It also brought the increasing dominance of material and economic interests in human activity at the expense of other factors. Again Weber recognised this first with the Junkers. Under the old system the landowners had been characterised by 'an absence of the profit motive',[19] and a width of political outlook that rendered them capable of national political achievements.[20] With the introduction of capitalism, material considerations became paramount,[21] and their political power was now placed 'in the service of economic interests'.[22] Although Weber did not always distinguish them explicitly, he was aware of two different factors at work here. One was the dynamic effect of capitalist competition, such that men either concentrated on making profit or went out of business. Whatever their personal inclination, the landowners had either to make profit, or see their estates decline into smallholdings; there was no room left for non-economic considerations.[23] Weber recognised this as a universal phenomenon wherever capitalism had taken root, whether at the level of the individual enterprise or that of national competition. This is what he had to say in an article on the strengthening of the German Stock Exchange.

> There is little room for a policy serving purely moral criteria, so long as the nations are engaged in an inexorable struggle for their national existence and economic power. . . . A strong stock exchange is no club for 'moral cultivation', and the capital of the large banks is no 'welfare institution', any more than are rifles and cannons.'[24]

The other effect of capitalism was that the pursuit of material goods assumed an ever-increasing importance. The 'dance around the golden calf' was becoming as dominant on the rural estates as in the towns; the claim of the landowners to be the custodians of the ancient Prussian aristocratic values was merely the façade for a pursuit of materialism as relentless as anywhere.[25] Weber's most eloquent passage on this aspect of bourgeois society occurs at the end of *The Protestant Ethic and the Spirit of Capitalism*, where he contrasts the motivation of the early capitalists with that of modern society:

> In Baxter's view the care for external goods should only be on the shoulders of the 'saint like a light cloak, which can be thrown aside at any moment'. But fate decreed that the cloak should become an iron cage. Since asceticism undertook to remodel the world and to work out its ideals in the world, material goods have gained an increasing and finally an inexorable power over the lives of men as at no previous period in history. Today the spirit of religious asceticism—whether

finally, who knows?—has escaped from the cage. But victorious capitalism, since it rests on mechanical foundations, needs its support no longer.[26]

It is ironic that *The Protestant Ethic* should have been read as providing a general justification for the independent power of ideas in social life, when the conclusion Weber himself drew for modern society was precisely the opposite.

These essential features of capitalism—the dominance of social relationships by class conflict, and of human activity by material and economic interests—found their expression in the political sphere also. They formed integral features of Weber's account of contemporary politics, as should be evident from the accounts given in the previous chapters. A few examples will suffice by way of summary.[27] The prime case was that of the Junkers themselves, whose transformation from landed patriarchs to capitalist business-men brought with it the inevitable decay of their 'national' political outlook and the subordination of politics to their sec-tional class interests. This was the distinctive feature of politics in capitalist society. Thus Weber insisted at the foundation of the National Social party that only a party based on class held any chance of success, and that a coalition across class lines, united only by their commitment to certain principles of social policy, would fail. Although he was impressed by the stronger movement of 'ideological' liberalism in Russia, his account showed that it could not survive the pressure of class interests. The success of the Kadets was illusory, based as it was on a rigged franchise and the boycott of the proletarian class parties. Once these participated, in the towns at any rate, 'the balance would fall entirely, as in Germany, between the socialist and the bourgeois class parties, and ideological democracy would be excluded'.[28] The landowners, for their part, were only too ready to jettison their liberal convic-tions once their property was threatened, and the masses were not to be won for a political programme going beyond their material interests. Whatever the ideal goals of Social Democracy in Ger-many, its actions were determined by the material interests of its followers, whether those who made their living directly out of the party, or the wider following who put their jobs and pay before socialist experiments and futuristic schemes. When Weber said that the materialist conception of history was no cab to be jumped on and off at will,[29] this was not merely a debating point. It was how he in practice interpreted contemporary politics, whether it was the monarchist and nationalist phraseology of the conservatives, which served merely to conceal the 'dance around the golden calf',[30] or the doctrines of the socialists, which served as an 'ethical legitimation of cravings for revenge, power, booty and spoils'.[31] Where he differed from the Marxists was that he had no hesitation in applying this canon of interpretation to the Social Democrats themselves. Even the process of revolution itself, far from transforming men's outlook as they imagined, only demonstrated the same pattern of motivation at work.

However, if the influence of class conflict and of material interests on the political behaviour of bourgeois society impressed Weber as a fact, it also confronted him as a problem. 'The period of economic development,' he said in the Inaugural Address, 'is threatening to undermine men's natural political instincts. It would be a misfortune if economic science contributed to the same goal, by encouraging a flabby pursuit of material well-being ... under the illusion of self-evident ideals of social policy.'[32] The only goals that Weber himself believed worth pursuing in politics were those which transcended the play of material interests. This was so not only in the sense that the particular values he espoused —liberal and national, cultural in the wide sense outlined—were specifically opposed to material values, and involved transcending a narrow class outlook. At a more general level he attributed to the activity of politics itself a significance in enabling men to rise above 'bread and butter' questions. If politics, in his view, should not be reduced to the pursuit of power as an end in itself, neither should it be regarded as a mere extension of economic life and of class or interest group activity. Politics was rather an arena where men could be lifted beyond their immediate self-interest to embrace wider conceptions. Thus Weber said of the working class, that if its collective activity were confined to the economic sphere alone, its outlook would remain 'banausic',[33] and 'the pressure of upward striving would disappear altogether from the masses'.[34] However, while Weber thus attributed to political activity an educative significance, he was only too aware that the reality tended to be different: political parties, even so-called 'Weltanschauungsparteien', concerned themselves with patronage,[35] economic interest groups were becoming increasingly influential in politics, ideal goals counted for little in the face of material and class interests.

This was not a problem which exercised Weber alone, but was recognised in common by most members of the Verein für Sozialpolitik. Despite all the conflict between the different standpoints in the association, wrote Marianne Weber, they were held

together by a 'common search for compromise between the economic demands of particular groups, and by the determination to
secure the supremacy of ideal interests over material ones'.[36]
It was here particularly that the conception held by the older
generation, of a system of government dominated by the bureaucracy, found its justification. They were particularly suspicious
of the institution of Parliament, and subscribed to the widespread
belief that it intensified the class conflict because it provided a
forum for the open expression of class and group interests.[37] To
make Parliament supreme would be to yield politics totally to this
element. Thus Gustav Schmoller argued that 'the darkest part of
our Parliamentary debates and votes is the class conflict, the
naked conflict of special economic interests with one another. It
poisons the parties. . . .' The chief question of politics was how
to bring to power 'men who stand above party and class'.[38] His
answer lay in an independent bureaucracy capable of imposing
a compromise on the class conflict and of acting as custodians of a
political outlook which went beyond the play of material interests. As we have seen, Weber would not accept this kind of
remedy. Not only was the civil servant no substitute for the
politician, but the bureaucracy was itself subject to the same class
pressures as Parliament. The play of class and economic interests
could not simply be abolished; any attempt to suppress it would
only result in its taking another form, the liaison behind closed
doors.

On the other hand Weber equally rejected the view that the way
to treat economic interest groups was to institutionalise them
within a kind of corporate state. Schemes of this kind, which
sought to resurrect the organic society of the past under modern
conditions, were a common part of wartime discussions for reform. One feature of such schemes was to make the occupational
group the basic organ for voting purposes, and so bring interest
group representation 'into the open'. Weber discussed this at some
length in his article on 'Wahlrecht und Demokratie', and raised a
number of objections.[39] One was a practical one, that there was
no way of defining economic functions adequately in modern
society, and that the continual transformation in the instruments
and circumstances of production, which was typical of capitalism,
would make any such classification a 'shifting sand'.[40] At the same
time such proposals would not produce the desired effect. Weber
poured scorn on the view that 'this is the way to ensure that the
power of material interests, which makes itself felt in a "disguised"
form in Parliamentary elections, is expressed instead in an "open"

and "honourable" manner "in the associations of fellow workers".'[41] On the contrary, the manifold hidden pressures of the economically powerful would simply be given another sphere of operation. 'A thousandfold are the strings,' Weber wrote, by which the capitalist powers would have the smaller businessmen dancing to their tune in such elections. The conflict of economic interests would play its part in this as in all other electoral bodies, 'but it would be much more a question of naked individual power relationships—debtors, clients—than, as at present, of long-term class position through the financing and influence of party electoral activities by interest groups.'[42]

The obverse side to such schemes Weber found equally unacceptable. This was to make the major interest groups, of employers and trade unions, into compulsory state organisations. Weber had attacked such proposals when put forward in the Verein on grounds of social policy.[43] He was even more scathing of it as an attempt to resurrect the 'organic' communities of the past. The proponents of such schemes had not learnt their sociological ABC. They failed to understand the character of modern capitalism, which was one of formally free economic activity and the free organisation of economic interests. This was what was 'organic' for modern societies, not compulsory regulation under police supervision:

> Economic interest groups in a capitalist economy are associations based upon (legally) *free* recruitment, which seek to use the private economic power of their members, whether this is based on ownership of wealth, market monopoly, or the trade union monopoly over the economically indispensable labour power of the workers, to compel a *compromise* over conditions for the price of goods or labours, which is favourable to their interests. . . . The attempt to organise them compulsorily in the manner of an official state institution would be a purely mechanical constriction, and would stifle their inner life.[44]

Weber thus rejected the view that the way to treat economic interest groups was either to subordinate them to bureaucratic direction or to integrate them into a corporate state. Both alternatives impeded the 'normal' course of capitalism, which consisted in the formally free association of economic interests. To this extent Weber accepted that the expression of such interests in the political sphere, both through parties and Parliament, was an inescapable part of politics in a capitalist society, and could not simply be eliminated by decree. Indeed, in this context, he attributed a positive significance to Parliament, as providing a means to achieve a compromise between class interests at a wider political level:

> Nowadays, as in former times, it is once more compromise which prevails as the means to settle the economic conflicts of interest, especially those between employers and workers; here it is unavoidably the only final form of settlement, and so it belongs to the essential character of all really vigorous economic interest groups. Naturally it prevails also in Parliamentary politics, between the parties: as electoral compromise or compromise over legislative proposals. The possibility of the latter, it should be said once again, belongs to the most important advantages of a Parliamentary system.'[45]

Nevertheless, while Weber recognised that the expression of economic interests formed an inescapable part of contemporary politics, the danger was that it would become its dominant feature. Just as he wished to preserve the economic sphere from supervision and control by the state, so he also sought to preserve the political from dominance by the economic. This was a characteristic concern of his political thought, from the earliest period onwards. It had found its typical expression in the Inaugural Address. There he had insisted that, far from material goals or economic development providing the self-evident standard for economic policy, it should be formulated rather according to *political* criteria.[46] It had been from the same standpoint that economic classes were to be judged. The important consideration was their political maturity—that is, their ability to rise above narrow class interests and adopt a wider political, or national, perspective.

It is in this same context of preserving the political dimension over against the economic that the emphasis on individual political leadership in Weber's later writings should also be seen. The Inaugural Address had emphasised the need for political education of the bourgeoisie as a whole, to help it rise above the petty-bourgeois limitations of material interest and a narrow class perspective. While a similar concern is evident at the end of the war—with this insistence that the success of Parliamentary government in Germany depended upon the capacity of the bourgeoisie to develop a more political spirit—it was primarily to the individual political leader that Weber now looked for the preservation of this distinctively political dimension. This was particularly true of the plebiscitary leader, whose ability to win the confidence of the masses in his personal qualities gave him a political basis which transcended that of class and interest groups.

The contrast is posed in an extreme form in Weber's postwar theory, in which a directly elected President with support of a mass vote stands over against the 'unpolitical' pursuit and compromise of economic interests in Parliament. Like Gustav Schmoller, Weber believed that politics should transcend such interests, but he looked to the political leader to achieve this rather than to an all-powerful and supposedly independent bureaucracy.[47]

The second part of the chapter will consider Weber's conception of political leadership from this standpoint.

THE PLEBISCITARY LEADER

In Chapters 3 and 4 Weber's emphasis on political leadership was discussed in the context of the problems raised by the bureau-cratisation of modern administration. His contrast between the politician and the official served to define both the specific failing of German politics and a general problem of the bureaucratised state: how to secure the goal-defining function of the politician in face of the increasing powers available to the official in the administration of policy. This is the context in which the emphasis on leadership in Weber's political writings has most frequently been discussed, not least because it fits in so neatly with the familiar contrast between bureaucracy and charisma of his academic sociology. There is a danger here, however. If it is mistaken to treat Weber's political situation as providing the key to the interpretation of his academic work, it is equally mistaken to imagine that his sociology provides the definitive framework for understanding his political writings, or to regard his political analysis as a kind of 'run up' to the achievements of his academic sociology. What this overlooks is the differences between the two contexts.

While there is no intention here of minimising Weber's contrast between political leadership and bureaucracy, nevertheless it is important also to recognise the significance he attached to political leadership in the context of his theory of society, and in relation to the problem of how to secure the realm of the political from dominance by the economic. In this context a different set of contrasts presents itself, not now between the politician and the official, but between the politician who pursues his work as a calling and the one who has no inner vocation, between the politician who seeks to exercise leadership in the service of a freely chosen cause, and the one for whom politics is simply an extension of economic activity, and who pursues it solely to improve his own personal economic position or as the agent of economic interests.[48] Only the former was capable of the transcendental role in relation to society that Weber's political theory demanded.

Weber's ideal conception of the politician, or political leader, was of someone with a capacity for independent judgement who was able to determine the goals of policy in the light of values he had freely chosen. The goals he pursued were not dictated from outside, from the pressures of a situation or a following, but from within, according to his own convictions, his 'daimon'. These qualities were expressed in an extreme form in the charismatic leader, of whom Weber wrote that 'he knows only inner determination and inner constraint'.[49] But how were such qualities possible under the conditions of modern politics? Weber considers this question in two different contexts, one where he discusses the personal situation of the politician, the other in his theory of plebiscitary democracy. These will be considered in turn.

The problem posed by the personal situation of the politician can be expressed in a simple question. How were the ideal qualities of independent conviction possible when the individual's outlook was so largely dependent upon his own class position and his need to secure his material existence? The answer Weber gave was that these qualities were more likely to be found where the individual's economic position was sufficiently secure for his political activity not to be subordinated to promoting it. The advantage of the traditional Junkers was that they had been what he called 'satte Existenzen';[50] their material wants had been so plentifully satisfied that they had had both the time and the capacity to look beyond them. They had formed the ideal of a 'political aristocracy'. Though Weber doubted whether a political class of this kind could be re-created under modern conditions, yet the principle on which it was based was still relevant to the individual politician: security of material existence encouraged independence of political outlook.

Weber argued the question at some length in his wartime article 'Wahlrecht und Demokratie',[51] and there is a parallel, though briefer, discussion in his articles on 'Parliament and Government'.[52] His argument can be summarised briefly. The question which formed his starting point was how far it was possible to re-create a political aristocracy under modern circumstances, and where individuals could be found capable of pursuing independent political goals. The necessary condition for an aristocracy in a *political* sense, he argued, was above all a 'storm-free economic existence'.[53] An aristocrat must be able to live *for* the state, not have to live *off* it. This meant that his economic activity must be such, not only that he could detach himself from it physically, but maintain an inner detachment from it also.[54] Of all modern economic positions, the industrialist was the least available for politics in this sense. This was not merely a question of the physical necessity of devoting himself full-time to his economic activities, but of a lack of inner distance from the class struggle:

> All those strata which are immediately involved in the struggle of economic interests as entrepreneurs lack something else, much more important: what one might call an inner detachment, a distance from the struggle of everyday interests in the private economic sphere. The modern entrepreneur ... is much too directly involved in this conflict as an interested party to be of much value politically.[55]

What Weber looked for in the politician was thus someone who stood at some distance from the struggle of economic interests, and was hence available for the pursuit of wider political goals. Historically, the typical figure with the necessary distance was the rentier, particularly the large rentier, whether he derived his income from land or industrial capital.[56] He was removed from the everyday struggle for existence, and this set free his powers to concentrate on the wider political issues affecting state and 'Kultur'. Not, Weber hastened to add, that he lived in a kind of social vacuum, free from economic interests; yet he was not a bearer of specifically *class* interests, but stood at some distance from them. Whatever Weber's disapproval of the rentier from an economic point of view, he clearly approved of the type in the political sphere, as providing a potential source of independent conviction, at least so long as his income was large enough to give him genuine security. Another figure, this time economically active, who was also 'available' for politics was the legal advocate.[57] Although engaged in a profit-making enterprise, he had the time to devote to politics, and enjoyed the additional advantage that he had a private, fully equipped office at his disposal and was trained to 'fight with the spoken word'. Lawyers had played a correspondingly significant role in all modern democracies, and it was desirable that they should be well represented in every Parliament.

There were two different aspects to Weber's argument here. The first was a question of detachment from the immediate class struggle. The people most likely to pursue a type of politics which transcended economic interest were those who occupied a relatively detached economic position. Thus the daughters of the aristocracy in Russia and other wealthy patrons had played an invaluable role in the democratic movement. They had proved themselves much more reliable and determined supporters of democratic ideals than those strata more immediately involved in the conflict of interests, because their economic position had not dictated their political attitudes, but rather provided the support for 'independent political conviction'.[58] The other question was that of not having to depend on politics itself as a source of livelihood. Anyone who depended on politics for a living could less afford to take an independent stand on a matter where his convictions were involved, for fear of losing his source of income. He was more likely to toe the party line. The significance of someone like Paul Singer in the SPD, Weber argued, was that, though intellectually limited, he had independent means which allowed him to live for the party, rather than off it. '"Political character" is much cheaper for the wealthy man; no amount of moralising can alter that.'[59]

The latter argument involved a distinction, recurrent in Weber's writing, between those who lived *for* politics, and those who lived *off* it.[60] The distinction first appeared in a short piece he wrote on Social Democracy in 1904.[61] The context was his discussion of the way in which the actions of the party were influenced by those paid officials who had a material interest in its perpetuation in its existing form. There are, he noted, two kinds of professional politician: 'the economically independent, who can live *for* their party, and others, whose economic position compels them to live *off* party politics.' Here, as elsewhere, the two types were presented as mutually exclusive. The former were able to act from independent conviction, whereas the latter had to subordinate their convictions to the need to secure their livelihood; they had to be subservient to the party. Only someone who lives *for* politics, he wrote later, 'can be a politician of great consequence; he can do that the more easily, the more his wealth enables him to be independent and hence "available".[62] When Weber came to give his lecture on 'Politics as a Vocation', under the immediate experience of a revolutionary situation, he modified the distinction to the extent of admitting that it was possible for the most reckless idealism to be found among the unpropertied strata, and that the rich rentier might also live *off* politics, in the sense that he would seek to use it for his economic advantage. 'According to all experience, a care for the economic "security" of his existence is consciously or unconsciously a cardinal point in the whole life orientation of the wealthy man.'[63] When the whole economic order was threatened, the rentier discovered that he was as much committed to a material foundation as anyone. In normal circumstances, however, Weber held that the rentier was able to be more detached and therefore it was vital that, so long as a system of private property remained, this type should be prepared to devote themselves to political activity.[64]

Although Weber's various discussions of this issue look like a search for some chimerical 'free-floating' social position, he recognised that the roles he saw as most valuable for politics, those of rentier and advocate, did not exist in a social vacuum. They were bourgeois figures, but at the same time more detached from the immediate circumstances of economic struggle and class conflict than the entrepreneur. As a consequence, they were less inclined to see politics as an extension of economic activity, and were capable of a wider and more independent political outlook. Weber's contrast between rentier and entrepreneur, in particular, showed the very different criteria he adopted in the economic and political spheres respectively. If economically the rentier was a parasite, politically he could perform a highly valuable function, whereas the dedicated pursuit of profit by the entrepreneur in the economic struggle made him unavailable for professional politics in both an external and an internal sense.

If part of Weber's conception of the political leader lay in the personal circumstances which allowed him to live *for* rather than *off* politics, and to devote himself to the wider issues of state and 'Kultur', the other part lay in the circumstances of mass democracy which enabled him to achieve a considerable measure of independent action and initiative. This was the significance of what Weber called 'plebiscitary' or 'leadership' democracy. His conception of leadership, as typified in the charismatic figure, was of a relationship of personal trust or faith in the *person* of the leader on the part of his following, which allowed him a wide range of freedom to pursue his own convictions.[65] The conception is well expressed in Weber's account of Gladstone:

> In 1886 the machine was already so charismatically oriented to his person, that when the question of Home Rule was raised the whole apparat from top to bottom did not ask: do we really stand on Gladstone's ground? It simply, on his word, fell in line with him and said—right or wrong we follow him.[66]

The conception of leadership expressed here is essentially individualistic. Weber's leader is an individualist; the source of his actions lies in himself, in his own personal convictions, and not in his following or associates. It is a conception which can be clearly distinguished from that according to which the leader's position depends upon his success in carrying out a programme laid down and accepted as a result of collective discussion and agreement within a group, and where this acts as a firm constraint upon his activity. In such a case the allegiance of members is primarily to the programme itself, only secondarily to the leader; the content is more important than the person. But this for Weber did not count as leadership. Someone who was elected to carry out a programme laid down by others was an official, not a leader:

> The elected official will conduct himself entirely as the mandated representative of his master the electors, whereas the leader will see himself as carrying sole responsibility for what he does. This means that the latter, so long as he can successfully lay claim to their confidence, will act throughout according to his own convictions (leader democracy) and not, as the official, according to the expressed or supposed will of the electorate (imperative mandate).[67]

The significant feature of mass politics to Weber was that it encouraged individual leadership of this kind.[68] This was the meaning of plebiscitary democracy. The extension of the suffrage brought with it the personalisation of politics, and weighted the scales in favour of the outstanding individual who was capable of securing the mass vote by force of personality and demagogic appeal. 'A Caesarist plebiscitarian element in politics—the dictator of the battlefield of elections—had appeared on the plain.'[69] Not that the supremacy of such individuals was by any means automatic. At first Weber believed that party officials were likely to regard them with suspicion, as posing a threat to their interests in the orderly conduct of party affairs and would seek to 'castrate the rise of charisma'.[77] Later he came to the view that this would be outweighed by their interest in having a leader who could prove himself successful at the polls.[71] It depended, however, on the character of the party. A party run by local notables rather than a bureaucratic machine would tend to resist the exceptional leader more vigorously, as they would see their own independence threatened.[72]

While circumstances would vary, the general direction in which the plebiscitary character of mass democracy worked was to increase the authority of the political leader, based on the direct confidence of the masses, and to accord him an important measure of independence, even from his own party.[73] The position of Lloyd George, Weber noted, in practice depended less on the confidence of Parliament and party than on that of the masses in the country and at the front.[74] Weber clearly welcomed this development as ensuring a strong political dimension not only against the civil service but also against the play of sectional interests in party and Parliament. If class and economic interests provided the necessary social and economic basis for political parties, the plebiscitary leader with mass support could ensure that these elements did not predominate over wider political and national perspectives.[75]

It is here that Weber's postwar constitutional proposals find their significance. In his wartime writings ('Parliament and Government' in particular) he had looked for a political leader to emerge from within Parliament itself. Contemporary British political theory, with its emphasis on the Caesarist character of the Prime Minister, as well as examples such as Lloyd George, had convinced Weber that a plebiscitary type of leadership was possible within a Parliamentary system. At the same time, the leader's responsibility to Parliament would provide a check on his activity and a means of removing him once he lost popular confidence. What Germany needed, therefore, was Parliamentary democracy. In the immediate postwar period Weber substantially revised this view. The necessity for a leader to provide decisive political direction and a focus for national unity could now only be met by divorcing him from Parliament and giving him a separate power base in a direct presidential election. What were the reasons for this change of view?

A directly elected president is first mentioned as a possibility in an article Weber wrote in November 1918 on 'Germany's Future Constitution',[76] but it was not till the following month, when he took part in Preuss's advisory committee on the constitution,[77] that he began to urge it with conviction, and thereafter it became a central feature of his political thinking. Besides being the only member of Preuss's committee not engaged full-time in politics or the civil service, Weber was also completely out of step with the other members on the issue of the president's powers, as the record of the committee meetings shows.[78] The other members regarded the president as a substitute for a constitutional monarch, filling the role of head of state and not playing an active part in government.[79] Weber in contrast argued that the tasks of national reconstruction required a strong president elected by direct suffrage, with a separate power base from Parliament and providing a counterweight to it. The scheme he proposed was one in which ministers would be chosen by the president from Parliament, to which they would be answerable; but the president would have his own right to appeal to the people over the head of Parliament by means of a referendum, and the right to dismiss it when he chose.[80] Weber still insisted as before on the necessity for Parliamentary committees of inquiry and other features which would provide training for political leadership.[81] But since the president would be elected directly, the initiative for his dismissal should not lie with Parliament but with the people; if ten per cent of the electorate demanded, a referendum could be held for his removal.[82]

The proposals marked a decided shift in Weber's views. It was not a momentary one, because, after failing to get his proposals accepted, he started to campaign publicly for a strong presidential system. Among other reasons for the change, Weber insisted that the needs of the time and the problems of economic and social reconstruction demanded more than ever a strong leader able to rise above sectional interests. But could this leadership not be met from Parliament? One disadvantage of the Reichstag under a federal system was that it would be limited by a second chamber composed of representatives from the individual states, and therefore a focus of national unity had to be provided from outside Parliament to counterbalance local particularism.[83]

However, this is not on its own a sufficient explanation for his change of view. To read Weber's speeches of this period is to be struck by his complete disillusionment with Parliamentary government itself. Even a Parliament with strong powers, which he had previously advocated so insistently, now seemed to him incapable of producing political leadership, and could only reproduce the defects of the 'unpolitical' assemblies of the previous era. One aspect of this was the compromise and horse-trading between parties. With Germany's social composition as it was, Weber believed that there would always be a number of minority parties, without any single one able to attain a clear majority. In practice this meant that a political leader dependent upon Parliament would be a creature of compromise between the parties, rather than able to attain an independent position above them.[84]

However, what concerned him more about Parliament was its inability to rise above the play of economic interests. This was exacerbated by the system of proportional representation, which made it possible for different interest groups to ensure their representatives a place on the party lists. This was what happened in the first elections in January 1919, and Weber feared that it would become a normal practice in the future:

> The effect of proportional representation makes this need [namely, for a directly elected president] more urgent. In the next elections we shall see established what has already appeared in embryo in the present ones: the various economic organisations . . . will compel the parties, purely for the sake of vote-getting, to place their paid secretaries at the head of the lists. It will be this kind of people, for whom national politics is an anathema, and even more, who in effect operate under an imperative mandate from economic interests, who will set the tone of Parliament. It will be a 'banausic' assembly, incapable in any sense of providing a selection ground for political leaders. This, together with the fact that the Bundesrat can extensively restrict the Chancellor by its resolutions, means an inevitable limitation on the political significance of Parliament, and positively demands a counterweight resting on the democratic will of the people.[85]

Part of Weber's disillusionment with the Parliamentary system no doubt also stemmed from his own experience in the elections and his failure to get selected for the Democratic Party list. The incident, as recorded by Marianne Weber, provides an instructive account of a conflict with the professional politicians who lived *off* politics.[86] In November 1918 Weber had joined the newly formed Democratic Party, and in the following month undertook a round of speeches on its behalf. One he gave in Frankfurt was so enthusiastically received that the local party members asked him on the spot to accept first place on their list of candidates. Weber eventually agreed. 'He knew,' writes Marianne, 'that it would be difficult to toe the line with others whose level of understanding was inferior to his own. And he had no intention of working his way up to a seat through the usual drudgery for the party. That would be quite out of place. But when they chose him as a political leader just like that, he recognised this as the "calling" for which he had been waiting deep down.'[87] Unfortunately for Weber, a party committee for the whole district subsequently 'corrected the will of the people' by substituting a local party worthy in his place. However, the offer of a last-minute nomination came from Heidelberg, where Weber received a tumultuous reception and was once more voted into first place. An agent was dispatched post-haste to Karlsruhe, but too late: the list was closed. Weber wrote afterwards: 'I only accepted the nomination in Frankfurt because of its strongly democratic character; naturally I couldn't sink to make any concessions whatever to the party bosses.'[88] So he renounced the chance of political leadership, concludes Marianne. 'The nation had no use for him at a time when everyone was calling for leaders.'[89]

While too much should not be made of any personal feelings of pique Weber may have had in the matter, the incident can only have reinforced his long-standing concern about the domination of politics by those who lived off it, whether in the sense that they saw it simply as a means of livelihood, or else that they used it for the promotion of wider economic interests. It was above all because Parliament continued to be dominated by these, and remained a place for the 'horse-trading' of interests, that Weber insisted on the need for a directly elected president, as a counterbalance to Parliament, in order to preserve a truly political element in face of the otherwise exclusively economically oriented character of politics. These concerns are clearly expressed in a passage from 'Politics as a Vocation', which will bear quoting in full:

> There is only the choice between leadership democracy with a 'machine', and leaderless democracy, in other words the rule of professional politicians without a calling, without the inner charismatic qualities which make a leader. And that means what the party malcontents are accustomed to call the 'rule of clique'. For the moment we have only the latter in Germany. Its continuance in the future, at least in the Reich, is facilitated, first, by the fact that the Bundesrat will raise its head again and will necessarily restrict the power of the Reichstag, and with it its significance as a place for the selection of leaders. And then there is the effect of proportional representation. This, in its present form, is a typical manifestation of leaderless democracy not only because it facilitates the horse-trading of notables for a place on the list, but also because from now on it gives organised interest groups the chance to compel the inclusion of their officials on the lists, and so create an unpolitical Parliament, in which genuine leadership finds no place. The only way the need for leadership could be met would be if the President of the Reich were elected in a plebiscitary fashion, and not by Parliament.[90]

The contrast between the strong leader elected by the people as a whole, and Parliament as the forum for the expression of sectional interests, is patent. In his campaign for a president elected directly on a plebiscitary basis, Weber went so far as to argue that only this, and not a Parliamentary system, was truly democratic. The right of the people to elect its own leader directly was the 'Magna Carta of democracy', whereas the supremacy of Parliament and its arrogation to itself of the power to elect the president was 'a mockery of the principle of democracy in the interest of the horse-trading between Parliamentarians'.[91] In her biography Marianne Weber records a conversation her husband had with Ludendorff in this period, which exemplifies his conception of leadership democracy.[92] Ludendorff had criticised Weber and the *Frankfürter Zeitung* for their part in bringing about a democratic system. Weber replied that the current 'Schweinerei' was no democracy. Then what, asked Ludendorff, did Weber understand by democracy?

> WEBER: In democracy the people elect a leader in whom they have confidence. Then the elected leader says: 'Now shut up and obey me.' People and parties may no longer meddle in what he does.
> LUDENDORFF: I should like that kind of democracy.
> WEBER: Afterwards the people can sit in judgement. If the leader has made mistakes—to the gallows with him.

The conversation was presumably retold at Ludendorff's expense, the last line being directed at him, but in the process it faithfully recorded Weber's own attitude. Having previously argued so insistently for a Parliamentary system, he was now at some pains to disassociate himself from the result, on the grounds that it involved an inadequate conception of democracy. A final quotation from his speech on the 'Reichspräsident' will demonstrate the character of this change:

> Previously, under the authoritarian state, it was necessary to argue for increasing the power of the Parliamentary majority, so that the importance and with it the whole character of Parliament would be raised. But now we have a situation where all constitutional proposals have degenerated into a blind faith in the infallibility and sovereignty of the majority—not of the people, but of the Parliamentarians: the opposite, but equally undemocratic, extreme. . . . True democracy means, not a helpless surrender to cliques, but submission to a leader whom the people have elected themselves.[93]

The change in Weber's attitude to Parliament is thus a marked one. Indeed, the haste with which he abandoned his earlier advocacy of Parliamentary democracy is remarkable. Despite the change, however, there is an important underlying continuity. What he had previously sought from a Parliamentary system was a strong leader to provide political direction and a focus for social unity. 'We demand the "democratisation" (as it is called) of German political institutions,' he wrote in 1917, 'as an indispensable means for securing the unity of the nation . . . and Parliamentary government as a guarantee of uniformity in the direction of policy.'[94] The experience of Parliamentary government in practice (even a few weeks of it!), and above all the circumstances in which it was instituted, convinced Weber that it could not achieve these ends; that a Parliamentary leader would be the creature of particular economic interests, and so unable to transcend existing social and political divisions. Therefore the leader had to be divorced from Parliament and given his own power base in the mass electorate, to provide, in Gustav Schmidt's words, an element of 'decisiveness' over against the 'compromises' of Parliament.[95]

Wolfgang Mommsen, and others after him, have interpreted Weber's theory of political leadership entirely from the perspective of the achievement of Germany's great power goals, to which it is seen as subordinate.[96] What this signally fails to explain, however, is that Weber's strongest insistence on a plebiscitary type of leadership came after the point of Germany's defeat, when Weber himself recognised that a world-political role was no longer possible for his country.[97] At this point it was the problems of internal reconstruction that were paramount: national ones, certainly, but not national*ist*. It is the internal context, therefore, and the internal 'tasks' that Weber saw facing the country, that must provide the basis for any interpretation. The winter of 1918–19 was a period of heightened social tension and class conflict, with social unity threatened particularly from the Left. Weber clearly regarded a Parliamentary system as incapable of providing decisive leadership in these tensions, or of sustaining the strong figure who would satisfy 'the need for leadership' and provide a focus for national unity over the divisions and 'cliques' of Parliament. In these circumstances, only a directly elected president could ensure decisive political direction in face of the horse-trading between particular interests, and preserve national unity in face of the social tensions consequent upon Germany's defeat.

It remains to consider, however, what became of the liberal

elements in Weber's theory under these circumstances. A central theme of this book has been to emphasise the liberal dimension in Weber's political thought. In Chapter 4 it was argued that the distinctive feature of his theory of Parliament was that he saw it as combining the function of leadership selection and the protection of liberties together. His reiterated critique of Bismarck's Caesarist rule was that he left behind 'a nation without any political education . . . a nation without the slightest trace of political will, used to having a great statesman at its head to direct its politics for it'.[98] Weber's theory of Parliamentary government was an attempt to secure the advantages of the Caesarist leader without the disadvantages associated with Bismarck's rule. Thus making the leader responsible to a Parliamentary following would provide the means for eliminating him peacefully when he lost public confidence. Equally important, the context of a working Parliament— the committee system, etc—would ensure that all other talent was not suppressed, and that there would be a continuity of political expertise when the individual leader went. Finally, a strong Parliament would provide 'a guarantee for civil rights in face of the leader's power'.[99]

Weber's theory of Parliamentary government thus attempted to hold a balance between elitist and liberal elements. The significance of his postwar constitutional proposals is that they upset this balance. The scheme for a plebiscitary president involved the erosion of some of the liberal constraints he had previously insisted on. In particular it threatened the independence of Parliament, what with the president's monopoly of patronage, his right of appeal over its head to the people and his power to dismiss the assembly when he chose. The only check in the system lay with the people themselves, but, as Weber must have known, their right to demand a referendum for the president's dismissal could only be a token one, since the initiative in such situations would be with the leader himself rather than with the disorganised mass. Far from the people 'sitting in judgement' on the leader's mistakes, they would be sent to the gallows first. In all these respects, Weber's proposals involved a significant shift of power to the head of state at the expense of Parliament and civil freedoms.

To point this out is not to present Weber as a precursor of Nazism, whether this is seen in terms of a similarity of ideas or, more implausibly, of a causal relationship. The issue has often been debated, and it cannot be answered simply either way.[100] On the one side it can be said that, whatever the similarities in Weber's emphasis on strong leadership and national goals, he would have opposed many of the manifestations of Hitler's rule: the total denial of civil liberties, the political interference in academic life, the racialist claptrap, the corporate state. This can be said, because Weber attacked all these things in his own time. On the other side, Weber's final constitutional scheme did not provide the guarantees against the negative aspects of Caesarism that he had previously insisted upon, and his strong leader was legitimated by a conception of democracy that was anything but democratic.

What Weber's postwar constitutional scheme demonstrates, in fact, is the characteristic dilemma of political liberalism in the face of social tension and class conflict. This was the same dilemma that he had himself analysed so acutely in the Russian context some thirteen years previously, when he showed how, under the pressure of social conflict and the threat to the security of their material existence, the bourgeois intelligentsia were only too ready to sacrifice their liberal values to the more pressing need for order and strong government. This is not to deny the genuineness of Weber's commitment to such values, whether in his insistence on a liberal social policy in Germany and his opposition to the authoritarian state, or in his support for the liberal movement in Russia and his conviction that life would not be worth living 'without the achievements bequeathed by the age of the "rights of man"'.[101] Even in anticipation of postwar troubles in Germany Weber could write early in 1918 that the antics of the Left should not be allowed to play into the hands of the old regime, and that the 'guarantees of a free order' should not be surrendered to the 'fear of the propertied' or the 'feeble nerves of the petty-bourgeoisie'.[102] When the threat to social unity came, however, and capitalism itself was jeopardised, Weber was only too ready to turn against Parliament in the search for a strong leader. To say that he had himself succumbed to the 'Feigheit des Burgertums' (cowardice of the bourgeoisie) would be an exaggeration. But in rejecting Parlimentary democracy for its feebleness—its subordination to cliques and sectional interests— and in posing the choice for German politics as between 'leadership democracy' and 'the rule of professional politicians without a calling', Weber was at the same time abandoning the checks on a Caesarist leader that he had previously regarded as an essential feature of a liberal Parliamentary system.

The circumstances of Weber's postwar constitutional proposals thus make clear a more general feature of his political theory: that his emphasis on strong individual leadership was not simply a means to a great power role for Germany, nor simply a response to circumstances of 'Beamtenherrschaft'. After the war both these were at an end, yet his insistence on a plebiscitary leader was stronger than ever. It was also a response to the inherent problems of capitalist society—the conflict of class and the pursuit of material interests—and the need for a strong political figure who would transcend these.[103]

MAX WEBER AND THE THEORY OF BOURGEOIS POLITICS

Most of the recent discussions of Weber's political thought, particularly by German writers, have been concerned with its specifically German context and significance. It is as a typical figure of Wilhelmine Germany, or as a symptom of the decline towards the Third Reich, that Weber is held to be important. This is particularly true of Wolfgang Mommsen's work, which holds the field in the interpretation of Weber's political thought. The standpoint of his book belongs to that of a generation of German scholars whose concern was to explore those features of German history and thought which could be seen as antecedents of Nazism. To say this is not to deny the fruitfulness of his perspective, but it is a standpoint which also has its characteristic limitations. One is to present Weber's 'Machtpolitik' as a striving for power in itself, and so to obscure the character of the ideology which Weber uses to justify that power, and the relation of this ideology to a distinctively bourgeois culture. A second is to underplay the extent of Weber's hostility to socialism, and to seek to make his theory of leadership intelligible mainly in a political, and not also a social, context.

One purpose of the present work, as should be clear, has been to demonstrate the wider significance of Weber's political writings, and to show how he is to be regarded as a representative bourgeois, and not merely a German national, figure. More than that, however, the purpose has been to show how implicit in these writings is to be found a coherent theory of bourgeois politics. The method of exposition has been systematic rather than historical, because only in this way is it possible to grasp the *structure* of Weber's perception of his contemporary society—both the empirical interrelationship between society and politics on the one hand, and the essential interconnection between his values on the other. At the same time the historical context has not been overlooked. Indeed, the theoretical significance of Weber's writing can only adequately be understood by paying careful attention to the particular historical problems he was engaged in.

In this sense a historical and a theoretical perspective must go hand in hand.

It should be evident that to regard Weber as a bourgeois thinker is nothing new in the history of Weber interpretation. From the early times Weber was dubbed a 'bourgeois Marx'.[104] Nevertheless, this characterisation is itself an ambiguous one, not only as to how far he can be regarded as 'bourgeois', but also in what sense he is to be seen as a counterpart to Marx. The material considered in the preceding chapters will help to clarify both questions. The evidence of Weber's political writings compels the conclusion that in a number of important respects the structure of his perception of his own society, at an empirical level, was similar to that of Marx. What differed was the practical standpoint he adopted as an actor in relation to that structure, the values in terms of which he perceived aspects of it as problematic, the goals towards which he sought to direct the process of interaction between society and politics. This can be most readily appreciated in relation to the concept of class. Weber's analysis of the class structure in both Germany and Russia, and its relationship to the state, could easily have come from a Marxist writer. But the problems raised by that analysis were defined in terms of a bourgeois class standpoint and its values: in Germany, how to secure the political independence of the bourgeois class from the conservative stranglehold of the authoritarian state; in Russia, how far the attainment of 'bourgeois democracy' was a realistic possibility. What differed here was not the terms of the analysis, but the particular class standpoint from which it was judged.

It may be objected that, if Weber's recognition of class was similar to Marx's, he nevertheless differed in emphasising certain distinctively political features, such as leadership and nationalism, which Marx ignored. It depends, however, on what is meant by 'emphasised'. On a purely empirical level, Marx yielded nothing to Weber in his recognition of the state as exercising a monopoly of the means of violence, or the effect of the 'great' political figure in establishing order in circumstances of class conflict, or the consequence of nationalism in diffusing proletarian class consciousness. The decisive difference, once again, was rather the point and direction in which each sought to intervene in this process of historical interaction. The aim of Marx's intervention was the creation of a specifically proletarian consciousness. The aim of Weberian political practice was rather to strengthen those elements which would help fuse the working class into a wider political identity, a national consciousness; it was to this end that he emphasised the national ideal, and the role of the individual leader who was legitimated by the direct support of a majority of the nation. Whereas in relation to the conservatives and the Junkers Weber wished to assert a distinctively bourgeois class consciousness, in relation to the proletariat he wished rather to assert those elements which would transcend class. If this conjunction seems paradoxical, it belonged to the particular character of German historical development that both had to be asserted simultaneously. Caught between the upper and the nether millstone, bourgeois political theory required both an attack against the Prussian conservatives on the one side, and a defence against the proletariat on the other. Hence Weber's insistence both on the attainment of an 'independent political will' on the part of the bourgeoisie, and also on the strong political leader, who would be independent of immediate class interests—though, as shown, the respective balance between the two differed according to the circumstance.

Both Marx and Weber, therefore, recognised the same power relationships, the same structure of power, in modern society; where they differed was the point at which they sought to apply the lever of political action to this structure. There remains, however, a more fundamental difference between the two thinkers, of a broad philosophical kind. Marx was committed to the belief that the particularism of class could only be transcended by the abolition ('Aufhebung') of capitalism itself; only by transcending capitalism as a system could the proletariat realise its inherent possibilities as a universal class. Weber, for his part, was committed to the contrary belief that the divisions of class could be transcended (though not abolished) *within* the capitalist system, and that the Marxian 'universality' was realisable within the existing social order (purged, it should be said, of its feudal trappings). As we have seen the significance of the political sphere to Weber was that it was here that the narrow pursuit of economic interests could be transcended. It was here that a national consciousness was created; here that, in submission to a great leader, men's sectional identity could be overcome. Where, for Marx, action in the political sphere was the necessary means to the development of a specifically class consciousness, its significance for Weber, in contrast, was a more transcendental one.

At the same time, however, Weber recognised that the political dimension—the force of a leader's personality, the sentiment of national consciousness—was not in itself sufficient to bring about a permanent transcendence of class divisions. This was only possible in as far as there could be shown to exist a common economic interest between the classes in the persistence of capitalism. An insistence on this underlying common interest can be seen in the political writing of all his periods. In his early speeches he argued that the German working class must be shown, as the English already recognised, that they had a common economic interest in the expansion of capitalism overseas.[105] In his wartime articles he wrote that, despite all their social antagonism, the workers and entrepreneurs had a common interest in the rationalisation of industry under capitalism.[106] After the war he argued that, only if capitalists were given a free hand in industry, could the nation's economic needs be met.[107] This is not to say that Weber approved the authoritarian form that capitalism took in Wilhelmine Germany. He wanted a more liberal type of capitalism, in which restrictions on trade union activity would be removed, and the balance of power in collective bargaining shifted more towards the workers. Given these conditions, however, he believed that capitalism could be shown to be in the best interests of the workers themselves, and could therefore be presented as non-ideological. It is in this spirit that he writes after the war:

> Democracy will reject *all* the slogans of the ideologues, of whatever kind they be: whether it is 'organisation' or a 'free economy', 'communal provision' or 'nationalisation'. The identification of a measure as 'socialist' or on the contrary as 'liberal' is neither a recommendation nor its opposite. For every sector of the economy the question must rather be one exclusively of the *actual* results: that is to say, how it is possible, on the one side, to improve the earnings prospects of the broad masses of the workers; on the other side to make a greater abundance of provision available to the population as a whole.[108]

Weber was confident that only within a capitalist order, in which a free hand was given to profit, could these non-ideological ('sachliche') demands be met.

It is here that Weber defined one of the essential tasks of 're-sponsible' political leadership, both within the labour movement and in society at large. This was to draw men away from an immediate class perception of society to an awareness of their common underlying interests in the perpetuation of a free enterprise system. In this sense Weber's plebiscitary leader was never a pure demagogue; he had also to possess the essential quality of 'Sachlichkeit', a recognition of the limits of the possible.[109] It was because they lacked this necessary quality that socialist leaders such as Eisner, whatever their charismatic relationship with a following, could never be other than mere demagogues,[110] since they played upon the emotional hostility of the masses towards capitalism, and their 'stupid hatred of the entrepreneur'.[111] What the proletarian movement and the nation needed, Weber had written during the war, was that the 'leadership of rational thinking politicians' should prevail over the 'politics of the streets' and the 'instincts of the moment'; and that the 'ordered leadership of the masses by responsible politicians' should 'break the hold of chance demagogues'.[112] Left to themselves, the masses were likely to develop an emotional outlook hostile to the existing social order; what was needed was a more 'independent' leadership, preferably from another class, to provide a counterweight:

> The propertyless masses, engaged as they are in the harsh struggle for their daily existence, are much more predisposed to all *emotional* motives in politics, to impulsiveness and momentary impressions of a sensational character, as compared to the 'cooler head' of the propertied man, who is freed from these cares. This makes it a pressing concern that democratic parties in particular should count among their *leadership* people in secure economic circumstances, who devote themselves to political activity from purely personal conviction, in order to provide a counterbalance to these emotional influences. . . .'[113]

Demagogic political leadership was thus not enough on its own to transcend class divisions; what was needed also was the quality of 'Sachlichkeit', the ability to recognise the objective necessity of capitalism, for the present at least.

Weber's theory of plebiscitary leadership, it may be said by way of conclusion, stood at the culmination of two concurrent processes of development in capitalist society, both of which can be contrasted with the traditional society of the Junkers, which provided the starting point for his political thought. The social structure of the Junkers, as described by Weber, had generated a distinctive type of politics. The landowners had been 'satte Existenzen', and had been able to devote themselves to the work of administration and national politics in a part-time capacity. At the same time the patriarchal economic structure had created a common interest with their workers and justified their claim to represent the general interest and a national point of view. Capitalism destroyed both aspects of traditional society. On the one hand it brought the professionalisation of administration and political activity,[114] and the bureaucratisation of political structures. In face of this development, Weber argued the need for men of strong leadership qualities ('Führernaturen') to give direction to policy over against the state bureaucracy and party officials. On the other hand capitalism also destroyed the ties of common interest in traditional society and brought class conflict and the pursuit of material interests to the fore. While a Parliamentary system could give expression to these features, it could only with difficulty surmount them. Hence the need for men of 'independent conviction', able to win the direct confidence of the masses through force of their personality, and at the same time give expression to the common interest which underlay men's immediate perception of class. Weber's theory of the plebiscitary leader was the response to both these developments.

At this point it is possible to recognise a clear relationship between Weber's political theory and his social science. The former was underpinned by two central postulates of Weberian social science: the demonstration of the 'rationality' of capitalism on the one hand, and the assumption that modern democracy could only be 'leadership' democracy on the other. These and other aspects of Weber's social science will be discussed in the final chapter, which will return to a theme of central importance mentioned in the introduction to this work: the relationship between Weber's political writings and his academic sociology.

REFERENCES

1 C von Ferber, op cit, p 33.
2 ibid, chs 3 and 4.
3 GPS, p 494; WG, p 29.
4 A Giddens, op cit, p 58.
5 O Stammer, ed, op cit, p 92.
6 This view is argued in E Fleischmann, 'De Weber à Nietzsche', *Archives Européennes de Sociologie*, vol V (1964), pp 190–238; also W G Runciman, op cit, pp 4–5.
7 GPS, pp 21–2.
8 SVS, vol 55 (1892), p 795; GASW, pp 455–6, 474. As Weber insisted, their 'national' outlook was not something they should be praised for as individuals; it was the product of their *social* organisation. GASW, p 456.
9 GPS, p 262.
10 See Chapter 5.
11 D Lindenlaub, op cit, pp 274–91.
12 ibid, p 289.
13 *Christliche Welt*, vol 8 (1894), col 475.
14 SVS, vol 55 (1892), p 780.
15 ibid, p 790.
16 'It is no longer a question of individuals confronting one another on the basis of individual psychological relationships, but of classes ready for

combat. . . . This makes it impossible to treat the relationship between rulers and ruled in ethical or religious terms.' *Christliche Welt*, vol 8 (1894), col 475.

17 *Verhandlungen des 5. Evangelisch-sozialen Kongresses* (1894), pp 71–2.

18 ibid, p 73. In the corresponding article in *Christliche Welt*, vol 8 (1894), Weber argued that the starting point for a realistic social policy must be a break with 'the sentimental fiction of the harmony of interests between ruling and subordinate classes' (col 473).

19 GASW, p 474.

20 The two went together: 'The absence of a purely economic viewpoint and the lack of a developed profit motive was their characteristic feature, and was politically valuable from the standpoint of the state.' *Verhandlungen des 5. Evangelisch-sozialen Kongresses* (1894), p 70.

21 'They are now agricultural businessmen, who pursue economic interests, and must do to survive,' ibid.

22 GASW, p 473.

23 GASW, pp 474–5. The capitalist estate 'must deny its nature if it does not put first what the landed aristocracy gave only a subordinate place: business profits'.

24 GASS, pp 321–2.

25 GASS, pp 384–7.

26 PE, pp 181–2; GARS, vol 1, pp 203–4.

27 The examples are sufficiently annotated in previous chapters.

28 *Archiv*, 23B, p 363.

29 GPS, p 545; GASS, p 405.

30 GPS, pp 300–1, 364.

31 GPS, p 545.

32 GPS, p 24.

33 An ancient Greek term of disapprobation for any activity or trade which was merely mechanical, a term frequently used by Weber.

34 GASS, p 405.

35 The distinction Weber drew between 'ideological' and 'patronage' parties was more apparent than real. See e.g. GPS, p 315. So too Mommsen, op cit, pp 124–5, where he argues that for Weber the 'Weltanschauungspartei' had 'had its day'.

36 *Lebensbild*, p 420.

37 D Lindenlaub, op cit, pp 243–4.

38 Quoted in ibid.

39 GPS, pp 243–51.

40 GPS, p 244.

41 ibid.

42 GPS, pp 244–5.

43 GASS, pp 397–9. This was a substantial point of difference between Weber and Brentano on the issue of trade union organisation.

44 GPS, p 250.

45 GPS, p 253.

46 GPS, p 14, and passim.

47 The difference between Weber and Schmoller was, in this respect, one of means rather than ends. As Lindenlaub shows, Schmoller was against universal suffrage because he believed this would mean a constant flux in government policy between the interests of employers and workers. Party politics could only be allowed if there came forward strong leaders

who would not be subservient to class interests. Where he differed from Weber was that he did not accept that conditions were ripe for this yet, whereas he was much more optimistic than Weber about the ability of the bureaucracy to transcend a class outlook. D Lindenlaub, op cit, pp 243–5.

48 GPS, pp 532–6; GM, pp 113–7.
49 WG, p 655; ES, p 1112.
50 GASW, p 471.
51 GPS, pp 260–6.
52 GPS, pp 352–3, 377–9.
53 GPS, p 260.
54 ibid.
55 GPS, p 262. The same also applied to the present-day Junkers, who were 'engaged in a social and economic conflict of interests as relentless as any industrialist'. GPS, p 265. To say that these figures were 'not of much value' politically was naturally not a judgement on the extent of their political influence, but rather on the use to which they could put it.
56 GPS, pp 262–3; cf 352, 502.
57 GPS, pp 260–1; cf 352–3, 378–9.
58 GPS, p 264.
59 GPS, p 263.
60 GPS, pp 260, 352, 377, 501, etc.
61 Archiv für Sozialwissenschaft und Sozialpolitik, vol 20 (1905), pp 550–3.
62 GPS, p 352.
63 GPS, pp 502–3; GM, p 86.
64 GPS, p 264.
65 The term Weber uses to describe the attitude of those subject to charismatic authority is not 'Glaube' (belief), as in the other types of legitimacy, but the more emotional 'Hingabe' (devotion). The leader is their 'Vertrauensmann', the one they trust. WG, p 124; ES, p 215, etc.
66 GPS, p 524; GM, p 106; cf WG, p 669; ES, pp 1132–3.
67 'Die drei reinen Typen der legitimen Herrschaft' in J Winckelmann, ed, Staatssoziologie (Berlin, 1956), p 110.
68 'All working of mass emotion necessarily carries with it charismatic elements.' WG, p 667; ES, p 1130.
69 GPS, p 523; GM, p 106.
70 So in the older part of WG, p 669; ES, p 1132.
71 GPS, pp 391, 521.
72 ibid.
73 'As a result of the Caesarist element in mass democracy, the parties are compelled to submit to the leadership of those with effective political temperaments and gifts, as long as they show themselves capable of winning the trust of the masses.' GPS, p 391.
74 GPS, p 383.
75 WG, p 668, points to the ability of a charismatic movement to transcend class and status distinctions.
76 GPS, pp 436–71, especially pp 456–9.
77 Lebensbild, pp 651–2.
78 'Aufzeichnung über die Verhandlungen im Reichsamt des Innern über die Grundzüge des der verfassungsgebenden deutschen Nationalversammlung vorzulegenden Verfassungsentwürfe, von 9. bis 12. Dezember 1918'

(Bundesarchiv, Nachlass Payer; copy in Max Weber Institute, Munich). Hereafter cited as 'Aufzeichnung'.

79 ibid, pp 31–4, especially 34.

80 ibid, pp 32, 35; cf GPS, pp 486–7. In the latter speech Weber argued that a popularly elected president was needed to bring about 'socialisation'. This did not mark his conversion to socialism, however. In this ambiguous term he included the 'indispensable financial measures' necessary to set capitalism on its feet again, as well as the more clearly socialist schemes for the reorganisation of industry which he considered a nonsense. The use of the term 'Sozialisierung' indicates, rather, that Weber was concerned to sell his presidential scheme to the Social Democrats. Indeed he went on to argue that their theory of the dictatorship of the proletariat required just what he was advocating: a 'dictator'. (GPS, p 487.)

81 'Aufzeichnung', pp 26–7.

82 ibid, p 36.

83 GPS, p 488.

84 This is the position Weber had taken in the committee. 'Aufzeichnung', p 32.

85 GPS, pp 487–8.

86 Lebensbild, pp 654–6.

87 ibid, p 655.

88 ibid, p 656.

89 ibid.

90 GPS, p 532; GM, pp 113–4.

91 GPS, p 489.

92 Lebensbild, pp 664–5.

93 GPS, p 488–9.

94 GPS, p 212.

95 G Schmidt, op cit, pp 79–80.

96 W J Mommsen, op cit, pp 386, 393–4.

97 See the passage quoted at page 143; also GPS, p 443, where Weber argues that, among other presuppositions of Germany's future constitution, must be a 'clear renunciation of imperialist dreams'.

98 GPS, p 307.

99 GPS, p 383.

100 The two opposing viewpoints can be assessed by comparing W J Mommsen, op cit, ch 10, especially pp 406–13, and Ernst Nolte, 'Max Weber vor dem Faschismus', Der Staat, vol 2 (1963), pp 1–24.

101 GPS, p 321.

102 GPS, p 393.

103 Mommsen makes a reference to this respect of Weber's theory of leadership in his final chapter when he writes that 'the true politician can, so Weber hoped, in virtue of his ability to win a following and acclamation by means of his demagogic gifts (in a good sense), come to override the pursuit of material interests'. W J Mommsen, op cit, p 398; cf pp 399, 411–12. This aspect, however, only forms a peripheral feature of Mommsen's analysis.

104 So A Salomon in Die Gesellschaft, vol 3 (1926), p 144.

105 Verhandlungen des 5. Evangelisch-sozialen Kongresses (1894), pp 81–2; 7 (1896), p 123; cf GPS, p 18.

106 GPS, p 239.

107 GPS, pp 446–8, 470–1, 473–5.

108 GPS, pp 448–9.
109 GPS, pp 525, 533–5; GM, pp 107, 115–16.
110 Because of his following, Eisner is included in Weber's list of charismatic figures, even though he is merely 'an ideologue, carried away with his own demagogic success'. WG, p 140; ES, p 243.
111 *Lebensbild*, p 653. 'Sterile excitation' Weber called it: GPS, p 533; GM, p 115.
112 GPS, p 275.
113 GPS, pp 263–4.
114 The passing of political power to the urban capitalist meant the domination of the professional politician, Weber wrote. GM, p 369.

Chapter 9

Social Science and Political Practice

The central purpose of this study has been to present a systematic account of Weber's political writings, so as to explore the theoretical assumptions they contain, and to elucidate the structure of his analysis of his own society and its politics. The question now to be considered is: what light can this enterprise throw on Weber's academic sociology? It was argued in Chapter 1 that it was mistaken to look for the key to this sociology in Weber's own personal or class situation and values, rather than first in the academic context of his time. This is not to deny that academic work in the social sciences is only properly intelligible in terms of the historical situation with which it is confronted, or that it is social life which poses questions for social science to answer. Rather it is to say that such questions are selected and interpreted according to an academic tradition which has the capacity to reflect independently on its own activity and methods. It is with this tradition that we must at least begin if we are adequately to understand Weber's academic work, because it is this that helps define the point of what he wrote. In the process it will also be necessary to look at the wider historical context, but not so as to provide a short cut to understanding. Such an enterprise is naturally far outside the scope of the present study.

No claim is being made, therefore, to provide the key to Weber's sociology. At the same time there are aspects of the latter which can usefully be illuminated by a consideration of his political writings. The purpose of this final chapter is to explore the way in which Weber's social science and political practice both interrelate, and also differ.

The chapter will concentrate on two points, both of which stem from Weber's own methodology. The first is that, in one direction, social science and political practice are closely interrelated. Science has important implications for practice.[1] This is because it provides some of the necessary empirical foundation for realistic action and policy, and for a coherent political standpoint. It by no means provides all this foundation; a good deal is also contributed by the accumulation of experience on the part of politicians, administrators and others, which may be unreflective and unsystematic. But at least one of the characteristics of social science is that it can contribute to effective political practice, both by providing a tool for realistic action and policy, and by serving as a weapon against the lack of realism and mistaken assumptions of others. In the light of this connection, knowledge of Weber's political writings can help to identify what aspects of his social science provided an underpinning for his own political standpoint, and were used as a weapon against his opponents. Of these aspects in particular it will be important to ask whether their claim to scientific validity is justified. This will form the subject of the latter half of the chapter.

On the other side, political practice can also pose questions to social science. However, the questions for social science are not necessarily drawn directly from this source. In Weber's case, apart from his early studies on East Prussia, they were not. The reason for his dissatisfaction with the Verein für Sozialpolitik on an academic level lay not merely in the confusion of many of its members between facts and values and between a scientific and a political role, but also because of the restriction of empirical research to questions defined from the practical standpoint of social policy. Weber's concern to free sociology from this limitation lay behind his support for the foundation of the German Sociological Association in 1909,[2] and it is also evident in the project on industrial sociology he organised for the Verein the previous year.[3] In his introduction to this project he argued that it broke new ground for the Verein in its orientation to 'exclusively scientific purposes'.[4] It stood aloof from any practical consideration of social policy, and its purpose was purely scientific. This meant not only that there was no question of passing judgement on the situation of the worker in industry, or of assigning blame, or of assessing possibilities for improvement, but also that the facts investigated stood far removed from areas and from problems which could form the subject of legislation. This was not to say that the study had no practical significance; only that this would be a secondary consequence, not its primary purpose.[5]

Weber thus set out a conception of 'purely scientific', 'socio-politically neutral' research. This is one reason why there is little immediate connection between the problems he is concerned with in his scientific and political writings respectively. The difference between them, however, goes deeper than the problems each is concerned with, to a difference in the structure of their analysis of social life. This difference can best be expressed as follows. Weber defined the activity of social science as taking one of two forms: either the causal analysis and explanation of *individual* actions, structures and personalities having cultural significance (this he called 'history', though it also included the present); or the construction of concepts and typologies, and the discovery of *general* laws of events ('sociology').[6] The two activities were to be seen as complementary. Political practice, however, requires besides these a form of analysis different from either of them: an understanding of the interaction between the major features of a particular social and political process, conceived as a whole, in order to identify the possibilities for change and the point at which action can be most effective. This involves a structure of analysis different from either of the above. This is why it is possible to find in Weber's political writings a sense of the interrelationship of forces in society which is frequently lacking in his academic work.

The present chapter will thus concern itself with two points. The first part will explore the difference in the type of question and the structure of analysis to be found in Weber's academic and political writings respectively.[7] The second part will consider those features of his social science which had a special bearing on his political standpoint.

PRACTICAL ANALYSIS AND HISTORICAL SOCIOLOGY

If one compares Weber's political and sociological writings, one notices, besides some obvious points of similarity in content, also a number of striking differences in the empirical treatment of politics. Thus, for example, though both deal with bureaucracy, they treat very different aspects of it. Where Weber's sociology demonstrates the achievements of bureaucracy, his political writings are concerned more with its inherent limitations and its tendency to exceed them; here is developed a distinction between the roles of official and politician which hardly appears in his sociological work. The treatment of politics in *Economy and Society* centres on the concept of authority and on a typology of authority, rather than on politics itself ('the struggle to alter the distribution of power, whether within states or between them');[8]

it is a sociology of 'Herrschaft' or a sociology of the state, rather than a sociology of politics. It is dominated by the category of order ('Ordnung'), where the political writings concern themselves with conflict and struggle ('Kampf'), whether between individuals, classes or nations. Of the concept of legitimacy, which is a hallmark of Weberian sociology, there is in the political writings hardly a mention; the emphasis is placed instead on the ability or failure of regimes to satisfy the interests of major social groups. The political writings lay much greater stress on the dependence of politics on class and economic factors than is generally assumed to be typical of Weber's sociology, and show a much greater scepticism about the place of 'ideal interests'. Finally, there is an important difference in the treatment of capitalism. In Weber's sociology, capitalism is subsumed under the wider concept of 'rationalisation', of which it is treated as one example, while in the political writings the feature of class conflict is much more evident.

Such differences only become explicable when one grasps the difference in the types of question and analysis Weber was concerned with in the two contexts. As pointed out above, the standpoint of Weber's political writings was a more practical one, concerned with assessing the possibilities for change from a particular value position. His interest was in questions such as the conditions for an effective German imperialism; what the obstacles were to achieving Parliamentary government; the chances for bourgeois democracy in Russia; how to ensure strong political leadership over bureaucracies and sectional interests. To answer such questions presupposed an account of the interrelationship between a society and its system of government, and an understanding of the structure of power in society, so as to assess where it was most open to change. Such an account, though it might embody some specific conclusions of science, differed from Weber's academic work both in terms of the questions asked and in its form of analysis. While this may seem self-evident, a brief account of what Weber understood by the activity of social science, both at the point of his resumption of academic work in 1903 and in his later period, will help to clarify the nature of the difference.

In his article on 'Objectivity' (written in 1904), Weber wrote that the kind of social science his journal was concerned with involved an understanding of the 'characteristic uniqueness of the social reality in which we are placed', and of the 'causes for its being historically so and not otherwise'.[9] This activity presupposed two different principles of selection from the infinite multiplicity of phenomena confronting the social scientist. First, it involved selecting as an 'object of scientific investigation' some aspect of contemporary society which was culturally significant. This significance was partly defined in terms of a contrast with other historical phenomena.[10] Secondly, it involved making a further selection from among the infinity of causes necessary to explain each such 'object'. The manner of this selection was determined partly by the practical need for specialisation; concentration on one aspect of social life and one type of cause (economic, political or whatever) had 'all the advantages of the division of labour'.[11] Specialisation was a condition for the advance of knowledge. But the necessity for selection was itself a logical one. Any definitive account of the causal interconnection of phenomena was a logical impossibility. It was for this reason that Weber rejected the claim of the materialist conception of history to integrate the 'unending flux of events' around the causal priority of the economic factor, a claim which was merely the 'rabid chauvinism of a specialised department of science'.[12] Where one stopped in the chain of investigation was a matter for choice; it was not given in the facts themselves:

> If we set out the causal lines, we see them run one moment from the technical to the economic and the political, at the next moment from the political to the religious and then the economic, and so on. Nowhere is there any resting point.[13]

Weber thus defined the task of the social scientist in this period as knowledge of particular causes of those phenomena which were culturally significant. This served as a programme for *The Protestant Ethic*, in which he singled out one significant feature of modern capitalism—its attitude to work—which formed a distinctive contrast to the attitudes of all other cultures, and sought to show how the ethic of reformed Christianity had helped to mould it. As he made clear, what he sought to explicate was only one particular but significant strand in the causal nexus. It would be important also to show, he wrote, not only how Protestantism had affected other aspects of modern culture, but also how it was influenced in turn by a variety of causal factors.[14] However, as he said in his later introduction to his study of the world religions, to demonstrate all these particular relationships—economic, political, social, geographical, national, etc—would be a 'pursuit of infinity'.

It is of some interest to compare this work on the Protestant ethic and its method, with Weber's articles on the Russian revolution, written almost contemporaneously. These were written from the standpoint of a practical interest in the likely course of development in Russia, and the outlook for bourgeois democracy there. Where the academic work was concerned with a 'universal' modern phenomenon (the spirit of capitalism), this was concerned with a particular society in the process of change. Where the one abstracted a particular causal relationship for examination, this sought to present an account of the complex interrelationship between society and politics together, a sense of the 'general social and political situation'[15] at a decisive historical moment. Particularly significant is to contrast the way ideas are treated in terms of the two frameworks. In *The Protestant Ethic* they are treated in a static, 'ideal-typical' form, abstracted from all social context. In the other work they are shown playing a variety of functions in a social and political structure undergoing change. Here, on the one side we see the role of religious ideas in sustaining Tsarist rule, and the close relationship between the structure of authority in state and church, whereby the priests in the rural areas co-operate with the police, and the police support the bishops against the radical clergy in the towns. On the other side we are shown how the ideas of liberal democracy serve as a temporary unifying factor in the challenge to Tsarism, and how these ideas collapse under the pressure of class conflict and the threat to the interests of the propertied intelligentsia. The power of material interests returns to its 'normal function'.[16]

The difference in Weber's treatment of ideas in the two works is a marked one. It is not merely a difference of situation, but a difference in the framework for analysis. *The Protestant Ethic* is the product of a conception of science which sees it proceeding by the isolation of particular causal relationships. The articles on Russia constitute an attempt to give an account of a 'general social and political situation', from the standpoint of a more practical analysis. The latter not only gives a different account from the former of the relationship between ideal and material interests; it also itself raises a question about Weber's particularist method of causal analysis, and that is how far it is possible to evaluate the influence of ideas unless we know their social background and the different purposes they may come to serve. At the end of *The Protestant Ethic* Weber writes that he has only given a partial account, and that it would be necessary also to investigate the influence of other factors in their turn, especially economic, on the development of Protestant asceticism.[17] But he writes as if such accounts would be merely complementary to the first, and not rather make a crucial difference as to how far Protestant asceticism was to be regarded as a promoter or a justifier of a particular economic way of life, and how much in different periods. And this would require, not merely an accumulation of different factors, but some understanding of a complex interrelationship in particular periods of change.[18]

A similar kind of question is raised about Weber's typology of legitimate 'Herrschaft' by the way he accounts for political stability and change in his political writings. In his sociology the persistence of regimes is explained primarily in terms of people's belief in their legitimacy.[19] In his political writings the persistence of regimes is explained rather in terms of their ability successfully to meet or play upon the interests of the dominant social classes, and in terms of a particular configuration of class support. Political change requires, or is the result of, a change in this configuration of support.[20] The two types of explanation are not mutually exclusive; the difference of emphasis is, however, an important one.

To understand this difference, it is necessary to say something about Weber's definition of sociology as a generalising science in his later writings,[21] and the place of the threefold typology of authority within his work *Economy and Society*. Even though the latter is a work of theory, it demonstrates the same particularist approach to causal analysis that characterised *The Protestant Ethic*. It contains a wealth of examples of particular causal relationships (economic-political, legal-economic, etc) within the separate sections devoted to the sociology of law, economics, the state respectively. But Weber's definition of this generalising science as a trans-historical, trans-cultural one prevented him giving any clear and sustained account of the causal or structural interrelationship between the economy, social structure and government of any particular historical epoch. The work contains an impressive kaleidoscope of historical examples, ranging from the ancient world to the present, which illustrate particular typologies and generalisations. But this very richness can itself limit the kinds of question that can be asked.

This is not to say that Weber's account of social institutions in *Economy and Society* is a totally disparate one. The different sectors that he treats—law, economics, administration, the state—do have an interconnection. But the integrating principle is primarily a conceptual rather than a causal one. In the case of modern society, where Marx, for example, had argued that the different aspects of state and civil society only became intelligible when their causal and structural relationship to capitalism was laid bare (the anatomy of civil society was to be found in political economy), for Weber they only became intelligible when they were shown to embody a common 'rationality'. Here we see Weber pursuing the same question that he posed in his article on 'Objectivity' and that formed a guiding theme of his research: 'What is the characteristic uniqueness of the reality in which we are placed?' Weber's answer was to point to those features which the different sectors of modern life held in common: a particular attitude, technique, form of activity which could be comprehended in the concept of 'rationality'. The question he asked was, in one sense of the term, a historical question, and the answer to it could only be given in terms of a contrast with other historical societies.[22] Only an understanding of traditional society could elucidate the distinctive character of the present; indeed it was the concept of 'traditional' that helped define the meaning of 'rationality'.

The conceptual contrast between the 'traditional' and the 'rational' thus provided the unifying element to the different sectors of life, the different sociologies, treated in *Economy and Society*. This contrast is defined most explicitly in the typology of legitimate 'Herrschaft', which can be regarded as providing a conceptual focus for the whole work. To this contrast Weber's historical reflection added a third category, which was recurrent throughout history in the different sectors of life, and cut across the other two: the distinction between the everyday and the exceptional, the routine and the charismatic:

> Bureaucratic and patriarchal structures, though antagonistic in so many respects, have in common the important characteristic of permanence; in this sense they are both institutions of everyday routine ('Alltagsgebilde'). . . . The provision of all demands that go *beyond* the everyday routine has typically been based on a very different principle, the charismatic one.[23]

The typology of authority, and the concept of legitimacy, thus had an important organising function for Weber's historical sociology; it provided an integration at a conceptual level to the different sectors of social life, and at the same time a means for defining those broad differences of social formation that, from a historical perspective, Weber regarded as most significant (traditional-rational; routine-exceptional).

This will help to explain why the concept of legitimacy plays such a central part in Weber's account of politics in *Economy and Society*, and why the analysis in his political writings is so different. This does not mean that there are not features in the latter, such as bureaucracy and political leadership, which find their obvious parallel in his types of authority. But legitimacy is not used as an explanatory concept, and when it appears it is in a persuasive context, such as when Weber urges the recognition of a national legitimacy, or even a natural law legitimacy[24]—types which do not fit at all readily into his threefold classification. The absence of the concept of legitimacy in an explanatory capacity in Weber's political writings becomes less surprising, however, once the point of its use in his historical sociology is recognised; its purpose is to provide an organising and differentiating principle, and a means for identifying a complex of elements in particular systems of rule (patrimonial-bureaucratic, leadership-bureaucracy) rather than to serve as a tool of explanation for the rise and fall of regimes.

To this it may be objected that in *Economy and Society* Weber provided an explanatory account of the German 'revolution' in 1918 in terms of the categories of legitimate 'Herrschaft' and that this gives an indication of how he would have handled the general chapter on revolution which he never lived to write. But this account itself demonstrates the problem of Weber's typology when used as an explanatory device, particularly when it is contrasted with the treatment of revolution in his political writings. Thus he writes in *Economy and Society* that the authority of tradition in Germany was broken down by war and defeat, and that the systematic habituation to illegal behaviour undermined the basis of discipline in both army and industry. At the same time there emerged charismatic leaders to establish a new legitimacy:

> It was only by the rise of charismatic leaders against the legal authorities and by the development around them of groups of charismatic followers, that it was possible to take power away from the old authorities.[25]

What is problematic about this account can be seen by comparing it with Weber's correspondence of that period. Here he was insistent that the only thing which could save the monarchical system was the timely abdication of the Kaiser.[26] Popular disaffection was so widespread, that, far from it needing an extraordinary leader to produce change, it required rather an extraordinary act of initiative to preserve the 'old authorities'. Weber's subsequent account in *Economy and Society* provides an illustration of the point frequently made in criticism of the concept of charismatic authority, that it makes the individual leader himself appear primarily responsible for the achievements of extra-ordinary periods.

The formalism of this account can be contrasted with Weber's analysis of the February revolution in Russia in his political writings. Although a formal break in authority had occurred, Weber insisted that all that had happened was the 'removal of an incompetent monarch'. It was not a real revolution, he wrote, since the same forces continued to exercise power as previously— the propertied bourgeois strata, the army officers, and above all the banks. These had been forced reluctantly to make common cause with the proletariat against the Tsar, because the latter could no longer guarantee order. But it would only be a revolution proper if the peasants, artisans and industrial workers won the 'real power' ('die reale Macht').[27] Such is Weber's account here. No doubt it would have been possible to produce a subsequent version according to the theory of legitimacy, showing how the traditional ruler came to be replaced by a legal constitutional order, with perhaps a charismatic leader to provide the transition. But this would have been an artificial account, which obscured the question of real power.

This contrast illustrates an important distinction between Weber's political and sociological writings. The former were concerned with power and the striving for power in particular societies. Only a class analysis was adequate to elucidate this. In his sociological work Weber was concerned rather with the broadest historical types of administration and authority, and the concept of legitimacy was more suited to distinguishing these. This is not to suggest that 'legitimacy' is unimportant as an explanatory concept; only that it is necessary to grasp the broad framework of *Economy and Society* in order to understand how Weber came to treat politics in it as he did. His conception of systematic sociology was historical, in two different senses. On the one hand it involved the development of political categories which were trans-historical and common to all periods of history (e.g. collegiality, separation of powers, etc). Cutting across this was a different historical purpose, that of elucidating the 'characteristic uniqueness' of the modern world in contrast with the past. Here Weber was concerned with those very general features of contemporary structures which constituted their distinctive modernity (e.g. legal, rational authority). It is in terms of this historical purpose that Weber's treatment of politics in *Economy and Society* needs to be both understood and assessed.

The argument being pursued here is thus that Weber's social

science and his practical political analysis differed both as to the kind of question asked and in the form of their analysis. The different questions posed meant that it was different aspects of contemporary politics that came to be of significance in the two contexts. Thus the treatment of bureaucracy in his sociology is concerned only with its most general manifestations: a definition of its character, and its typical presuppositions and consequences. From the standpoint of political practice Weber was concerned more with the problem of bureaucratic power, its inherent limitations and the practical question of how it could be controlled—questions which are touched on in *Economy and Society*, but not treated as central. More significant is the difference in his treatment of capitalism. From the standpoint of social policy and practical politics alike, the class conflict remained for Weber an 'integral feature of the modern social order'.[28] From the standpoint of universal history, and the concern to elucidate the common qualities of modern social structures as a whole, Weber concentrated on those features of capitalism which could be presented in terms of their 'rationality', of which the class conflict was certainly not one. The change in the way capitalism is presented between Weber's writings on East Prussia for the Verein für Sozialpolitik and *Economy and Society* respectively cannot thus be interpreted merely as a change in his views about its nature. It represented rather a change in his conception of sociology: its divorce from questions of social policy on the one hand, and its integration into a universal-historical perspective on the other. It is not enough therefore to ask how Weber conceived his own society. It is also necessary to ask through what conception of social science he came to present it as he did.

If the questions asked in Weber's sociological and political writings were different, so also was the form of analysis necessary to answer them. Here one must avoid exaggeration. *The Protestant Ethic* was an extreme example of Weber's particularist approach to causal analysis, while on the other hand *Economy and Society* did not set out to offer an account of social and political interaction in any particular society, but only the tools for such an account. Nevertheless, the treatment of the different sectors of social life in isolation from one another, and the trans-historical framework of inquiry, ruled out the systematic consideration of certain kinds of question at a theoretical level, such as the relationship between economy and social stratification, between social structure and forms of government, between leadership and social context, etc. Here a consideration of Weber's political writings can help to dispel certain misconceptions about how he conceived such relationships, for example, that he saw the 'political' as independent from the 'economic' or the 'social'. At the same time they suggest the possibility of a different kind of political theorising from that to be found in *Economy and Society*.

To point to a divergence between Weber's politics and his sociology is nothing new. It is widely accepted that the question of the relationship between science and practice forms one of the most fundamental points of difference between Weber and Marx. Yet the full implications of this divorce for Weber's own work have never adequately been explored, and it is only from a comparison of his political and sociological writings that its extent becomes apparent. However—and this brings us to the second part of the question outlined at the start of the chapter—to underline the differences between Weber's practical analysis and his systematic sociology is not to suggest that the latter held no consequences for his own political standpoint. As he himself recognised, because society was studied for 'purely scientific purposes' did not mean that the conclusions of such study could not have important implications for policy and practice. The second half of the chapter will therefore look at those substantive conclusions of Weber's social science which provided support for his political standpoint and a weapon against opponents.

SOCIAL SCIENCE AS IDEOLOGY

It will be argued in the second part of the chapter that certain features of Weber's social science (but only certain features) are to be seen as ideological. The term 'ideology' will be used here in a critical sense, similar though not identical to the Marxian use. A theory or a work or a conclusion will be called 'ideological' when both its subject matter has a direct bearing on controversy about the structure of social and political power, and it is false or misleading (either it is empirically untrue, or makes claims to an objectivity or universality which is unwarranted).

Any analysis of Weber's work which seeks to show aspects of it as ideological in this sense, should at least begin by recognising the extent to which he sought to free social science from ideology. A familiar feature of this was his constant criticism of the older members of the Verein für Sozialpolitik for their confusion of facts and values, and for their belief that a middle political course was objective in a way that more extreme positions were not. 'The constant confusion of the scientific discussion of facts with their evaluation,' he wrote, 'is still one of the most widespread and damaging traits of work in our field.'[29] The consequence of this confusion was to clothe with the authority of science conclusions which were matters of personal preference, though they were not recognised as such. That Weber realised the effect this could have in making science the supporter of the existing social order, is well attested by his wife:

> Weber observed that often in the field of his specialism the academic, without realising it himself, spoke not only as the servant of the truth, but as servant of the established order, that is, pleaded 'between the lines' for a policy coloured by the interests of his own class, so that Karl Marx's slogan about 'bourgeois science' was in this respect not all that wide of the mark.[30]

Weber's answer was to demand that the social scientist should keep 'unconditionally separate' the establishment of facts from the evaluation of them, and should maintain a clear distinction between an academic and a political role.[31]

At one level this distinction between pursuing science and playing a political role is an obvious one. At another level it is more difficult to sustain. Weber himself recognised that even purely factual conclusions could have important consequences for politics, for example in demonstrating the necessary means, or unavoidable consequences of given policies.[32] The same holds for political standpoints at a more general level. Although values cannot be deduced from facts, yet the political positions that men hold are underpinned by a variety of empirical assumptions about society and human nature.[33] To provide support for such assumptions, or else to demonstrate their falsity, can be as effective a form of political persuasion as an appeal to men's moral sentiments, as Weber himself was aware. In the same way the choice of exposing particular aspects of social life to investigation, or leaving them unexposed, can have significant political consequences. In such cases the distinction between doing science and engaging in political activity becomes more difficult to sustain.

This is not to say that such science is necessarily ideological, only to show how it can be so in those cases where its claim to scientific truth is also unjustified. A simple illustration can be given from a contemporary of Weber's, Gaetano Mosca. Mosca believed that socialism was based on a democratic 'metaphysic', on false empirical assumptions about the nature of power in society, whether the existing or any conceivable future one. It was the task of science to demonstrate that oligarchy was inevitable, that political power 'always has been, and always will be, exercised by organised minorities, which have had, and will have, the means to impose their supremacy on the multitudes'.[34] Science could thus show that man's striving for a more democratic society was based upon an illusion; it provided an essential political weapon:

> In the world in which we are living, socialism will be arrested only if a realistic political science succeeds in demolishing the metaphysical and optimistic methods that prevail at present in social studies—in other words, only if discovery and demonstration of the great constant laws that manifest themselves in all human societies succeed in making visible to the naked eye the impossibility of realising the democratic ideal. On this condition, and on this condition only, will the intellectual classes escape the influence of social democracy and form an invincible barrier to its triumph.[35]

Mosca's example shows in an explicit way how science and politics can coincide. It also makes clear how theorising which remains on a purely empirical level can be ideological, when it is itself false or misleading. Mosca's definition of scientific method was questionable, his concept of oligarchy imprecise, his conclusions stretched well beyond the evidence.[36] Yet they were presented with the authority of science. This is a rather more subtle way in which the social scientist can come to act as 'servant of the established order' than by the intermingling of empirical statements and evaluations that Weber was attacking.

It is important at this point to make clear what is being argued. It is not Mosca's intention of seeking to pursue and make use of science for political purposes that is being called into question. To pursue science for self-consciously political purposes is no more ideological (in the sense used here) than to pursue it for any other purpose; to use one's political values as organisers for defining problems for research no more ideological than any other criterion of selection. What can be called 'ideological' about Mosca's work is rather the uncritical claim to scientific status for conclusions which were questionable, at least, and which, as Mosca very well knew, had important consequences for contemporary controversy about the structure of power in society. It is in this sense that aspects of Weber's sociology can also be criticised, even though he did not pursue it with the same conscious political purpose.

The concept of 'ideology' presented here is thus one which seeks to bypass the elusive question of the social scientist's motives in engaging in a particular study, or arriving at a particular conclusion, not to mention his unconscious motives. What is at issue is the validity of the conclusions themselves and the nature of their political consequences. This is to recognise that aspects of a writer's work may be inadvertently ideological. This should not leave him immune from criticism, however. There are certain areas of empirical inquiry and theorising which are more sensitive than others, because of their bearing on questions of political controversy and on the structure of economic and social power. When a social scientist deals with these areas, we have a right to expect from him that, in so far as he is claiming to be objective or 'scientific', he will be at his most self-critical about the implications of selecting one aspect to treat rather than another, about the validity of the evidence he uses, about the choice of terms in which he presents it, about the hardness of the conclusions at which he arrives. What makes aspects of Weber's work open to question is that he is least self-critical in those areas of his sociology which have a direct bearing on the controversy between capitalism and socialism: his presentation of democracy, and his account of capitalism itself. Not only did his own political position draw support from this presentation; it was also used as a weapon against political opponents.

The above argument should help to clarify what kind of light Weber's political writings, and the definition of his political standpoint as a 'bourgeois' one, can throw on his academic sociology. It is not so much that they show how he arrived at his sociological conclusions or categories, much less that they define the 'real' purpose of his academic work. Rather these writings can show in what way aspects of his sociology served to support his political standpoint, and help to explain why at certain points in his sociology he was less self-critical than others. The subsequent discussion will concentrate on two aspects of this: his treatment of democracy and capitalism respectively.

Democracy
The conception of democracy presented in *Economy and Society* is one which serves to rule out certain kinds of democracy as impractical for modern societies, and the striving for a more genuine democratisation of social and political institutions as unrealistic. Weber's theory achieves this effect in a variety of ways: by a conceptual framework in which the concepts of leadership, bureaucracy, mass, set the terms of discussion for modern politics; by the explicit assertion that 'leadership democracy' is the

only viable form for mass states; by an insistence on the universality of the 'law of the small number'; finally, by the presentation of bureaucracy as the inevitable and irreversible form of organisation in all spheres of life.

The conceptual framework of Weber's account involves a further consideration of his typology of authority.[37] The significant feature of this for the present discussion is that it explicitly excludes a form of legitimacy which had appeared earlier in Weber's writings: belief in the ultimate legitimacy of substantive values ('Wertrationalität'). This exclusion has been a matter of some debate in the German literature on Weber. In his book *Legitimität und Legalität in Max Webers Herrschaftssoziologie*[38] Professor Winckelmann tried to show that a belief in the legitimacy of substantive values was part of what Weber meant by legal or rational authority, but this conclusion has been rejected by the majority of scholars.[39] This type of legitimacy makes a brief appearance at the outset of *Economy and Society* in the section on the legitimacy of a system of order, where natural law beliefs are presented as its most typical example. But it is dismissed from there with the statement that 'today the most usual basis of legitimacy is the belief in *legality*: the readiness to conform with rules which have been enacted according to the *formally* correct and accepted procedures.'[40]

The reasons for this exclusion are various, and are to be found not only in Weber's belief that natural-law concepts were a fiction and that instrumental attitudes were becoming increasingly prevalent in modern society, but also in the organising function the typology performs in *Economy and Society* already referred to. Whatever the reason, however, the consequence of Weber's typology is clear. A counterbalance to the formal legality of a bureaucratic administration cannot be sought in the values of society, but only in a leader and the values which he 'announces'. Even democracy itself comes to be presented in Weber's sociology as a sub-variant of charismatic authority.[41] Admittedly, the discussion takes place under a heading entitled the 'anti-authoritative development of charisma', but this Weber shows to be a misnomer. The only anti-authoritative form of democracy he considers is administration by elected officials, but these are dismissed as inefficient, and 'there is no place for such a type in a technically rational bureaucratic organisation'.[42] The only alternative to this 'leaderless democracy', as Weber calls it, is 'leadership democracy' or 'plebiscitary democracy'; and this, as Weber makes clear, is only in appearance democratic and anti-authoritative.

> 'Plebiscitary democracy'—the most important type of leader-
> ship-democracy—is in its genuine sense a kind of charismatic
> authority which conceals itself under the *form* of a legitimacy
> which is derived from the will of the ruled and only sustained
> by them.[43]

Having dismissed the concept of popular sovereignty as a fiction,
Weber is unable to consider it as anything else than a means of
providing an aura of legitimacy to an outstanding individual
whose qualities are really to be seen as self-authenticating.

The consequences of the limited conceptual framework in terms
of which Weber discussed democracy, and of his insistence that in
modern society it can only be 'leadership-democracy', are thus
twofold. The first is to direct all the emphasis in a theory of
democracy away from the contribution which different groups or
sectors of society can make to decision making, and from the
possibility of extending the areas of popular participation in the
political process, on to the character and quality of the leader, and
the 'genuineness' of his charisma. It is this that becomes all-
important. The second consequence is to present under the title of
democracy something which has very little to do with democracy
at all. Indeed, Weber's charismatic figure, although he requires
popular acclaim, is the opposite of democratic, as Weber himself
admits; the source of what he does lies in himself, not in his
following. 'The leadership of parties by the plebiscitary leader,'
Weber writes, 'entails the "soullessness" of his following, their
intellectual proletarianisation, one might call it.' However, he
adds, 'this is simply the price to be paid for guidance by leaders.'[44]
This is a situation, nevertheless, which he still seeks to describe as
'democratic'.

Both these consequences of Weber's presentation can be clearly
demonstrated from his political writings. The inevitability of
leadership, in Weber's sense, means that the quality of the leader
himself becomes the all-important consideration:

> It is not the politically passive 'mass' which produces the leader,
> but the political leader who recruits a following and wins the
> mass through 'demagogy'. This is so under even the most
> democratic political arrangements. Therefore it is the opposite
> question that is much more immediate: do the parties in a fully
> developed mass democracy permit the rise of men with real
> leadership qualities?[45]

The ambivalence of Weber's conception of the 'mass' has already been indicated in a previous chapter.[46] Here it is sufficient to observe that the use of the term 'mass' itself limits the conception of the people's role in politics to that of objects; it prevents them ever being seen as the potential subjects of political action except in a dangerous capacity. And since there is no other acceptable possibility for the mass than an ordered response to a leader's initiative, this becomes the meaning of democracy for modern society, and the concept of popular sovereignty (albeit fictional) can be used to legitimate the necessary directing role of the leader. The right of the people to elect their president directly, Weber says in his speeches at the end of the war, as opposed to having him chosen by Parliament, is the 'Magna Carta of democracy'— more, even, it is the 'Palladium of true democracy'.[47]

Weber's conclusions about leadership were related to another set of conclusions about the inevitability, the inescapability of the bureaucratic type of administration in modern society.[48] As he never tired of insisting, the onward march of bureaucracy, not only in the state, but in all sectors of social life, was *irreversible*.[49] The only way those subject to it could challenge its existence was by setting up a counter-bureaucracy of their own.[50] The idea of dispensing with such forms of administration was increasingly Utopian. Without the consistent functioning of the bureaucratic machinery, only chaos could result.[51]

Just as with democracy Weber had posed the alternatives of 'leadership' or 'leaderless' democracy, so here the only alternatives were bureaucracy or chaos. The 'objective indispensability'[52] of the bureaucratic machine became the 'first fact' with which socialism had to come to terms.[53] This was particularly true of organisation at the work place, which socialists sought to change.[54] The circumstances of modern technology and the conditions of 'rationalised' production required, not only a bureaucratic hierarchy of technical experts, but the adjustment of the worker in every detail to the machine:

No special proof is necessary to show that military discipline is the ideal model for the modern capitalist factory, as it was for the ancient plantation. In contrast to the plantation, organisational discipline in the factory is founded on a completely rational basis. . . . The final consequences are drawn from the mechanisation and discipline of the plant, and the psychophysical apparatus of man is completely adjusted to the demands of the outer world, the tools, the machines—in short, to an individual 'function'.[55]

This ever-widening grasp of discipline, he concluded, was proceeding as a universal phenomenon 'irresistibly onwards'. Socialism, as he pointed out in his lecture of that name, was itself born out of the subjective experience of this discipline.[56] But the dilemma of socialism was that its hopes of changing it could not be realised.[57] Nor could it ever break the bureaucratic hierarchy of industrial life; indeed, the consequence of socialism could only be to make the power of bureaucratic administration in society more extensive.[58]

Amongst other assumptions which lay behind these statements, Weber took it as self-evident that the exercise of technical skill at the work place must involve a bureaucratic hierarchy, that mass needs could not be met except by drawing the 'final conclusion' from the mechanisation of the plant, that the 'rationalisation' of production was the primary value to which any future society must commit itself. That socialism could be no different from capitalism in these respects was in fact a necessary presupposition for carrying out 'socio-politically neutral' research into industrial life, of the kind Weber planned for the Verein für Sozialpolitik.[59] The investigators could report the complaints of the workers, Weber wrote, but there was no question of sitting in 'moral judgement' upon the entrepreneur, much less of treating these complaints as the symptom of a practical question to be solved. Rather, they should seek to explain the particular causes of such complaints (technical, economic, psychological) as objectively as possible.[60] However, if Weber's investigation was to be socio-politically neutral, one thing had to be ruled out, and that was the consideration that the cause of such complaints might lie at a more structural level, in the nature of capitalism itself. Thus Weber wrote at the end of his introduction that the factory structure being investigated—its bureaucratic hierarchy, its discipline, its chaining of the worker to the machine, its rigorous calculation of the minutest detail of the worker's movements—stood independent of the question of capitalism or socialism.[61] Socialism could at the most alter the spirit, but not the structure, of this work place.[62]

Weber's presentation of future possibilities is thus a deterministic one, in which the existing organisational realities of a capitalist society are allowed to dictate the limits of the possible in any future social order. Men should adjust to these rather than seek to change them. What is open to objection in this, it should be clear, is not so much Weber's descriptive account of the actual developments in political leadership or bureaucracy taking place in his own time. It is rather that what is given in a particular society is explicitly made to prescribe the bounds of what is possible in any future one, and that this is then presented authoritatively as the 'facts' which any realistic political theory and practice (particularly socialist theory) must accept. Yet, as Weber himself remarked in a different context, historical experience shows that men have only attained the possible by striving again and again for the impossible.[63] The least we should expect of a social science which claims to be socio-politically neutral is that it should remain open to future possibilities, not seek to close them prematurely.

Capitalism

Weber's social science provided the basis not only for a critique of socialism, but for a defence of capitalism also. Central in this was his treatment of profit and the activity of profit-making. His work *The Protestant Ethic and the Spirit of Capitalism* showed how this activity could be seen in an ethical light. His later work *Economy and Society* demonstrated its 'rationality'. Each of these will be considered in turn.

Weber recognised with Marx that one of the most distinctive features of modern capitalism was, besides the employment of free labour, the pursuit of profit and forever *renewed* profit on a cumulative basis.[64] However, the account which he gave of this phenomenon in *The Protestant Ethic* stood in marked contrast to that of Marx. First, he showed it to have an ethical significance. The pursuit of profit was associated with a variety of ethical qualities; the accumulation of profit itself demonstrated that men had laboured hard in their calling. Secondly (and related to the first), he sought to differentiate this systematic acquisition of profit from a number of other attitudes to gain and forms of capitalism known to history: those of the adventurer, the speculator, the profiteer. All these stood in marked contrast to 'sober bourgeois capitalism'.[65] Whatever Weber's intention of engaging in a purely historical study, one consequence of his presentation was to provide a contemporary justification for capitalism against its critics: first, because it endowed profit with a moral significance; secondly, because it provided a way of dismissing various more reprehensible forms of profit-making as aberrations, as not the 'essence' of modern capitalism.

It was argued earlier that a problem about Weber's historical method was the impossibility of evaluating the causal significance of the Protestant ethic in abstraction from a wider context. What is important here, however, is rather Weber's account of the capitalist spirit itself, which is what the work seeks to explain.

This is already, prior to the examination of the link with Protestantism, presented in ethical terms which predispose the reader to see the capitalist in a highly favourable light.[66] The following is a characteristic example:

> Along with clarity of vision and decisiveness of purpose, it was only by virtue of very definite and highly developed ethical qualities that it was possible for him to command the absolutely indispensable confidence of his customers and workmen. Nothing else could have given him the strength to overcome the innumerable obstacles, above all the infinitely more intensive work demanded of the modern entrepreneur. . . . They were men who had grown up in the hard school of life, calculating and daring at the same time, above all temperate and reliable, shrewd and completely devoted to their business, men of strict bourgeois opinions and principles.[67]

By already defining the spirit of capitalism solely in ethical terms, Weber has already prepared us for his conclusion: it comes as less of a surprise to discover that such sterling qualities have their origin in a religious way of life.

It is, however, the contemporary significance of Weber's account that concerns us here. Weber recognised, of course, that contemporary capitalism differed in a number of respects from the earlier one. The motive of the early capitalists, according to his account, had been a sense of religious vocation and a desire to demonstrate that they were among the saved. Capitalism was now a self-sustaining system which required the support of religion no longer; men had to pursue profit or go to the wall.[68] Further, capitalism now took a bureaucratised form which left less scope for the earlier individualism. Despite these differences, however, the pursuit of profit could still be presented in a moral light; indeed, it was precisely in the moral terms of *The Protestant Ethic* that Weber himself sought a justification for the capitalist in his own society. On the one hand profit could be seen as a proof of 'hard work in a calling', which Weber described as the 'highest economic ethic known to history'.[69] On the other hand were those qualities of character that the risk of the market place and the struggle for competition helped to develop. These features have been discussed in previous chapters. They were the features which Weber wished to see preserved in the German bourgeoisie, some of whom were deviating towards a rentier existence. The same ethical features could also provide a defence against the critics of capitalism. Here is a passage from a wartime article, in which

Weber seeks to demonstrate the difference between income received from state bonds and from dividends. What is the significance of dividends? he asks.

> [They signify] that in the office and the technical bureau, and in the machine shops of the factories . . . hard and persistent *work has been done*, goods have been produced for mass needs, men have been provided with wages and bread, and all this with the degree of perfection and imperfection allowed by the existing economic order, which must be valid for a long while to come. Further, it means that the economic and social power and status of the directors and executives, and the livelihood of their employees and workers, have been placed at risk in the struggle of the market, and that this struggle has been won. *This* is the significance of dividends.[70]

These are the same qualities that are celebrated in *The Protestant Ethic*. What is not at issue is whether these terms could not legitimately be applied to particular capitalists in particular situations. It is rather a question of whether an account of the 'spirit of capitalism' which is limited to these terms can be accepted as adequate.

This brings us to the second feature of Weber's account mentioned above. The reason for his defining the 'spirit of capitalism' as he does is partly to be found in his conception of historical method. The concern of the historian, as he defines it in his article on 'Objectivity', is with phenomena which are culturally unique; in their uniqueness lies their significance from a historical point of view.[71] Weber's concern was similarly to identify what was distinctive about the ethos of the modern capitalist, and this required it to be contrasted with other historical attitudes to profit: those of ruthless acquisition, unscrupulous profiteering, adventurist speculation, the *auri sacra fames* such as that of the Dutch sea captain who 'would go through hell for gain, even though he scorched his sails'.[72] All these attitudes were to be found throughout history. The unique feature of bourgeois attitude was to be found where it differed from these. The consequence of Weber's method is clear: it is to suggest that these other motives are unimportant to modern capitalism, because they do not define its *distinctive* spirit.

In Weber's later writing this distinction between motives becomes a distinction between different forms of capitalism. In *Economy and Society* Weber draws a fundamental distinction between 'rational capitalism' on the one hand, in which profit-making is pursued on the basis of continuous production and exchange in a free market using systematic calculation, and various forms of 'irrational' capitalism on the other: for example, those based on purely speculative opportunities for profit, or dependent on a connection with political bodies ('politically-oriented capitalism'). The two types are 'qualitatively different' in character. The latter have existed universally: the former is unique to the modern Western world.[73] In his introduction to the volumes on the world religions Weber acknowledges that the 'irrational' forms also existed in modern society. But they did not define what was distinctive about it, nor what was significant from the perspective of universal history:

> In a universal history of culture the central problem for us is not, in the last analysis, even from a purely economic view point, capitalist activity as such, which appears everywhere, differing only in form: the adventurer or trading type, or capitalism oriented towards war, politics or administration as sources of gain. It is rather the origin of this systematic bourgois capitalism. . . .[74]

The effect of Weber's 'historical' standpoint was thus first, that all the emphasis in his account of modern capitalism came to be put on one set of features: one set of motives, one type of pursuit of profit. Secondly, where the other (from Weber's standpoint) ethically more dubious forms of profit-making were recognised in modern society, they were conceived as separable from the first. Modern capitalism was shown to consist of a variety of different forms of capitalism, qualitatively different from one another, with no structural interconnection between them. The polemical implications of this account should be obvious. It enabled Weber to present the more dubious types of profit-making as aberrations, as not properly representative of bourgeois capitalism, even though they were the product of one and the same economic system. Here is another example of his answer to wartime critics who saw capitalism as the 'father of all evil':

> It is above all the profound ignorance of our ideologues about the essence of capitalism that makes anyone at all acquainted with the facts so impatient. The least of their marvellous naïvety is to lump together the war profits of the firm of Krupp with the war profits of some arrant profiteer, simply because both are the product of 'capitalism'. More important is that they have not the slightest conception of the fundamental

antithesis that exists between all forms of capitalism that depend upon political opportunities (supplying the state, financing wars, illicit trade, and all similar opportunities for booty which have escalated to such gigantic proportions because of the war), and the bourgeois *rational* undertaking, which depends upon the careful calculation of profit. . . . They have no conception that the one (politically oriented booty capitalism) is as old as the history of military states itself, while the other is a specific product of modern European man.[75]

Weber's justification for capitalism was, in important respects, a moral one. Despite all the bureaucratisation of modern society, which was itself a consequence of capitalism, Weber still believed that the accumulation of profit in 'rational' undertakings could be given an ethical significance. But this presupposed that it could be sharply differentiated from other, more reprehensible forms of profit. Weber's universal-historical approach to social science provided a means for making such a distinction, by concentrating on that form of profit-making which was historically unique to modern society. What this approach produced was not only a one-sided account of the capitalist himself. It also overlooked the structural connections between this 'rational' capitalism and various forms of speculative, politically-oriented capitalism (finance capitalism, imperialism, etc) in modern society. But such connections Weber's historical method was unable to elucidate. As argued in the first part of this chapter, Weber's historical approach to sociology involved separating off his theoretical discussion of the state, capitalism, class, etc from each other. It also involved separating off capitalism from itself. The consequence, if not the intention of this method, both in *The Protestant Ethic* and in *Economy and Society* was to produce a one-sided version of capitalism, and one which contributed to its ideological defence.

This brings us to a final point about Weber's presentation of capitalism: its 'rationality'. Weber wrote in *Economy and Society* that the modern capitalist system embodied the height of economic 'rationality' in a purely formal or technical sense, in that it allowed for the maximum degree of numerical calculation in all aspects of the economic process: the maximum calculability of accounting procedures, of technical processes, of human functions within the enterprise.[76] The necessary conditions for achieving this degree of calculability were a profit-oriented system of production operating in a free competitive market, with modern technology, advanced specialisation of functions, and employment of free labour under rigorous selection and sanction of dismissal.[77] These features could themselves be described as formally 'rational' in that they contributed to the calculability of economic action. Weber argued that to call a system 'formally' or 'technically' rational was to say nothing about its capacity to satisfy human wants or fulfil other substantive purposes. This involved a judgement of 'substantive' rationality—a judgement from a particular value standpoint.[78] However, Weber believed that modern capitalism was in fact substantively rational also, from the standpoint both of the production of goods and the satisfaction of wants:

> If the standard used is that of the provision of a certain minimum of subsistence for the maximum size of population, the experience of the last few decades would seem to show that formal and substantive rationality coincide to a relatively high degree.[79]

Equally, however, formal and substantive rationality could conflict, as in a socialist planned economy, which would produce an 'inevitable reduction in the formal rationality of calculation' and hence of productive efficiency.[80]

The way Weber uses the concept of rationality in this discussion, as throughout the economic section of *Economy and Society*, is of some importance. He insisted that he was using the term in a purely formal, technical sense, and that this implied no evaluation from any substantive viewpoint. Indeed, in his political writings, and in other areas (e.g. bureaucracy and science),[81] Weber showed himself to be critical of the extension of formal rationality as an end in itself. Nevertheless, such a criticism could only be made from a substantive value standpoint, and thus could not form the subject of science, since there were 'an indefinite number of positive standards of value which are "rational" in this sense'.[82] There could be no question of making a judgement from such a standpoint in a scientific work.[83] The result of this exclusion, however, is that the concept of formal rationality becomes by default the sole consideration in terms of which economic activity is considered in *Economy and Society*. The calculability of economic processes becomes the standard in terms of which everything is assessed. Thus the expropriation of the workers is presented as a means to improved calculability;[84] their traditionalist attitudes become so many 'hindrances' to rationality.[85] For the workers to have a say in management produces all kinds of 'technically irrational obstacles and economic irrationalities';[86] whereas, on the other hand, to adjust their psycho-physical apparatus in every detail to the machine represents the 'supreme triumph' of scientific management.[87] The concern is to know what are the 'conditions for the maximum calculability of labour productivity'; what the conditions for the 'maximum rationality of capital accounting'.[88] Technical calculability becomes here both the standard of achievement and the criterion for defining what is problematic. Because any substantive position would involve a value judgement, technical rationality is left holding the field; it becomes the definitive standpoint from which everything is assessed.

As Herbert Marcuse has argued, what Weber is discussing here is not simply technical rationality, but capitalist technical rationality.[89] It is attained at its highest in the capitalist market economy. But the motivating force for this rationalization—the 'pursuit of profit and forever renewed profit' as an end in itself—which dictates that the capitalist entrepreneur must continually intensify the process of rationalisation whether he like it or not, and whether or not the result can be justified from the standpoint of human needs,[90] this motivating force remains unexplicated in *Economy and Society*. Weber notes in passing some of the paradoxical consequences of this rationalisation, for example, that the entrepreneur's desire to eliminate all that is incalculable from the process of production produces a situation where 'to a large degree the consumer's wants are "awakened" and "directed" by the entrepreneur'.[91] But the motivating force of profit remains unexamined. This enables Weber to pass off the 'substantive' irrationalities of capitalism simply as matters for extra-scientific value judgement, rather than as something which is persistently problematic. Instead, where in *The Protestant Ethic* profit was presented as a sign of faithful work in a calling, now it is itself described as 'rational' because of the technical rationality which it encourages.

The argument being presented here, it should be emphasised, is not that Weber either consciously or unconsciously engaged in social science as a means to support the existing social order. Sociology is not simply the modern intellectual's substitute for the novel as a means of self-expression, as Steding put it. The explanation for Weber's work is to be found in the first instance in a particular conception of what social science involved. As argued at the outset of this section, Weber sought to free sociology from one particular kind of ideology—the belief that value judgements, if judicious and balanced enough, could have the authority of science—and also from a narrow subordination to social policy and practice. But this did not prevent him in his own work from presenting as objective truths, categories and conclusions which were themselves more one-sided than was claimed for them, and whose effect was to reinforce a particular image of the world convenient to bourgeois capitalism. In this sense Lukacs is right, though the form of his argument is exaggerated.[92] It is not that Weber's social situation produced a particular historical or sociological method; it is rather that his social situation explains why he was so uncritical about some of the conclusions arrived at as a result of that method.

This has had its consequences in our own time. The impact of Weber's undoubted brilliance as a scholar and thinker, and his obvious concern to distinguish between the logical status of facts and value judgements, itself contributed powerfully to the illusion of an epoch of social science which believed that to avoid the open expression of values in its work was sufficient to make the conclusions objective and value-free. No such claims, it should be clear, are being made for the present study. Its assumption is rather that to take up a clearly defined value standpoint can be a help in providing a coherent account of Weber's political theory, which is the main purpose of this book, as it can also contribute to a more just assessment of his academic sociology. In this sense the critical discussion of values must be a work, not only for political philosophy, but for a reflective social science also.

REFERENCES

1 GAW, pp 494, 577; MSS, p 18; GM, p 138.
2 See Weber's address to the first meeting in 1910, and the programme of research outlined there. GASS, pp 431–49.
3 'Auslese und Anpassung der Arbeiterschaft der geschlossenen Gross-industrie.' Weber's introduction to the study is in GASS, pp 1–60.
4 GASS, p 2.
5 GASS, pp 2–3.
6 WG, p 9; ES, p 19.
7 It is taken as self-evident here that there is an important difference between the persuasive purpose of much of Weber's political writing and the (in this sense) value-free character of his sociology. The first part of the chapter seeks to take the discussion of the difference beyond this obvious point.
8 GPS, p 494.
9 GAW, pp 170–1; MSS, p 72.
10 'We seek knowledge of a historical phenomenon, meaning by historical: significant in its individuality.' GAW, p 177; MSS, p 78.
11 GAW, p 170; MSS, p 71.
12 GAW, p 169; MSS, p 71.

13 GASS, p 456.
14 GARS, vol 1, p 205; PE, p 183.
15 GPS, p 103.
16 GPS, p 55.
17 GARS, vol 1, ibid.
18 In the articles he wrote in reply to critics Weber frequently appeared defensive about this aspect of his method. His answer was that he was not arguing a causal hypothesis, but rather answering the question: assuming Protestantism had the effect it did, how did it come to do so? It remains true, however, that in the work he makes causal assertions which need other evidence to evaluate properly. The critical articles and Weber's replies are assembled in J Winckelmann, ed, *Max Weber: Die protestantische Ethik II* (München, 1968). For the point mentioned here see especially pp 163–4.
19 e.g. WG, p 122; ES, p 213.
20 See Chapters 6 and 7.
21 The fullest account of the development in Weber's conception of sociology is to be found in Egbert Tellegen, *De Sociologie in het Werk van Max Weber* (Meppel, 1968). It is reviewed by Constans Seyfarth in *Kölner Zeitschrift*, vol 22 (1970), pp 595–7.
22 This formed a major purpose of his studies on the world religions. 'It is our prime concern to understand the unique character of modern Western rationalism. . . . . In every culture those elements are deliberately emphasised which differ from Western civilisation.' GARS, vol 1, pp 12–13; PE, pp 26–7.
23 WG, p 654; ES, p 1111.
24 For public effect, not because he believed in it. GPS, p 439.
25 WG, p 155; ES, pp 265–6.
26 GPS, 1st edn, pp 477–9.
27 GPS, pp 200, 205.
28 See page 219.
29 GAW, p 157, cf pp 485–7; MSS, pp 60, 10–12.
30 *Lebensbild*, p 330.
31 GAW, pp 486, 585.
32 GAW, p 494; MSS, p 18.
33 This is well illustrated by W G Runciman in his book *Social Science and Political Theory* (Cambridge, 1965), and in the article 'Sociological Evidence and Political Theory' in P Laslett and W G Runciman, eds, *Philosophy, Politics and Society*, 2nd series (Oxford, 1964), pp 34–47.
34 G Mosca, *The Ruling Class* (New York, 1939), p 326.
35 ibid, p 327.
36 See G B Parry, *Political Elites* (London, 1969), pp 20–7.
37 This part of the discussion follows Mommsen. See particularly his article 'Zum Begriff der "plebiszitären Führerdemokratie" bei Max Weber', *Kölner Zeitschrift*, vol 15 (1963), pp 295–322.
38 J Winckelmann, op cit (Tübingen, 1952).
39 So W J Mommsen, *Max Weber und die deutsche Politik*, pp 414–19; A Karsten, *Das Problem der Legitimität in Max Webers Idealtypus der rationalen Herrschaft* (Hamburg, 1960); *Fritz Loos, Zur Wert- und Rechts-lehre Max Webers* (Tübingen, 1970), pp 113–42.
40 WG, p 19; ES, p 37.
41 WG, pp 155–8, 666–7; ES, pp 266–71, 1127–30.

42 WG, p 157.
43 WG, p 156. Weber is writing here of the 'purest' types, who win power and subsequently legitimate their position by means of a plebiscite. However, he sees little distinction between this and an election proper in which a number of 'pretenders' are presented to the people. WG, p 667.
44 GPS, p 532; GM, p 113.
45 GPS, p 389.
46 See Chapter 4.
47 GPS, p 489.
48 WG, pp 128-9, 569-71; ES, pp 223-4, 987-9.
49 WG, ibid; GPS, pp 318, 321; GASS, pp 497-8.
50 WG, p 128; ES, p 223.
51 WG, p 569; ES, p 988.
52 ibid.
53 GASS, p 498.
54 A central argument of Weber's lecture on socialism is the impossibility of this. See especially GASS, pp 498-9.
55 GM, p 261; WG, p 686.
56 GASS, p 501.
57 It was determined by the nature of modern technology. GASS, p 499, cf pp 59-60.
58 WG, p 128; ES, pp 223-4.
59 See page 251.
60 GASS, p 3. The kind of cause Weber had in mind was the effect a change in the speed of machinery had on the physiology of the worker. GASS, pp 16-17.
61 GASS, pp 59-60.
62 The distinction is a difficult one to sustain. Weber recognised that it was the pursuit of profit and the existence of competition which subjected the worker to such a harsh 'selection process' at the work place (GASS, p 501). Yet he wanted to maintain that a change in this could only affect the spirit ('Geist') of the work situation, while its structure ('Apparat') must remain unchanged.
63 GPS, p 548; GM, p 128.
64 GARS, vol 1, p 4; PE, p 17.
65 GARS, vol 1, p 10; PE, p 24.
66 Wolfgang Lefèvre calls Weber's account 'idyllic'. W Lefèvre, op cit, p 42.
67 GARS, vol 1, pp 53-4; PE, p 69. It should be emphasised that this passage occurs in the chapter where Weber is defining the spirit of capitalism. In fact Weber is drawing here on examples known to him personally.
68 GARS, vol 1, pp 36-7; PE, pp 54-5.
69 GPS, p 242.
70 GPS, p 237.
71 To quote again: 'We seek knowledge of a historical phenomenon, meaning by historical: significant in its individuality.' GAW, p 177; MSS, p 78.
72 GARS, vol 1, pp 41-2, 53; PE, pp 56-7, 69.
73 WG, pp 95-7; ES, pp 164-6.
74 GARS, vol 1, p 10; PE, pp 23-4. This introduction was written at the end of the war, i.e. long after The Protestant Ethic itself.
75 GPS, p 241.
76 WG, pp 44-5, 58-9, 86-7, 94-6; ES, pp 85-6, 107-9, 150-3, 161-4.
77 ibid.

78 WG, pp 44–5; ES, pp 85–6.
79 WG, p 59; ES, pp 108–9.
80 WG, p 60; ES, p 111.
81 GPS, p 320; GAW, p 582.
82 WG, p 45; ES, p 86.
83 ibid.
84 WG, pp 77–8; ES, pp 137–8.
85 WG, p 72; ES, p 129.
86 WG, p 78; ES, p 138.
87 WG, p 686; ES, p 1156.
88 WG, pp 86–8, 94–5; ES, pp 150–3.
89 H Marcuse, 'Industrialism and Capitalism in the Work of Max Weber', in H Marcuse, *Negations* (London, 1968), pp 201–26.
90 'Capitalism is identical with the striving for *profit*, in a continuous, rational capital enterprise, a striving after ever *renewed* profit, after profitability. It must be so. In a wholly capitalist economic order, an individual enterprise which did not orientate itself to the chance of making profit would be doomed to extinction.' GARS, vol 1, p 4; PE, p 17.
91 WG, p 49, cf p 53; ES, pp 92–99–100.
92 See Chapter 1, p 27.

Bibliography

The following bibliography is not intended to be definitive. It simply indicates the works drawn on directly in the writing of this book. It is, however, based on the complete bibliography of Weber's works and secondary literature being compiled at the Max Weber Institute, Munich. In the section on Weber himself, only those articles are listed which do not appear in the collected editions of his work. In the book itself, references have been based on the second editions of both Weber's political and methodological writings, since these are the most convenient to use; the other editions have, however, been used for additional material (e.g. GPS, 1st edn, for a number of political letters).

WRITINGS OF WEBER

Gesammelte Aufsätze zur Religionssoziologie, 1–3 (Tübingen, 1920–1).
Gesammelte Aufsätze zur Soziologie und Sozialpolitik (Tübingen, 1924).
Gesammelte Aufsätze zur Sozial- und Wirtschaftsgeschichte (Tübingen, 1924).
Gesammelte Aufsätze zur Wissenschaftslehre, 2nd edn (Tübingen, 1951); 3rd edn (Tübingen, 1968).
Gesammelte Politische Schriften, 1st edn (München, 1921); 2nd edn (Tübingen, 1958); 3rd edn (Tübingen, 1971).
Wirtschaft und Gesellschaft, 5th edn (Tübingen, 1972).
Wirtschaftsgeschichte, 1st edn (Tübingen, 1923).
Jugendbriefe (Tübingen, 1936).
Die Protestantische Ethik II, ed J Winckelmann (München, 1968).
Soziologie, Weltgeschichtliche Analysen, Politik, ed J Winckelmann (Stuttgart 1968).
'Die Verhältnisse der Landarbeiter im ostelbischen Deutschland', *Schriften des Vereins für Sozialpolitik*, vol 55 (1892).
'Privatenqueten über die Lage der Landarbeiter', *Mitteilungen des Evangelisch-sozialen Kongresses*, nos 4–6 (April–July, 1892).
'Die Erhebung des Vereins für Sozialpolitik über die Lage der Landarbeiter', *Das Land*, vol 1 (1893), pp 8–9, 24–6, 43–5, 58–9, 129–30, 147–8.

'Die Erhebung des evangelisch-sozialen Kongresses über die Verhältnisse der Landarbeiter Deutschlands', *Christliche Welt*, vol 7 (1893), cols 535–40.

'Die deutschen Landarbeiter', *Verhandlungen des 5. Evangelisch-sozialen Kongresses* (1894), pp 61–82, 92–4.

'Was heisst Christlich-Sozial?', *Christliche Welt*, vol 8 (1894), cols 472–7.

' "Römisches" und "deutsches" Recht', *Christliche Welt*, vol 9 (1895), cols 521–5.

'Die Arbeitslosigheit', *Verhandlungen des 7. Evangelisch-sozialen Kongresses* (1896), pp 122–3.

'Deutschland als Industriestaat', *Verhandlungen des 8. Evangelisch-sozialen Kongresses* (1897), pp 105–13, 122–3.

'Stellungnahme' zur 'Flottenumfrage' der *Münchner Allgemeinen Zeitung* (13 Jan 1898).

Bemerkungen zu R Blank, 'Die soziale Zusammensetzung der sozialdemokratischen Wählerschaft Deutschlands', *Archiv für Sozialwissenschaft und Sozialpolitik*, vol 20 (1905), pp 550–3.

' "Kirchen" und "Sekten" in Nordamerika', *Christliche Welt*, vol 20 (1906), cols 558–62, 577–83.

'Zur Lage der bürgerlichen Demokratie in Russland', *Archiv für Sozialwissenschaft und Sozialpolitik*, vol 22 (1906), Beiheft, pp 234–353.

'Russlands Übergang zum Scheinkonstitutionalismus', *Archiv für Sozialwissenschaft und Sozialpolitik*, vol 23 (1906), Beiheft, pp 165–401.

'Die Handelhochschulen', *Berliner Tageblatt* for 27.10.1911.

'Rundschreiben zur Sozialpolitik', 15.11.1912.

'Die drei reinen Typen der legitimen Herrschaft', *Preussische Jahrbücher*, vol 187 (1922), pp 1–12.

Translations

Economy and Society (New York, 1968).

From Max Weber: Essays in Sociology, ed H Gerth and C Wright Mills (London, 1948).

General Economic History (London, 1923).

Methodology of the Social Sciences (New York, 1959).

The Protestant Ethic and the Spirit of Capitalism (London, 1930).

SECONDARY LITERATURE

ABRAMOWSKI, Günter, *Das Geschichtsbild Max Webers* (Stuttgart, 1966).

ALBROW, Martin, *Bureaucracy* (London, 1970).

ANTONI, Carl, *From History to Sociology* (London, 1962).

ARON, Raymond, *Main Currents in Sociological Thought* (New York, 1967).

—— 'Max Weber und die Machtpolitik' in Stammer, Otto, ed, *Max Weber und die Soziologie heute* (Tübingen, 1965), pp 103–20.

BAUMGARTEN, Eduard, *Max Weber, Werk und Person* (Tübingen, 1964).

BENDIX, Reinhard, *Max Weber. An Intellectual Portrait* (New York, 1962).

BENDIX, Reinhard and ROTH, Guenther, *Scholarship and Partnership* (Berkeley, 1971).

BERGSTRAESSER, Arnold, 'Max Webers Antrittsvorlesung in zeitgeschichtlicher Perspektive', *Vierteljahreschefte für Zeitgeschichte*, vol 5 (1957), pp 209–19.

BLAU, Peter, *Bureaucracy in Modern Society* (New York, 1956).

BOESE, Franz, *Geschichte des Vereins für Sozialpolitik 1872–1932* (Berlin, 1939).

BRUUN, Hans, *Science, Values and Politics in Max Weber's Methodology* (Copenhagen, 1972).

BUSSHOFF, Heinrich, 'Ein offener politik-soziologischer Begriff des Politischen?' *Politische Vierteljahresschrift*, vol 10 (1969), pp 108–15.

DIBBLE, Vernon, 'Social Science and Political Commitments in the Young Max Weber', *Archives Européennes de Sociologie*, vol 9 (1968), pp 92–110.

DIECKMANN, Johannes, *Max Webers Begriff des 'modernen okzidentalen Rationalismus'* (Düsseldorf, 1961).

DRONBERGER, Ilse, *The Political Thought of Max Weber* (New York, 1971).

ELDRIDGE, J E T, *Max Weber* (London, 1971).

ENGISCH, Karl, PFISTER, Bernhard, WINCKELMANN, Johannes, eds, *Max Weber, Gedächtnisschrift* (Berlin, 1966).

FERBER, Christian von, *Die Gewalt in der Politik* (Stuttgart, 1970).

—— 'Der Werturteilsstreit 1909–59', *Kölner Zeitschrift für Soziologie und Sozialpsychologie*, vol 11 (1959), pp 21–37.

FLEISCHMANN, Eugène, 'De Weber à Nietzsche', *Archives Européennes de Sociologie*, vol 5 (1964), pp 190–238.

FRANCIS, Emerich, 'Kultur und Gesellschaft in der Soziologie Max Webers', in Engisch, Pfister, Winckelmann, eds, op cit.

FREUND, Julien, *The Sociology of Max Weber* (New York, 1968).

FRYE, Bruce, 'A Letter from Max Weber', *Journal of Modern History*, vol 39 (1967), pp 122–5.

GIDDENS, Anthony, *Capitalism and Modern Social Theory* (Cambridge, 1971).

—— 'Marx, Weber and the Development of Capitalism', *Sociology*, vol 4 (1970), pp 289–310.

—— *Politics and Sociology in the Thought of Max Weber* (London, 1972).

GRAB, Hermann, *Der Begriff des Rationalen in der Soziologie Max Webers* (Karlsruhe, 1927).

GREEN, Robert, *Protestantism and Capitalism* (New York, 1959).

HABERMAS, Jürgen, *Technik und Wissenschaft als Ideologie* (Neuwied, 1968).

HÄTTICH, Manfred, 'Der Begriff des Politischen bei Max Weber', *Politische Vierteljahresschrift*, vol 8 (1967), pp 40–50.

HENRICH, Dieter, *Die Einheit der Wissenschaftslehre Max Webers* (Tübingen, 1952).

HONIGSHEIM, Paul, 'Max Weber und die deutsche Politik', *Kölner Zeitschrift für Soziologie und Sozialpsychologie*, vol 13 (1961), pp 263–74.

—— *On Max Weber* (New York, 1968).

HUFNAGEL, Gerd, *Kritik als Beruf* (Frankfurt, 1971).

HUGHES, H. Stuart, *Consciousness and Society* (New York, 1958).

JANOSKA-BENDL, Judith, *Methodologische Aspekte des Idealtypus* (Berlin, 1965).

JASPERS, Karl, *Max Weber, Politiker, Forscher, Philosoph* (München, 1958).

JELLINCK, Georg, *Allgemeine Staatslehre* (Berlin, 1905).

KARSTEN, Alfred, *Das Problem der Legitimität in Max Webers Idealtypus der Rationalen Herrschaft* (Hamburg, 1960).

KOCHAN, Lionel, *Russia in Revolution* (London 1966).

KOCKA, Jürgen, 'Karl Marx und Max Weber. Ein methodologischer Vergleich', *Zeitschrift für die gesamte Staatswissenschaft*, vol 122 (1966).

LACHMANN, Ludwig, *The Legacy of Max Weber* (London, 1970).

LANDSHUT, Siegfried, *Kritik der Soziologie* (Neuwied, 1969).

LEFEVRE, Wolfgang, *Zum historischen Charakter und zur historischen Funktion der Methode bürgerlicher Soziologie* (Frankfurt, 1971).

LEICHTER, Käthe, 'Max Weber als Lehrer und Politiker', *Kölner Zeitschrift für Soziologie und Sozialpsychologie*, Sonderheft 7 (1963), pp 127–40.

LENK, Kurt, 'Das Werturteilsproblem bei Max Weber', *Zeitschrift für die gesamte Staatswissenschaft*, vol 120 (1964), pp 56–64.

LINDENLAUB, Dieter, *Richtungskämpfe im Verein für Sozialpolitik* (Wiesbaden, 1967).

LOOS, Fritz, *Zur Wert- und Rechtslehre Max Webers* (Tübingen, 1970).

LÖWENSTEIN, Karl, *Max Webers staatspolitische Auffassungen in der Sicht unserer Zeit* (Frankfurt, Bonn, 1965).

—— 'Max Weber als "Ahnherr" des plebiszitären Führerstaats', *Kölner Zeitschrift für Soziologie und Sozialpsychologie*, vol 13 (1961), pp 275–89.

LÖWITH, Karl, 'Max Weber und Karl Marx', *Archiv für Sozialwissenschaft und Sozialpolitik*, vol 67 (1932), pp 53–99, 175–214.

MAIER, Hans, 'Max Weber und die deutsche politische Wissenschaft', in H. Maier, *Politische Wissenschaft in Deutschland* (München, 1969), pp 69–88.

MARCUSE, Herbert, 'Industrialisation and Capitalism in the Work of Max Weber', in H. Marcuse, *Negations* (London, 1968), pp 201–26.

MARX, Karl and ENGELS, Friedrich, *Selected Works*, 2 vols (Moscow, 1962).

MAYER, Jacob, *Max Weber and German Politics* (London, 1956).

MICHELS, Robert, *Political Parties* (Glencoe, 1958).

MITZMAN, Arthur, *The Iron Cage* (New York, 1970).

MOMMSEN, Wolfgang, *Max Weber und die deutsche Politik, 1890–1920* (Tübingen, 1959).

—— 'Zum Begriff der "plebiszitären Führerdemokratie" bei Max Weber', *Kölner Zeitschrift für Soziologie und Sozialpsychologie*, vol 15 (1963), pp 295–322.

—— 'Universalgeschichtliches und politisches Denken bei Max Weber', *Historische Zeitschrift*, vol 201 (1965), pp 557–612.

—— 'Die Vereinigten Staaten von Amerika im politischen Denken Max Webers', *Historische Zeitschrift*, vol 213 (1971).

MOORE, Barrington, *Social Origins of Dictatorship and Democracy* (London, 1967).

MOSCA, Gaetano, *The Ruling Class* (New York, 1939).

NISBET, Robert, *The Sociological Tradition* (New York, 1966).

NOLTE, Ernst, 'Max Weber vor dem Faschismus', *Der Staat*, vol 2 (1963), pp 1–24.

OBERSCHALL, Anthony, *Empirical Social Research in Germany, 1848–1914* (The Hague, 1965).

OSTROGORSKI, M, *Democracy and the Organisation of Political Parties* (London, 1902).

PARRY, Geraint, *Political Elites* (London, 1969).

PATEMAN, Carole, *Participation and Democratic Theory* (Cambridge, 1970).

PIPES, Richard, 'Max Weber und Russland', *Aussenpolitik*, vol 6 (1955), pp 627–39.

REX, John, *Key Problems of Sociological Theory* (London, 1961).

RINGER, Fritz, *The Decline of the German Mandarins* (Cambridge, 1969).

ROSCHER, WILHELM, *Politik* (Berlin, 1908).

ROSENBERG, Arthur, *Entstehrung der Weimaren Republik* (Frankfurt, 1961).

ROTH, Guenther, *The Social Democrats in Imperial Germany* (Englewood Cliffs, 1963).

RUNCIMAN, W G, *A Critique of Max Weber's Philosophy of Social Science* (Cambridge, 1972).

—— *Social Science and Political Theory* (Cambridge, 1965).

SAHAY, Arun, ed, *Max Weber and Modern Sociology* (London, 1971).

SCHÄFER, Bernard, 'Ein Rundschreiben Max Webers zur Sozialpolitik', *Soziale Welt*, vol 18 (1967), pp 261–71.

SCHELTING, Alexander von, *Max Weber's Wissenschaftslehre* (Tübingen, 1934).

SCHLUCHTER, Wolfgang, *Wertfreiheit und Verantwortungsethik* (Tübingen, 1971).

SCHMIDT, Gustav, *Deutscher Historismus und der Übergang zur parlamentarischen Demokratie* (Hamburg, 1964).

SCHORSKE, Carl, *German Social Democracy, 1905–17* (Cambridge, Mass, 1955).

Schriften des Vereins für Sozialpolitik, vol 132 (1910).

SCHULZ, Gerhard, 'Geschichtliche Theorie und politisches Denken bei Max Weber', *Vierteljahreshefte für Zeitgeschichte*, vol 12 (1964), pp 325–50.

SCHUMPETER, Joseph, *Capitalism, Socialism and Democracy* (London, 1954).

SHEEHAN, James, *The Career of Lujo Brentano* (Chicago, 1966).

SIMEY, T S, 'Max Weber: Man of Affairs or Theoretical Sociologist', *Sociological Review*, vol 14 (1966), pp 303–27.

STAMMER, Otto, ed, *Max Weber und die Soziologie heute* (Tübingen, 1965).

—— *Max Weber and Sociology Today* (Oxford, 1971).

STEDING, Christoph, *Politik und Wissenschaft bei Max Weber* (Breslau, 1932).

—— *Das Reich und die Krankheit der europäischen Kultur* (Hamburg, 1938).

TELLEGEN, Egbert, *De Sociologie in het Werk van Max Weber* (Meppel, 1968).

TENBRUCK, Friedrich, 'Die Genesis der Methodologie Max Webers', *Kölner Zeitschrift für Soziologie und Sozialpsychologie*, vol 11 (1959), pp 573–630.

TÖNNIES, Ferdinand, *Der englische Staat und der deutsche Staat* (Berlin, 1917).

WEBER, Marianne, *Ein Lebensbild* (Tübingen, 1926).

WINCKELMANN, Johannes, *Legitimität und Legalität in Max Webers Herrschaftssoziologie* (Tübingen, 1952).

—— *Staatssoziologie* (Berlin, 1956).

WRONG, Dennis, ed, *Max Weber* (Englewood Cliffs, 1970).

Index

Abramowski, G. 27–30
Agricultural workers 17, 37–8
Aron, R. 14, 120, 133, 216
Authoritarian government 23, 152–64, 177–9, 192–8, 205
Authority 68, 252, 257–9
Autonomy 42–3, 169–70, 185, 228–9

'Beamtenherrschaft' 75–6, 240
Bismarck 38–9, 51, 109, 157, 216, 238
Bolshevism 201–3
Bourgeoisie 26, 38–9, 40, 53, 57–8, 83, 110, 116, 157–61, 165–6, 173, 176–7, 190–1, 197, 199, 204–5, 209
Bourgeois values 55–9, 143–4, 165–6, 190–1, 209–10, 240–5
Brentano, L. 19, 168, 170
Britain 21, 78, 135, 139, 145
Bruun, H. 133
Bureaucracy, bureaucratisation 15, 16, 23–4, 44, 47, 49, 50–5, 57, 63–89, 100, 107, 183, 185, 191, 194, 223, 226, 244, 252, 267–8
Bureaucracy, Prussian 64, 66, 73–4, 84–5, 155

Calling 55, 57, 226, 234
Capitalism 16, 19, 20, 23, 24, 37, 44–7, 55–8, 82–4, 153–4, 157–8, 164, 178, 184, 187, 198, 202, 204–5, 207–10, 218–26, 242–5, 253, 269–76
Charisma 26, 227, 230–1, 235, 243, 257–9, 265–6

China 69, 122
Class, class conflict 19, 20, 37, 39, 41, 53, 58–9, 63, 66, 80, 109–10, 144–7, 152–64, 175–9, 185, 186–91, 195–8, 200–2, 204–5, 215–26, 229–30, 237, 239, 241–2
Communism, peasant 45, 184
Constitutional Commission 21, 232–3
Culture 37–8, 40, 43, 57, 78, 125–38, 140–4, 146–7

Demagogy 100, 103–4, 110, 171, 243
Democracy, democratisation 14, 15, 21, 24, 70, 95–112, 119, 123, 160–1, 172, 177, 184–91, 195–7, 199, 204–10, 236, 263, 264–9
Democratic Party, German 13, 173, 234–5
Dictatorship 71, 104, 199
Dragomanov 130, 141
Dronberger I. 16
Duma 190, 191, 194–7

East Prussia 17, 36–9, 42, 123, 131–2, 153–6, 218
Economic interests 40, 47, 58, 154–6, 188, 191, 197, 209, 217, 222–5, 228–9, 233–7
Economic policy 37–8
Egypt 53, 69, 86–7
Elections 70, 107–9, 195–7, 232–5
Elites 41, 103–12, 217, 238
Entrepreneurial qualities 48, 57, 82–3, 173, 228, 270
'Evangelisch-soziale Kongress' 17, 20–1, 44, 58, 134–5, 219

Ferber, C. von 133, 215
'Fideicommissum' 154–5, 158–9, 166, 170
Foreign policy, German 21, 52, 78, 138–44, 155
France 78, 101, 124, 135, 139, 145, 159
Francis, E. 144
Freedom 24, 37, 44–9, 71, 83, 113–16, 165–6, 176, 183, 193–4, 198

German Sociological Association 14, 18, 41, 122, 146, 251
Germany, political institutions 49–55, 72–8, 98–102, 104, 152–64, 170–2, 178, 232–40
social structure 36–9, 151–79.
Giddens, A. 26
Gladstone 107

Ideal interests 44, 185, 202, 223, 229
Ideology 23, 97–8, 138, 161–2, 186, 195–6, 201–3, 221–2, 261–4
Imperialism 134–8, 140–7
Individualism 47–8, 54, 56, 112, 185, 187–8, 204–7, 231
Industrial relations 19, 158, 224–5
International order 15, 50, 133, 138–43, 173, 193, 200

Junkers 38, 53, 58, 109, 152–6, 216–20, 244

Kadets 195–7
Kaiser Wilhelm II 26, 78, 172
Kerensky 199
Kompert, P. 85

Lachmann, L. 178
Landowners 17, 37–8, 132, 153–5, 165, 185, 188, 195–6, 220
Leadership 15, 23, 24, 38, 39, 40–1, 50–4, 57–8, 77, 98–102, 107–12, 202, 215–18, 226–40, 243–5, 265–6
Legality 68, 265
Legitimacy 115, 133, 253, 256–9, 265–6
Lenin 175–6, 189–90
Liberalism 14, 26, 45–7, 54, 113, 183–91, 195–6, 198, 204–10, 238–9
Liebknecht, K. 173
Lindenlaub, D. 19, 63, 218

Lloyd George 107, 232
Löwith, K. 27–30, 71
Ludendorff 236
Lukacs, G. 27, 276
Luxemburg, R. 18, 173

'Machtstaat' 23, 131–44, 237
Maier, H. 22, 120
Marx, Marxism 14, 19, 20, 28, 71, 86, 160, 189, 216, 218, 241–2, 262
Mass, masses 16, 52, 57, 103–12, 126, 146, 199, 219, 231, 244, 267
Material interests 43, 162–3, 166, 188, 195–6, 201–4, 210, 220–6, 245
Mayer, J. P. 16, 173
Methodology 23, 30, 250–2
Michels, R. 71, 111, 162, 167
Mitzman, A. 26, 120
Modernisation 67
Mommsen W. J. 14, 16, 26, 54, 113–14, 119, 133, 237, 240
Monarchy 50–1, 63, 75, 102, 199
Mosca, G. 262–3

National interest 18, 38, 39–40, 56, 132, 139–41, 154
Nationalism 14, 40, 54, 57, 119–47, 241
National Socialism 54, 238–9
Nation state 16, 21, 119–47
Naumann, F. 20–1, 50, 96
Negative politics 97–9
Nietzsche 216

Officials, officialdom 51, 65–70, 76–9, 197, 229, 252
Ostrogorski, M. 21, 107–8

Parliament, parliamentary government 24, 51–4, 74, 95–102, 113–16, 171–2, 188, 194, 204–5, 209, 217, 223, 225, 232–41
Paternalism 19, 20, 43, 168
Patriarchalism 56, 153, 218
Peasantry 45, 186–8, 195–6, 198, 200–1
Petersen, K. 13
Petty-bourgeoisie 145, 190
Pipes, R. 183
Plebiscitary democracy 52, 108, 114, 231–40, 265–6
Plekhanov, G. 189

Poland, Poles 17, 37, 38, 41, 123, 126–8, 131, 141–2
Political education 39, 41, 52, 58, 144, 147, 189–90, 225
Political parties 13, 21, 107–10, 155, 162–4, 166–7, 170, 173, 195–7, 221, 224, 229, 231, 233–4
Political practice 22, 23, 250–2, 259–61
Politicians, role of 51, 65, 76–9, 98, 228–30, 252
Power 44, 65, 70, 74–5, 130–1, 133–44, 153–4, 174, 192–3, 199, 222, 242, 259
Presidential government 21, 232–40
Prestige 73, 78, 80, 133–4, 141–2, 192, 197–9
Prime Minister 52, 107

Race 123
Rationality, rationalisation 28–9, 46, 48, 68–9, 71, 194, 218, 257, 273–5
'Reichstag' 20, 51, 98, 101, 205, 233–5
Religion 46, 185–6, 205–7, 219, 254–5
Rentiers 57, 159, 228–30
Responsibility, personal 44, 48, 76, 219, 231
    political 51, 53, 76-8, 137, 142, 171
    ethic of 174–6
Revolution 44–5, 172–4, 188–90, 192–203, 222, 258–9
Roman Empire 69, 86–7, 192
Russia 22–4, 44–9, 66, 70, 72, 95, 113, 129–30, 140–3, 183–210, 221, 229, 241, 259

'Sachlichkeit' 23, 95, 243
Schelting, A. von 23
Schmidt, G. 114–15
Schmoller, G. 18, 19, 63, 208, 223, 226
Schumpeter, J 111–12
Selection 41–3, 51, 98–9, 108–10, 234
Social Darwinism 43
Social Democracy 45, 98, 146, 161–4, 166–7, 173, 176, 189–90, 195–6, 199, 202, 222, 229
Socialism 23, 48, 55, 82–9, 173–5, 198, 202–3, 207–8, 267–8

Social science 16, 23, 24–5, 251, 253–4, 261–4, 269, 275–6
Social unity 58, 144, 217, 232–3, 237
Sociology 15, 20, 22, 24, 25, 27–31, 115–16, 226, 250, 252–3, 256–61, 264
Sombart, W. 19
State 128–31, 162–3, 207–8, 216
Status, status stratum 79–82, 122, 155, 159–60
Steding, C. 25–6, 54
Stolypin 198
Struggle 15, 41–3, 51, 56, 77, 82, 110, 132, 253
Struve, P. 184
Suffrage reform 19, 74, 166
Suffrage, universal 96, 103–8, 161, 205, 209

Tönnies F. 19
Token constitutionalism 100, 152, 191, 192, 194–5, 199
Trade unions 19, 146, 167–70, 224
Traditional authority 68, 70, 257–9
Tsarist rule 45, 70, 183, 188–9, 192–8, 203

United States of America 21, 69–70, 78, 124–5, 143, 205–6

Value freedom 39, 251, 262
Values, value judgements 16, 22, 23, 24–5, 28–30, 36, 42, 49, 54–5, 89, 120–1, 125, 136–7, 143–4, 222, 239, 261–2, 276
'Verein für Sozialpolitik' 17, 18–20, 21, 41, 44, 63–4, 66, 78, 81, 84–5, 96, 162–3, 166–70, 208–9, 218, 222–3, 268
Vitte, Count 193, 197

Wagner, A. 19
War aims, German 21, 139–40
Weber, Alfred 19, 64, 66, 84–5
Weber, Marianne 13, 21, 44, 173, 222, 234–6
Winckelmann, J. 24–5, 265
Working class 17, 19, 45, 58, 134–5, 144–7, 161–4, 167, 176, 189–90, 199, 201, 204–5, 243–4
World War 21, 81, 138–44, 170–2, 200

Zemstvos 185, 190, 195–6, 199